Structures of Grace

Structures of Grace

Catholic Organizations
Serving the Global Common Good

KEVIN AHERN

ORBIS BOOKS

Maryknoll, New York 10545

ORBIS BOOKS
Maryknoll, New York 10545

Fathers and Brothers
MARYKNOLL.

Founded in 1970, Orbis Books endeavors to publish works that enlighten the mind, nourish the spirit, and challenge the conscience. The publishing arm of the Maryknoll Fathers and Brothers, Orbis seeks to explore the global dimensions of the Christian faith and mission, to invite dialogue with diverse cultures and religious traditions, and to serve the cause of reconciliation and peace. The books published reflect the views of their authors and do not represent the official position of the Maryknoll Society. To learn more about Maryknoll and Orbis Books, please visit our website at www.maryknollsociety.org.

Library of Congress Cataloging-in-Publication Data

Ahern, Kevin.
    Structures of grace : Catholic organzations serving the global common
    good / Kevin Ahern.
        pages cm
    Includes bibliographical references and index.
    ISBN 978-1-62698-120-1 (pbk.)
    1. Church work—Catholic Church. 2. Catholic Church—Charities. 3.
Common good—Religious aspects—Catholic Church. I. Title.
BX2347.A34 2015
267'.182—dc23
                                                    2014046229

Contents

Part II
THEOLOGICAL CONSIDERATIONS—
MISSION, CHARISM, AND GRACE

Part III
DISCERNING GOD'S SPIRIT
IN ACTION—IDENTITY, MISSION, AND ORGANIZATION

Frequently Used Acronyms

CDF	Congregation for the Doctrine of the Faith
CIJOC	Coordination Internationale de la Jeunesse Ouvrière Chrétienne / International Coordination of Young Christian Workers
ECOSOC	United Nations Economic and Social Council
GC	General Congregation of the Society of Jesus (Jesuits)
GE	General Electric
ICO	International Catholic Organization
ILO	International Labor Organization
IMCS	International Movement of Catholic Students (Pax Romana)
IYCW	International Young Christian Workers / Jeunesse Ouvrière Chrétienne Internationale
JOC	Jeunesse Ouvrière Chrétienne
JRS	Jesuit Refugee Service
NGO	Nongovernmental organization
UN	United Nations
UNHCR	The Office of the United Nations High Commissioner for Refugees
YCW	Young Christian Workers

Frequently Cited Church Documents and Abbreviations

SELECTED DOCUMENTS OF THE SECOND VATICAN COUNCIL AND POST-CONCILIAR PERIOD

LG   *Lumen Gentium, Dogmatic Constitution on the Church* (1964)

UR   *Unitatis Redintegratio, Decree on Ecumenism* (1964)

PC   *Perfectae Caritatis, Decree on Renewal of Religious Life* (1965)

AA   *Apostolicam Actuositatem, Decree on the Apostolate of the Laity* (1965)

GS   *Gaudium et Spes, Pastoral Constitution on the Church in the Modern World* (1965)

ET   *Evangelica Testificatio, Apostolic Exhortation on the Renewal of the Religious Life*, Paul VI (1971)

Note: Quotations from Austin Flannery, ed. *Vatican Council II: The Basic Sixteen Documents: Constitutions, Decrees, Declarations.* 2nd ed. Northport, NY: Costello, 1996.

SELECTED DOCUMENTS FROM CATHOLIC SOCIAL TEACHING

MM   *Mater et Magistra, Christianity and Social Progress,* John XXIII (1961)

PP   *Populorum Progressio, On the Development of Peoples,* Paul VI (1967)

OA   *Octogesima Adveniens, A Call to Action,* Paul VI (1971)

JM   *Justitia in Mundo, Justice in the World,* World Synod of Bishops (1971)

EN   *Evangelii Nuntiandi, Evangelization in the Modern World,* Paul VI (1975)

SRS   *Sollicitudo Rei Socialis, On Social Concern,* John Paul II (1987)

CV   *Caritas in Veritate, Charity in Truth,* Benedict XVI (2009)

Note: Quotations from David J. O'Brien and Thomas A. Shannon, eds. *Catholic Social Thought: The Documentary Heritage.* Expanded edition. Maryknoll, NY: Orbis Books, 1987.

OTHER CHURCH DOCUMENTS

CIC   *Codex Iuris Canonici,* Code of Canon Law (1983)

RP   *Reconciliatio et Paenitentia, On Reconciliation and Penance,* John Paul II (1984)

RM   *Redemptoris Missio, On the Mission of the Redeemer,* John Paul II (1990)

VC   *Vita Consecrata, On Consecrated Life and Its Mission in the Church and in the World,* John Paul II (1996)

DCE   *Deus Caritas Est, God Is Love,* Benedict XVI (2005)

EG   *Evangelii Gaudium, On the Joy of the Gospel,* Francis (2013)

Note: Unless otherwise noted, other texts from Catholic teaching can be found online at www.vatican.va.

Introduction

Experiences of Grace
in a World of Suffering
and Indifference

On July 8, 2013, Pope Francis embarked on his first official visit
outside of Rome to the Italian island of Lampedusa. The event was
both highly symbolic and deeply pastoral. Much to the surprise
of those who plan and follow papal trips, the Argentinian pope's
request came at the last minute. His decision was in response to
an increasing number of people seeking refuge in Europe by taking
overcrowded and dangerous boats to Lampedusa, Malta, and other
European points in the Mediterranean. The crisis was powerfully
illustrated by the dramatic images of dozens of African migrants
clinging desperately to tuna cages in late June.

Deeply moved by the recent death of hundreds of migrants in their
attempt to cross into Europe, the pope sought to express the church's
solidarity with some of the world's most desperate people. For over a
decade the small Italian island, which is closer to North Africa than
continental Europe, has borne witness to one of the most tragic human dramas of this century. Fleeing poverty, conflict, and dehumanizing injustice, hundreds of thousands of people from Africa, Asia,
and the Middle East have crossed the perilous Mediterranean Sea
in hopes of securing a better life in Europe. In 2013, the number of
migrants attempting to cross into Europe rapidly increased as many
sought to escape new social, political, and economic conflicts in
North Africa, the Middle East, and Asia.

Tragically, the desperate plight of migrants heading toward Europe
is not an isolated experience. Similar human dramas are taking place
in other regions of the world, including the increasingly militarized

border of the United States and Mexico and the waters around Australia. For far too many of these—mostly young—people the journey has ended too soon. According to the International Organization for Migration, 2013 was the deadliest year on record for migrants. More than seven thousand people are estimated to have died on their journeys across deserts, oceans, and dangerous militarized borders.[1] At the time of this writing, the number of migrant deaths for 2014 has already surpassed this number.

The global phenomena of migration and forced displacement illuminate what can be described as the Janus-faced nature of globalization. On the one hand, the human family is more deeply connected than ever before, linked together in a complex web of technological, cultural, and economic ties. This was very evident, for example, in the recent crisis surrounding the 2014 outbreak of Ebola, which resulted in scores of deaths. In a global context a virus originating in an impoverished rural community in Guinea can spread to urban centers in the United States within months, and the impact of the disease on local communities in West Africa can influence economies, political races, and the price of commodities (for example, chocolate) across the world.

On the other hand, serious divisions and gaps appear to be widening. According to a recent study by the British organization Oxfam, the eighty-five richest people on the planet possess as much wealth as the poorest 3.5 billion![2] For millions of women, men, and children, everyday life in the era of globalization is marked by the reality of poverty and inequality. While progress has been made in some important areas, the situation remains dire for many. For example, the World Bank has recently estimated that there are more than 400 million children who live in extreme poverty—a dehumanizing reality that for most will mean an early death from preventable causes.[3] The increasing interconnection of the global economy, in other words, does not mean that we are coming closer together as a human family. Even in New York, one of the world's wealthiest

---

[1] Stephanie Nebhay, "2013 Believed to Be Deadliest for Desperate Migrants—IOM," *Reuters*, December 17, 2013, UK edition, uk.reuters.com.

[2] Daniel Tencer, "85 People Hold As Much Wealth As Poorest 3.5 Billion," *The Huffington Post*, January 20, 2014, www.huffingtonpost.ca.

[3] "Report Finds 400 Million Children Living in Extreme Poverty," *The World Bank*, October 10, 2013, www.worldbank.org.

cities, close to half of the people, more than four million human beings, live below or near the poverty line and over fifty thousand people, including thousands of children, are homeless. How should Christians and other people of good will respond to so much suffering and preventable death?

In a passionate homily during his visit to Lampedusa, Pope Francis seeks to respond to this question as he laments the loss of life and the failure of the international community to respond seriously to the phenomenon of migration and its root causes. Drawing from the biblical account of Cain and Abel, Francis condemns what he describes as "the globalization of indifference," an attitude that prevents people from responding to the plight of their brothers and sisters.[4] Even if we see the suffering of others, we seem unwilling or unable to do much to address it. In his apostolic exhortation on evangelization, *Evangelii Gaudium*, Francis elaborates on this problem:

> The excluded are still waiting. To sustain a lifestyle which excludes others, or to sustain enthusiasm for that selfish ideal, a globalization of indifference has developed. Almost without being aware of it, we end up being incapable of feeling compassion at the outcry of the poor, weeping for other people's pain, and feeling a need to help them, as though all this were someone else's responsibility and not our own. The culture of prosperity deadens us; we are thrilled if the market offers us something new to purchase. In the meantime all those lives stunted for lack of opportunity seem a mere spectacle; they fail to move us (EG, no. 54).

Tragically, despite his popularity and global presence, the strong call of Pope Francis for the international community to take action to protect the lives of people seeking refuge in places like Lampedusa has been ignored. In October 2013, a ship carrying migrants from Eritrea, Somalia, and Ghana sank, killing over 350 migrants on their way from Libya to Lampedusa. Less than a year later, on September 6, 2014, more than 570 people died in two separate incidents in the Mediterranean. In one incident more than 500 people perished when the boat carrying them from Egypt to Malta was deliberately sunk

---

[4] Pope Francis, *Visit to Lampedusa: Homily of Holy Father Francis* (Rome: Libreria Editrice Vaticana, 2013).

by human traffickers. What does it say that far more attention was paid to the announcement about a new smartphone that week than the death of hundreds of people?

In the face of this globalization of indifference, how should Christians and other people of good will respond? What can any one person do to make a difference, especially when the root causes of so much human suffering are a result of complex systems and social forces? Recently, a student in one of my courses summed up the frustration felt by so many of us. "I don't want to hear these stories," he said, "because there is nothing I can do to change it."

Thankfully, this is not the whole story. There *are* ways that people and communities can take a stand against systemic violence and preventable death. In the face of structural poverty, indifference, and dehumanization, there are profound experiences of compassion, justice, and charity. Inspired by the Holy Spirit and the gospel mission, Christian social movements and organizations, in many forms, are among the most active groups involved in the promotion of the global common good. Their social engagement includes service to marginalized people, humanitarian aid, the promotion of peace and democracy, human rights advocacy, healthcare, education, and efforts to reform the structures of global governance. As organized entities distinct from the official leadership structures of their churches, these various associations, at their best, are transforming the globalization of indifference into a globalization of solidarity and social justice. Consider the following examples:

- The *Young Women's Christian Association* (YWCA) is an international network of women and girls that works for "women's full and equal participation in society." Inspired by the Christian tradition, the YWCA reaches over 25 million women and girls in over 120 countries.
- Each year over 400 young adults give a year or two of their lives in volunteer communities in over sixty cities sponsored by the *Jesuit Volunteer Corps* (JVC) and *JVC Northwest*. Often inspired by their Christian faith, these young adults commit themselves to the values of spirituality, simple living, community, and social justice.
- *World Vision*, an evangelical Christian humanitarian aid organization, provides services to thousands of children in over

ninety countries around the world with the stated goal to "work toward a world where every child experiences life in all its fullness. Where they are protected, cared for and given the opportunities to become all God meant them to be." Immediately following the devastating effects of Typhoon Haiyan in the Philippines, for instance, World Vision supplied over 600,000 people with emergency food aid.

- Thousands of women in more than forty countries, inspired by the legacy of Catherine McAuley, are members or associates of the *Sisters of Mercy*. They serve tens of thousands of people in a multitude of ministries including hospitals, schools, and advocacy at the United Nations. In addition to the three traditional vows of poverty, chastity, and obedience, religious Sisters of Mercy take a fourth vow of service.

Occupying a middle position between individual believers and institutional church structures are thousands of Christian social movements and social movement organizations. These agents of social transformation gather and inspire millions of people for social change in a world marked by suffering and injustice. They have been described in different ways, including para-ecclesial or para-church groups, faith-based organizations, and Christian nongovernmental organizations (NGOs). While the focus of this book is generally on collective agents originating within the Roman Catholic tradition, I use the broader and more inclusive term *Christian social movement* to highlight the transformative potential of the wide range of Christian groups involved in the promotion of human dignity and the common good.

The experience of Christian communal life is certainly not new to the church. Originating as a community within Judaism, Christianity can in many ways be understood as a movement or, more precisely, as a movement of movements. Almost from the very beginning of the church, dynamic groups of socially engaged Christians took shape among the community of believers to witness to the word of God *(martyria)*, celebrate their faith in sacraments *(leitourgia)*, and respond to the gospel through acts of service *(diakonia)*. Christianity is at its core a communal religion.

Today, however, Christian social movements are taking on innovative roles in the church and in the world. The dynamic forces of globalization are creating new problems that call for concerted responses on the part of Christian collectives. At the same time, the increased interconnectedness of the world is offering fresh and exciting opportunities for Christians to gather beyond the local level. Though not without problems, these movements are shaping the lives of millions of people and, in turn, the life of the church.

The presence of Christian social movements at the intersection of the church and global public life raises several questions. What is the theological significance of Christian social movements and their organizational structures? Are there any resources from theology that can aid social movements as they seek to live out their mission in a rapidly changing world? How do the experiences of Christian social movements shape our understanding of the nature of God, the nature of the church, and the nature of ethics?

In my own experience as both a theologian and a member of several Christian social movements, these are questions that receive little sustained reflection by either activists or academics. From 2003 to 2007, for example, I served as president of the International Movement of Catholic Students (IMCS–Pax Romana). In that capacity I worked with national student organizations in more than seventy countries and served on the coordination team for several networks of Christian and non-Christian international organizations. In these distinctive spaces questions frequently surfaced concerning organizational structures, the relationship between identity and fundraising, and debates on how best to engage other actors in the church—including Vatican officials. Rarely, if ever, did I see organizations apply a thick theological lens to these important deliberations. Mission statements, organizational plans of action, fundraising, and the development of structures were far too often pragmatic decisions made in the midst of busy schedules, financial pressures, and competing demands.

At the same time, the contribution of Christian social movements is also often overlooked in scholarly writings in theological ethics, which tends to focus on either the personal and heroic witness of individual Christians such as Dorothy Day, Martin Luther King, Jr., and Oscar Romero, or the official actions and teachings of the institutional church. There is much more to the church's public social engagement, however, than the pope's latest statement and the witness of heroic and saintly individuals.

From the civil rights movement in the United States to human rights campaigns in Latin America, experience shows that organized movements are necessary in order to overcome oppressive and unjust social structures. In the face of massive injustice and powerful political, corporate, and criminal forces, education, charitable gifts, and individual actions, though extremely important, are not sufficient.

Communities, movements, and nongovernmental organizations are essential agents in the church's efforts to serve the global common good and witness to the gospel in a desperate world. But what is the theological value of these structures and how can they be better organized to embody the values that they seek to instill in society?

Recognizing both the possibilities and shortcomings of any human community, this project aims to highlight the theological significance of Christian social movements in three steps. Part I situates the experience of transnational Christian social movements in the present global context. Drawing from the work of sociologists and political theorists, Chapter 1 begins by laying out a framework to understand the contribution of these groups to the global common good. After looking at the broader reality, I then look specifically at three very different case studies: Jesuit Refugee Service, a movement organization of the Society of Jesus involved in humanitarian efforts; the Young Christian Workers, a global youth movement of specialized Catholic action with two conflicting international structures; and Plowshares, a radical pacifist movement with no structured organization. Clearly, other examples of Christian social movements could have been studied, including those known as new ecclesial movements, communities associated with the new monasticism, and movement organizations involved in higher education or healthcare. Choosing case studies that would encompass the totality of all Christian social movements is not possible here. Despite these limitations, the three case studies do offer important perspectives on the reality of Christian social movements. From each case study several questions surface. These can be grouped broadly in three categories: movement identity, mission, and organization.

After taking stock of the reality of Christian social movements, Part II considers the missiological, pneumatological, and ecclesiological dimensions of these collective agents by placing their experience into conversation with official Catholic teaching. Christian social movements, I contend, would benefit from a more robust theological lens. A framework of social or structural grace can assist movements to better situate themselves in relation to the broader church, the reign of God, and God's loving action in the world.

Like all institutions of the church, Christian social movements are imperfect and always in need of reform. One must acknowledge that no organization or movement, not even the most faithful Christian community, is perfect. Many important Christian thinkers, notably among them the American theologian Reinhold Niebuhr, have pointed to the destructive behaviors (that is, sin) inherent to all social entities.[5] Without question, groups of people, including those that identify themselves as Christian, can fall victim to the collective egoism that Niebuhr warns about.

Nevertheless, it is my contention that collective egoism, while present and real, should not be seen as the only or even the primary way to understand collective social agents.[6] A deeper theological and ethical analysis of these organizations will help to illuminate the sinful shortcomings while also naming the ways in which these communities, at their best, embody God's grace and concern for the plight of human beings in a complex world of suffering and indifference.

Drawing from the case studies and theological analysis, Part III concludes by offering several tools for movement discernment. If Christian social movements can be considered as structures of grace and participants in the mission of the church, what should that mean for how they live out that mission?

This project does not aim to address all the theological and practical questions surrounding Christian social movements and movement organizations. Such a task is impossible for one volume, and each movement needs to undertake its own process of discernment and renewal. Rather, this project seeks to be a resource for both theologians and members of Christian social movements to help them better understand what God may be doing in their midst.

---

[5] Reinhold Niebuhr, *The Nature and Destiny of Man: A Christian Interpretation*, vol. 1 (Louisville, KY: Westminster John Knox, 1996), 208; see also Reinhold Niebuhr, *Moral Man and Immoral Society: A Study in Ethics and Politics* (Louisville, KY: Westminster John Knox, 2001).

[6] Though he is often portrayed as having a rather negative view of human collectives, Reinhold Niebuhr does see an important role for communities and organized life. See Reinhold Niebuhr, *Man's Nature and His Communities: Essays on the Dynamics and Enigmas of Man's Personal and Social Existence* (New York: Scribner, 1965).

Part I

The Experience of Christian Social Movements Today

Chapter 1

Voices in the Wilderness

Christian Social Movements
in a Globalized World

*We can only praise the steps being taken to improve
people's welfare in areas such as health care, education and
communications. At the same time we have to remember
that the majority of our contemporaries are barely living from day to day, with dire consequences. A number
of diseases are spreading. The hearts of many people are
gripped by fear and desperation, even in the so-called rich
countries. The joy of living frequently fades, lack of respect
for others and violence are on the rise, and inequality is
increasingly evident. It is a struggle to live and, often, to
live with precious little dignity.*

—POPE FRANCIS, *EVANGELII GAUDIUM* (NO. 52)

The daily experience for far too many people today, as Pope
Francis laments in the above quotation, is marked by a dehumanizing and desperate struggle. What else would lead people to take
to dangerous seas in overcrowded boats and trust their lives to un-
scrupulous human smugglers in search for a better life in a foreign
land? Ultimately, to paraphrase Gustavo Gutiérrez, the consequence
of the desperate reality of poverty and extreme inequalities is death:
"unjust death, the premature death of the poor, physical death."[1]

---

[1] Gustavo Gutiérrez, *Essential Writings*, ed. James B. Nickoloff (Maryknoll, NY:
Orbis Books, 1996), 144.

As with the biblical accounts of Abel and the enslaved Hebrew people in Egypt, the collective blood of the millions of people who suffer preventable death in a global system filled with an abundance of wealth cries out to God. Their voices are all the more profound when we recognize that this is not the way the world has to be. It is not inevitable, for instance, that women and girls are forced into contemporary forms of slavery. It is not inevitable that people who are poor are more likely to perish from natural disasters. It is not inevitable that people have to suffer injustice. Christians, as Pope Francis reminds us, cannot remain indifferent to cries of the poor and the marginalized. Christians, in other words, cannot be on the sidelines in the hopeful struggle for a new way of living.

The conviction that change is possible is at the heart of many movements for social action, both Christian and non-Christian. This was very evident in January 2001 when tens of thousands of social activists and representatives of social movements opposed to neoliberal globalization gathered in Porto Alegre, Brazil, for the first World Social Forum. The event was conceived and organized by a group of movements and civil society leaders—with Christian social movements playing a leading role—as an alternative to the World Economic Forum, the annual meeting of the world's most influential corporate and political figures. Since 2001 the World Social Forum and related events have become important spaces to gather the hopes and visions of those seeking alternatives to the dehumanizing effects of globalization. Championing the principles of solidarity, human rights, and social justice, the gatherings have been organized with the prophetic slogan: Another world is possible. This is a wonderful and inspiring conviction, but how do we go about transforming the structures and relationships that define our human family?

A central argument of this book is that Christian social movements have an enormous potential to bring about some of the social changes needed to create a more just world. Indeed, it is difficult to overstate the contribution of Christian communities in global civil society.[2] Nearly every major process of social change over the past

---

[2] See Douglas M. Johnston and Cynthia Sampson, eds., *Religion: The Missing Dimension of Statecraft* (New York: Oxford University Press, 1994); J. Bryan Hehir, "Overview," in *Religion in World Affairs* (DACOR Bacon House Foundation, 1995), 11–24; J. Bryan Hehir, "Religious Activism for Human Rights: A Christian Case Study," in *Religious Human Rights in Global Perspective: Religious Perspectives*,

century, from the anti-slavery movement to the global campaigns on human rights and the environment, has involved socially engaged Christian communities. Today, Christian social movements remain on the frontlines of some of the most important efforts at social change. Returning to the drama of global migration, as mentioned in the Introduction, Christian social movements are actively engaged in both providing for the immediate needs of migrants in places like Lampedusa and working to address the root causes of forced displacement in the communities of origin.

What are Christian social movements, and what role do they play in the present struggle for a more just world? This chapter examines the nature of Christian social movements by considering their significance within global civil society. This will help set the stage for the following chapters, which offer a more detailed look at three very different examples or case studies of Christian social movements.

ANOTHER WORLD IS POSSIBLE

But first, how are Christian social movements involved in transforming what Pope Francis describes as a "globalization of indifference" into what might be called a globalization of social justice? At their greatest, Christian social movements and organizations, often operating in concert with other social agents, counteract the deleterious effects of globalization in at least three broad ways.

Engendering a Sense of Social Responsibility among Christians

First, Christian social movements form people with moral and ethical visions that challenge the cultural assumptions underlying the globalization of indifference. Social movements have a tremendous potential to shape the way people understand God, the world, and themselves. This has most certainly been my experience. My thinking, worldview, and faith have been deeply formed by my experience in social movements, where I have learned about new ideas and encountered people from different cultures. Through my own experiences in these movements, I have learned about Catholic social teaching,

---

ed. John Witte and Johan David Van der Vyver, 97–119 (Boston: Martinus Nijhoff Publishers, 1996).

liberation theology, and the Second Vatican Council. Though these movements I have developed friendships with people who come from different countries and social contexts. All of this shapes my own social engagement. For example, the experience of working with Syrian Christians on several projects in the past made it impossible for me to ignore the reality of the Syrian conflict. It may seem obvious, but we must recognize that Christian social movements shape people in ways that traditional educational and official church structures generally do not.

At their best, one of the ways that Christian social movements transform the ways in which people think is by helping them to overcome the destructive forces of individualism and indifference. Long critiqued by leading Christian social thinkers, the notion of individualism, which is at the center of the dominant culture of consumerism, stands in contrast to the Christian values of solidarity, communion, reciprocity, and social responsibility.

This worldview is all the more dangerous in the ways it supports compliancy in the face of the suffering of other human beings and an attitude of detachment from the processes for social change. An overly individualistic worldview, as Pope Francis warned in Lampedusa, "makes us live in soap bubbles," which, while beautiful to look at, ultimately cut us off from one another and make us indifferent to realities of others.

In recent years many philosophers and sociologists have joined religious leaders in forcefully critiquing the dangers posed by individualism to the social fabric of civil society. While certain Christian beliefs can be (mis)used to support an individualistic worldview, scholars point to the important role of religious institutions in helping to move people beyond themselves and form communities. Robert Bellah and his team of researchers, for example, outline the dangers of certain types of individualism and highlight the important role of religious groups in sparking civil engagement and social responsibility.[3]

Laws and political platforms can only do so much to change this individualistic mindset. What is needed, as Pope Francis pointed out in his "Message for the Celebration of the World Day of Peace: Fraternity, the Foundation and Pathway to Peace," is a "conversion of hearts" that enables "everyone to recognize in the other a brother

---

[3] Robert N. Bellah et al., *The Good Society* (New York: Vintage, 1992), 219.

or sister to care for, and to work together with, in building a fulfilling life for all" (no. 7). Christian social movements are one of the spaces in the world that enables this conversion to take place.

Proposing Social Alternatives

Second, Christian social movements transform globalization as they publicly communicate religious, moral, and ethical visions that support alternatives to unjust and oppressive social arrangements. Consider the significant presence of Christian social movements, such as the Southern Christian Leadership Conference, in denouncing the institutionalized forms of racism in the struggle for civil rights in the United States. Christian images and biblical themes permeate the writings, speeches, and visions of the major leaders of the US civil rights movement, including Dr. Martin Luther King, Jr., who often drew from scripture and Christian tradition in denouncing racism and injustice.

Another prominent example is the Jubilee 2000 Campaign, believed by many to be one of the most successful efforts by global civil society. Inspired by the moral and ethical vision of the jubilee forgiveness tradition outlined in the Jewish and Christian scriptures, Christian social movements spearheaded a wide coalition of support, from Pope John Paul II to Bono, to push wealthy nations to cancel or reduce the highly burdensome debt owed by poorer counties.

In the process of publicly communicating religious visions, Christian social movements are challenging many aspects of the secularization thesis, a cultural assumption that has dominated Western political thought for centuries. Originating with the Peace of Westphalia following the European (inter-Christian) wars of religion in 1648, the secularization thesis generally assumes that religions ought to and will eventually be marginalized from political and public life. According to Eva Bellin, the strong influence of the secularization thesis among Western intellectuals, coupled with a realist vision of the world that looks only at "hard power" (for example, economic and military), has led many scholars to overlook the contribution of religious actors in public life.[4]

---

[4] Eva Bellin, "Faith in Politics: New Trends in the Study of Religion and Politics," *World Politics* 60, no. 2 (January 2008): 315–47.

Despite the dire predictions offered by major Western intellectuals such as Jean-Jacques Rousseau, Karl Marx, Max Weber, and Sigmund Freud, religious actors have not faded away; neither have they accepted a role limited to the private sphere. Since the 1980s religious actors have surprised many observers in their continued attempts to "go public" with their faith. In *Public Religions in the Modern World*, sociologist José Casanova offers several case studies to show some of the distinctive ways in which religion has affected public life since the 1970s.[5]

Religion, Casanova argues, has not disappeared; nor has it been privatized. As such, the only valid understanding of secularization is the differentiation between the state and religion. Paradoxically, instead of inhibiting religion, secularization—if understood as a distinction between the roles of church and state—may actually free religious groups to play a more public role.

In fact, according to Casanova, the Second Vatican Council's "voluntary disestablishment" of the church from the state actually led to a more active form of Catholic engagement in public life.[6] Vatican II's groundbreaking *Dignitatis Humanae (Declaration on Religious Freedom)*, in particular, helped to free Christians and Christian organizations from the constraints imposed on the church in a model where the church is formally established in a particular country. With this document the Catholic Church adopted a stance in favor of democracy and public participation that would have been unimaginable in the nineteenth century.

Monica Duffy Toft, Daniel Philpott, and Timothy Samuel Shah have further explored this point in *God's Century: Resurgent Religion and Global Politics*. Building on Samuel Huntington's work on the "third wave of democracy," the authors analyze the role of religion in the promotion of democracy over the past forty years.[7] While they affirm the presence of pro-democratic forces in most religions, they particularly highlight the transformative role of the Christian organizations, especially Catholic groups, in the emergence of democratic governments since the 1960s:

---

[5] José Casanova, *Public Religions in the Modern World* (Chicago: University of Chicago Press, 1994).

[6] Ibid., 62.

[7] See Samuel P. Huntington, *The Third Wave: Democratization in the Late Twentieth Century* (Norman, OK: University of Oklahoma Press, 1991).

The fact is that religious actors from the Catholic tradition accounted for an overwhelming proportion of religious activism on behalf of democracy between 1972 and 2009. In three-quarters of the cases where religious actors played a role in democratization—36 of 48 countries—at least one of the prodemocratic religious actors was Catholic. In 18 of 48 cases, the *only* religious actors that played a leading or supporting democratizing role were Catholic actors.[8]

Admittedly of course, the social engagement of religious actors, including Catholic organizations, is not always constructive. Not all Christian social movements have benevolent or charitable intentions. Moreover, the paths paved by even the best of intentions, as the old adage reminds us, do not always lead to positive outcomes.

In *The Ambivalence of the Sacred*, R. Scott Appleby critically explores the varied ways in which religions and religious believers seek to understand and respond to the sacred. Employing vivid examples from several religious traditions, Appleby illustrates how people's response to the sacred in the world is neither inherently destructive nor purely constructive. Rather, religion has the potential to move people and communities to engage in both social transformation and social destruction.[9]

Facilitating Social Action

Finally, Christian social movements are transforming globalization through direct collective action. Consider the many ways in which Christian social movements are active agents within civil society. For example, I have recently been working with several vowed women religious involved in the campaign to end contemporary forms of human slavery or human trafficking. I have been deeply moved by their many different prophetic and effective actions to address this evil. For years, these women, many of whom are senior citizens, have been devoting their time to this cause by praying for social change,

---

[8] Monica Duffy Toft, Daniel Philpott, and Timothy Samuel Shah, *God's Century: Resurgent Religion and Global Politics* (New York: W. W. Norton and Company, 2011), 101.

[9] R. Scott Appleby, *The Ambivalence of the Sacred: Religion, Violence, and Reconciliation* (Lanham, MD: Rowman and Littlefield, 2000).

educating the public about the issues surrounding human slavery, leveraging their investments in large multinational corporations to address the issues of forced labor in the global supply chain, and by lobbying congress and the United Nations for sensible laws to address the problem. Perhaps most powerful, since it involves risk to their own safety, they also directly challenge contemporary slave masters by setting up shelters and safe houses for women and girls who have been in situations of slavery.

In her comparative study of Catholic social engagement in the United States, Kristin Heyer highlights two distinct approaches or styles of Christian collective action, each with its own interpretations of the role of the church, church communities, and government structures.[10] One approach, the "public style," is deeply inspired by Catholic social teaching and perceives the church as having a responsibility to engage actively in academic discourse, governments, and the structures of civil society. Often this approach seeks long-term goals by working within existing social structures. The work of women religious in lobbying a UN meeting for a resolution to support women as they leave situations of slavery illustrates this public style.

In contrast to the public style, Christian movements also employ more radical approaches to social action. Drawing heavily from the biblical tradition, the "prophetic style" of Christian action in its attempt to witness to the gospel seeks to avoid being coopted by the dominant structures of society. This approach is less optimistic about the possibility of transforming the world through existing structures. Rather than directly engaging governments and civil society through direct lobbying (for example, status with the United Nations), this model is often involved in direct service to the poor, radical witness, civil disobedience, and symbolic actions to raise attention to injustice and suffering. In the United States the Catholic Worker movement is a prime example of this approach. Unlike the movements with a more public style, those in the prophetic tradition generally avoid the creation of robust movement organizations.

Occasionally, some Christian social movements will employ both styles in their social actions. In addition to lobbying congress or the

---

[10] Kristin E. Heyer, *Prophetic and Public: The Social Witness of US Catholicism*, Moral Traditions Series (Washington, DC: Georgetown University Press, 2006).

United Nations, for example, women religious involved in movements to end human slavery also adopt a more prophetic approach
by taking to the streets in protest or by undertaking high-risk actions
to save human lives.

Despite their differences, movements of both "prophetic" and
"public" styles are involved in transforming society through direct
action that challenges a second major legacy of Westphalia, the
principle of absolute state sovereignty. The idea of the state as a
sovereign entity emerged fairly recently with the work of the French
political philosopher Jean Bodin (1576) and was later formalized in
the Peace of Westphalia.[11] This model envisions a world composed of
primarily independent sovereign states, which alone possess authority
over political questions. Borders clearly delineate who is in and who
is out. It is the purview of the state, then, to control borders, wage
war, regulate the economy, and make the major decisions regarding
public life.

Until recently, when considering international social and political
questions, the focus of both scholars and political leaders has centered largely on the role of the state and the more than 230 intergovernmental organizations sponsored and directed by states.[12] Even
the most active and inclusive of these, however, such as the United
Nations, are founded on the basic principle that member states are
the primary sovereign entity in the world. Little can be done without
their direction and approval.

Within the context of globalization this model of a world stage
consisting primarily of sovereign states is challenged both positively
and negatively by a wide array of non-state actors. Along with other
civil society groups, Christian social movements challenge concep-
tions of absolute state sovereignty and the unregulated free market
through both public and prophetic actions.

---

[11] See Jean Bodin, *Les Six Livres de la République* (Aalen, France: Scientia, 1961).

[12] According to Margaret Karns and Karen Mingst, an intergovernmental organization is any organization "whose members include at least three states, that
have activities in several states, and whose members are held together by a formal
intergovernmental agreement. These organizations range in size from three members
(North American Free Trade Agreement) to more than 190 members (Universal
Postal Union)." Margaret P. Karns and Karen A. Mingst, *International Organizations: The Politics and Processes of Global Governance* (Boulder, CO: Lynne Rienner
Publishers, 2004), 7.

Movements with a more prophetic style often directly confront the state. For these movements, working within the system is not enough to enact the change needed. Instead, they have been moved prophetically to take to the streets or engage in acts of civil disobedience to call for social reform. Peace vigils, boycotts, and civil disobedience are frequently planned to witness against sinful state-supported polices and practices. Consider the anti–School of the Americas movement that has organized annual protests against the US Army training facility at Ft. Benning, Georgia, for over twenty years. More than three hundred people have been arrested and sentenced for acts of civil disobedience and radical witness during these protests.

Movements that adopt a more public style of collective action challenge the power and the role of the state through other methods, including educational projects that seek to empower and raise awareness among citizens and consumers (for example, voter guides, study sessions, and fair trade) and advocacy efforts for changes in specific policy issues (such as lobbying, petitions, and mobilizing shareholders).

Internationally, the UN system offers an important space for Christian social action, with many social movements lobbying and holding governments to account in their role as nongovernmental organizations. In the meetings that drafted the United Nations Charter, several NGOs, including a number of Christian and Jewish organizations, successfully lobbied for a provision (Article 71) that created a consultative status for NGOs within the UN Economic and Social Council (ECOSOC). This status enables accredited organizations, within certain parameters, to observe meetings alongside governmental delegations and present oral and written interventions on agenda items.

Since the 1990s the participation of NGOs in the intergovernmental system has increased significantly. NGOs, including many Christian groups, dynamically engaged the major UN conferences of the 1990s and 2000s on issues ranging from the environment and women to technology and small arms. Although sovereign states remain the lead agents in the UN system, NGOs have become an integral part of nearly every UN process today.[13]

[13] See Thomas G. Weiss and Leon Gordenker, "Pluralizing Global Governance: Analytical Approaches and Dimensions," in NGOs, the UN, and Global Gover-

The public actions of Christian social movements in holding governments and corporations to account is perhaps most dramatically illustrated by their human rights advocacy. In their activities at the United Nations and in the streets around the world, communities of Christians are speaking out in defense of human dignity. They are "naming and shaming" governments in the official sessions of the UN Human Rights Council. They are raising awareness about violations and urgent problems taking place in different parts of the world. They are helping to propose changes to international human rights law. And they are working to support and develop structures to monitor and enforce international ethical agreements.

One of the primary aspects of advocacy is to bring the concerns and experiences of underrepresented groups to national and global attention. Often this involves bringing actual victims of abuse to speak on their own to positions of power. This has proven to be important especially when individual states involved fail to respond to the needs of their citizens. Margaret Keck and Kathryn Sikkink describe this as the "boomerang pattern of influence" whereby organizations with local ties "bypass their state and directly search out international allies to try to bring pressure on their states from the outside."[14]

At times, however, Christian social movements, such as the Plowshares movement or the movement to close down the School of the Americas, have found that working only within the system is not enough to enact the change needed.[15] Instead, they have been moved to prophetically take to the streets or engage in acts of public civil disobedience to call for social reform.

From empowering rural women to changing the language in a human rights treaty, Christian social movements are actively engaged in shaping the world in which we live. Taken as a whole, these groups represent a significant source of social capital that can be more effectively applied to address some of the major challenges facing humanity today.

---

nance, ed. Thomas G. Weiss and Leon Gordenker, Emerging Global Issues Series (Boulder, CO: Lynne Rienner Publishers, 1996), 18.

[14] Margaret E. Keck and Kathryn Sikkink, *Activists beyond Borders: Advocacy Networks in International Politics* (Ithaca, NY: Cornell University Press, 1998), 12.

[15] James Hodge and Linda Cooper, *Disturbing the Peace: The Story of Father Roy Bourgeois and the Movement to Close the School of the Americas* (Maryknoll, NY: Orbis Books, 2004).

MEDIATING THE GLOBAL COMMON GOOD

What gives Christian social movements their transformative potential? Perhaps the answer lies in the four ways in which they mediate for the global common good. The following graphic may help illustrate this role. First, social movements mediate between people and communities (line 1). Participating in a social movement connects people and local communities across borders and cultures to other people and communities in profound ways. Social movements have the capacity to engender both global solidarity and intercultural dialogue as people connect with one another in shared affinity groups. For instance, in the face of a disaster or conflict on the other side of the planet, it can make a difference if you know that there are other members of your ecclesial movement there. When the recent pro-democracy protest movement took to the streets in Ukraine, I could directly connect with people in that city, even people directly engaged in the protests. My contacts through a global Christian movement helped me to understand the events in ways that went far beyond what the local media was reporting.

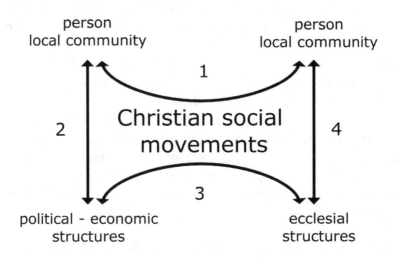

Figure 1–1. Four ways Christian social movements mediate for the global common good.

Second, as nongovernmental actors, Christian social movements operate in intermediary positions between persons and political and economic power structures (line 2). For example, hundreds of Christian social movements are involved in advocacy work with the UN system, sometime through a formalized NGO consultative status. As president and representative of IMCS, I attended several UN meetings at which I helped to share the experiences of our student members on the ground in global deliberations on youth policy, education, development, and human rights. Many Christian social movements are also demanding changes from transnational corporations by seeking to leverage their collective power as investors (for example, corporate social responsibility, divestment strategies) and consumers (for example, fair trade, boycotts).

In this mediating position social movements and social movement organizations empower local people and communities while also working to transform those political and economic structures often seen as beyond the reach of individuals alone. Drawing partly on the work of Peter Berger and Richard John Neuhaus on this point, David Hollenbach, SJ, writes:

> Movements, therefore, empower people. They mediate between individuals and large social structures, giving the individuals who work together in the movement greater power to bring about social change than they could have alone. Different movements can empower individuals in different domains of social interaction depending on the type of movement. They can play this mediating role in local, national, and even international settings.[16]

Christian social movements also operate in a similar way within the church (line 3). As intermediary agents they mediate between local believers and those in official ecclesial positions. This is particularly important in churches, like Roman Catholicism, with robust

---

[16] David Hollenbach, "Sustaining Catholic Social Engagement: A Key Role for Movements in the Church Today," ed. Cheryl Handel and Kathleen Shields, *Journal of Catholic Social Thought* 10, no. 2 (2013): 434. See also Peter L. Berger and Richard John Neuhaus, *To Empower People: The Role of Mediating Structures in Public Policy*, Studies in Political and Social Processes 139 (Washington, DC: American Enterprise Institute for Public Policy Research, 1977).

institutional structures. Global ecclesial structures, such as the Pontifical Council for Justice and Peace or the Assembly of the World Council of Churches can appear as impersonal and detached from the local reality of believers. Movements within the church can go a long way in helping to bridge those gaps.

Finally, Christian social movements mediate between economic and political structures and religious institutions (line 4). For example, those movements that have formal status with the United Nations frequently communicate the concerns of the church to the intergovernmental institutions and the issues on the international agenda with the church. Movements, in other words, bridge between faith and politics or church and state.

MEDIEVAL CHRISTIAN PEACE MOVEMENTS

Christian social movements are not a new element in the church. The medieval period, for example, saw the creation of many innovative movements, including the movements of Benedictine monasticism; the military and hospitaller orders created to care for the wounded, imprisoned, and sick; the Franciscans, Dominicans, and other mendicant movements; and the movements of ecclesial reform that eventually sparked the Reformation. Among the lesser-known movements in Medieval Christendom are a number of peace movements.

Contrary to popular imagination, the European Middle Ages was not defined only by war, conflict, and the brutality of the Crusades. In the face of violence among conflicting feudal knights, lords, and kings, Christians formed movements to limit conflict, curtail the violence of battle, and create peace. In his study on the Catholic peace tradition, Ronald Musto highlights the actions of some of these organized Christian efforts to transform the social context. Initially linked to popular millennialism in the ninth and tenth centuries, large groups of people, often peasants, called for efforts to limit war with decrees and oaths. Responding to the private wars among feudal lords in the tenth century, religious leaders sought to counteract the devastating realties of war by establishing limits on protected peoples (for example, monks, cloistered religious, women, clerics, the poor), places (for example, monasteries, churches) and times (for example, Sundays, Holy Days, Lent). Such regulations, if followed, would restrict fighting to only a few days throughout the year.

The agreements were decreed at councils called for by local church leaders who would invite all the people, especially the nobility, to attend. Relics of saints were used to convene people into mass rallies demanding an end to feudal warfare. According to Musto, more people were involved in these movements than those involved in the military campaigns of the Crusades: "Peace demonstrators at the Plain of the Pasquara on one day (August 1233) reportedly totaled 400,000. . . . A penitential army estimated at 200,000 thronged Rome. . . . The councils of the Peace of God, which convened every year throughout Europe, attracted thousands of laypersons to each meeting."[17]

CHRISTIAN SOCIAL TEACHING FROM BELOW

Given their intermediary role between individual believers and ecclesial officials, Christian social movements help to translate between official church teaching on social issues and the experiences of people dealing with those issues on a daily basis. In this way they aid in both the reception and the development of official Christian social teaching.

On the one hand, these organizations play an important role in sharing the rich tradition of Christian reflection and analysis on social issues. Perhaps more so than the weekly worship service or catechetical classroom, Christian social movements are well suited to form and educate people about Christian ethical teaching and to offer people opportunities to get involved in acting for justice. For many, it is only through socially engaged communities that they hear about official church statements on labor, human rights, war, and other social issues. The *Compendium of the Social Doctrine of the Church* explicitly recognizes this:

> The Church's social doctrine must become an integral part of the ongoing formation of the lay faithful. Experience shows that this formative work is usually possible within lay ecclesial associations. . . . The various specialized associations that gather people together in the name of their Christian vocation and mission within a particular professional or cultural field have a precious role to play in forming mature Christians.[18]

---

[17] Ronald G. Musto, *The Catholic Peace Tradition* (Maryknoll, NY: Orbis Books, 1986), 87.

[18] Pontificium Consilium de Iustitia et Pace, *Compendium of the Social Doctrine of the Church* (Washington, DC: United States Conference of Catholic Bishops, 2004), nos. 549–50.

On the other hand, Christian social movements are actively involved in shaping the content of the church's official social teaching—though this role is almost never explicitly recognized. With their intimate connection to the social reality, Christian social movements are well placed to help develop and refine the church's response to social realties. Commenting on this, David Hollenbach describes such groups as "innovators" that "seek to create responses that are not presently happening and are perhaps not yet envisioned as necessary by higher church leadership."[19]

In other words, in their application of Christian moral principles to lived realities, Christian social movements are often laboratories for Christian ethical thinking. At times, their analysis of a social reality in light of the Christian tradition will provide feedback to ecclesial officials and help to shape subsequent official ecclesial teaching. In fact, virtually all statements from Christian churches over the past fifty years reflect in some way—even if this is not explicitly noted—the innovative ideas of Christian social movements on the ground. Gordon Zahn describes this dynamic as "Catholic social thought from below." This does not mean, of course, as Zahn points out, "that such organizations or their efforts have always been welcomed or even approved by the institutional church and its leadership."[20] In fact, many of the groups whose efforts would later shape official teaching were once mistrusted by church officials.

Nevertheless, it is possible to discern a dialectical relationship between the innovative work of Christian movements and the official positions of the church. While this is true in most churches, the following examples from Catholic social teaching highlight this role:

- Birth of modern Catholic social teaching: *Rerum Novarum* (1891), the groundbreaking encyclical of Pope Leo XIII's reflects many of the experimental initiatives by nineteenth century social Catholicism.
- The method of Catholic social teaching: Blessed John XXIII's encyclical *Mater et Magistra* (1961) lays out a specific method of Catholic social teaching in encouraging people to observe,

---

[19] Hollenbach, "Sustaining Catholic Social Engagement," 443.
[20] Gordon C. Zahn, "Social Movements and Catholic Social Thought," in *One Hundred Years of Catholic Social Thought: Celebration and Challenge*, ed. John A. Coleman (Maryknoll, NY: Orbis Books, 1991), 52.

judge, and act (MM, no. 236). The use of this method was developed decades earlier by the movement of the Young Christian Workers and their chaplain, Joseph Cardjin.

- Liberation theology: The emergence of what would later be known as liberation theology originated largely with social movements of the church in Latin America. While it was heavily critiqued by John Paul II, several key themes were later employed by the pope in *Sollicitudo Rei Socialis* (1987) and subsequent papal teaching.
- Economy of communion: Pope Benedict XVI included insights on the economy of communion as articulated by the Focolare movement in the 2009 encyclical *Caritas in Veritate* (CV, no. 46).

Whether or not this dialectical relationship between teaching and action can effectively take shape in ecclesial contexts with strong hierarchical arrangements is less clear, as Ellen Van Stichel has recently pointed out:

As with every hierarchical institution, however—certainly with one the global size of the Church—it is not unthinkable that the Church overlooks local developments and insights stemming from its practical wisdom. In such cases, the question is not so much what the official teachings add but rather what ideas and reflections they lose sight of and consequently delete from the Catholic social thought from below.[21]

Despite the tendency for official Catholic teaching to ignore or reject the reflections and experiences on the ground, Christian social movements are still shaping the official positions of their churches, even if only in subtle and limited ways. Thus, the influence of socially committed groups of Christians on global institutions is not limited to political and civil society. Christian social movements are also shaping the internal life of the church. But what exactly constitutes a Christian social movement, and how can they be more effective in positive social change?

[21] Ellen Van Stichel, "Movements Struggling for Justice within the Church: A Theological Response to John Coleman's Sociological Approach," ed. Cheryl Handel and Kathleen Shields, *Journal of Catholic Social Thought* 10, no. 2 (2013): 291.

CHRISTIAN SOCIAL MOVEMENTS:
IN SEARCH OF A DEFINITION

A clear-cut definition of such a heterogeneous set of actors is not easy to articulate. The wide range of styles, scopes, sizes, and missions makes it difficult, if not impossible, to construct a neat box that can comfortably hold all Christian social movements, especially when it is not a label that most groups self-consciously articulate. Moreover, given the wide range of social and political concerns, it is not uncommon to find specific Christian social movements sharing more in common with non-Christian partners than with other groups from the same faith tradition. Nevertheless, these organizations generally do possess common threads in their missions and how they function. The categorization itself provides three defining characteristics, which help to set the stage for the following chapters.

Christian

A first characteristic concerns Christian identity. Although some groups, such as Church Women United and Church World Service, are ecumenical and draw members from different Christian denominations and churches, many groups, such as Pax Christi International or United Methodist Women, are constituted primarily by members from one denomination or church. At the same time, there are other groups and movements that were founded as Christian movements and/or were deeply inspired by Christian principles, such as the Fellowship of Reconciliation, ATD Fourth World, and Emmaus movement, but have grown to identify themselves as interfaith or nonsectarian. Whether these groups ought to be defined as Christian today is debatable, and one may defer to their own self-understanding.

To be clear, Christian identity does not—and should not—limit the concerns of Christian social movements to intra-ecclesial issues and only the needs of other Christians. For most major Christian organizations involved in direct service to others, including those with a very explicit Christian mission or focused membership, the faith identity of those in need does not have an impact on the services provided. For example, Catholic Relief Services, while explicitly a Roman Catholic agency, does not limit itself only to Catholic staff members or to serving the needs of people who are Christian.

A separate but related question concerns official recognition. More than any other church or denomination, the Roman Catholic tradition expects communities and movement organizations to obtain recognition from formal ecclesial structures. For instance, within its Code of Canon Law, there are certain requirements for associations and institutions that want to identify themselves as Catholic. The Code, revised in 1983, details requirements for a number of types of groups within the church, including institutes of consecrated life, societies of apostolic life, public and private associations of the faithful, and other juridical persons established by church authorities.[22]

At the international level different pontifical dicasteries have specific competencies for recognizing different types of groups. The Congregation for Institutes of Consecrated Life and for Societies of Apostolic Life, for instance, has competency over movements and organizations of vowed. The Pontifical Council for the Laity, by contrast, is responsible for international associations of the faithful. These lines of division are then continued at the national and diocesan levels. Not all movements, however, fit into the neat boxes outlined in Canon Law, as Jean-Paul Durand, OP, and Brendan Leahy note.[23]

Some lay movements, such as Focolare or Communauté Emmanuel, have sparked the creation of societies for their own priests. Others have led to the creation of institutions of vowed religious or a quasi-religious community of consecrated laity. The relationship between non-lay members and lay members is further complicated because, at least according to the Catholic Church, lay people cannot be superiors of ordained men or vowed religious.

Conversely, many movements of vowed religious have sparked the creation of lay associations and/or other institutes of vowed religious. The Vincentian movement, for instance, began with St. Vincent de Paul (1581–1660) founding the Ladies of Charity in 1617 for lay women, the Congregation of the Mission in 1625 for vowed priests

---

[22] Code of Canon Law (Vatican City: Libreria Editrice Vaticana, 1983), nos. 298–329 and 113–23.

[23] Jean-Paul Durand, "Catholic Movements and Communities of the Faithful Which Arose in the Twentieth Century: Some Challenges to Canon Law," in "Movements" in the Church, ed. Alberto Melloni, Concilium 2003/3 (London: SCM, 2003), 94–105; Brendan Leahy, Ecclesial Movements and Communities: Origins, Significance, and Issues (Hyde Park, NY: New City Press, 2011), chap. 17.

and brothers, and the Daughters of Charity in 1633 for vowed women. This inspired other international movement organizations, including the Sisters of Charity in 1809, the Society of St. Vincent de Paul in 1833, and most recently the Lay Vincentian Missionaries in 1999—not to mention a multitude of schools, hospitals, and other charitable organizations. There are even Vincentian associations of religious women and men in the Anglican Communion. The relationship between all these movement organizations must be frustrating to anyone who perceives the church through clearly defined canonical and denominational categories.

In cases where there are multiple movement structures it is also not uncommon to find different understandings of how each entity relates to the movement mission and Christian identity. Despite these regulations, however, not all self-identified Catholic groups seek formal recognition, and there are some, such as the St. Joan's International Alliance and the International Young Christian Workers, that have lost official recognition. The issue of recognition highlights challenges faced by Christian social movements as they seek to reconcile the sometimes conflicting demands of their members, donors, church officials, and the people they serve. The case studies and theological analysis in the following chapters will illuminate some of these issues.

Social

Second, Christian social movements, for the purposes of this study, are those groups concerned with questions that have relevance beyond what is often considered the strictly religious sphere. While all groups and collectives that exist are at some level social, some faith-based groups appear to shirk their obligations to society. Despite the social demands intrinsic to the Christian faith, not all Christian movements and groups are concerned with social issues, even indirectly. But what constitutes a social concern? A clear delineation of what groups maintain or fail to maintain a social focus is nearly impossible. Should an international community of cloistered nuns whose members regularly pray for those who are poor, for instance, be considered a social movement? What about an organization that exists only to promote the reading of the Bible or a specific devotion to Mary devoid of any social concern?

At a very basic level it is possible to identify ecclesial movements and groups whose mission *directly* includes concerns relating to the wider society including, but not limited to, social justice, peace, human rights, the needs of those who are poor, the sick, children, education, and immigrants. Again, while social concerns ought to factor in some way into the mission of every Christian community by virtue of the gospel demands, they need not be an explicit concern for all groups. In other words, one can still maintain the intrinsic value of social justice to the Christian faith without reducing everything in the church to social concerns. In the Pauline tradition the body of Christ includes many interrelated, yet distinct gifts, offices, and roles that are necessary for the building up of the common good.

Nevertheless, balancing between the social and spiritual demands of the gospel and Christian faith is not always easy even for the most experienced Christian community. Pope John Paul II, among others, frequently warned about the dangers of what he called horizontalism, or the reduction of the Christian mission to only its social dimensions. His concern is not without merit as the following chapters will show. Some Christian social movements and institutions have, in effect, de-Christianized and lost their connection to the faith tradition that inspired their creation. At the same time, I argue, there is also a risk of an opposing verticalism, which reduces the Christian mission to only its spiritual dimensions. A more robust theological and ethical analysis, as developed in the following chapters, can help Christian organizations strike a balance between the horizontal and vertical dimensions of Christian faith.

Movement

The term *movement*, according to Alberto Melloni, originated in the seventeenth century "to indicate a collective social agitation."[24] While not new, the phenomenon of people from the grassroots joining together for collective social action "underwent a qualitative transformation" in European modernity with the rise of the nation state, capitalism, and the urban working class.[25] The role of social

---

[24] Melloni, *"Movements" in the Church*, 9.

[25] Steven M. Buechler, *Social Movements in Advanced Capitalism: The Political Economy and Cultural Construction of Social Activism* (New York: Oxford University Press, 2000), 5.

movements in the anti-establishment revolutions of the early modern period deeply shaped the way the social movement theorists first described the phenomenon.[26] Since religion in the modern period was largely perceived as being linked to the conservative power structures, religious social movements received little scholarly attention until recently.

The category of social movement, however, can be very useful to understand the significance—even the theological significance—of religious organizations. For example, writing from their respective disciplines of theology and sociology, both Sandra Schneiders and Patricia Wittberg apply social movement theory to movements of vowed religious life. Approaching religious life with this lens, they argue, can help to put the phenomenon into a broader perspective than by simply addressing questions of structure and canonical status.[27] A social movement theory approach, for example, contextualizes the present reality of Roman Catholic religious orders into a wider historical and sociological pattern of growth, institutionalization, decay, and renewal. It also draws attention to the fact that the movements of religious life are far more dynamic than the institutions and movement organizations they created.

At its most basic level a "social movement is a purposive and collective attempt of a number of people to change individuals or societal institutions and structures."[28] Movements arise when individuals or preexisting groups come together for a common cause.[29] They may

---

[26] See John A. Hannigan, "Social Movement Theory and the Sociology of Religion: Toward a New Synthesis," *Sociological Analysis* 52, no. 4 (Winter 1991): 311–31.

[27] See Patricia Wittberg, *The Rise and Fall of Catholic Religious Orders: A Social Movement Perspective* (Albany: State University of New York Press, 1994); Sandra M. Schneiders, *New Wineskins: Re-Imagining Religious Life Today* (New York: Paulist Press, 1986).

[28] Mayer N. Zald and Roberta Ash, "Social Movement Organizations: Growth, Decay, and Change," *Social Forces* 44, no. 3 (March 1, 1966): 329. See also Jackie Smith, Charles Chatfield, and Ron Pagnucco, "Social Movements and World Politics: A Theoretical Framework," in *Transnational Social Movements and Global Politics: Solidarity beyond the State*, ed. Jackie Smith, Charles Chatfield, and Ron Pagnucco (Syracuse, NY: Syracuse University Press, 1997), 59–80.

[29] Canon Law constructively distinguishes between those actors that bring together individuals directly and those that primarily gather other groups (for example, national affiliates, institutions, other movements) united by a common mission: "They are aggregates of persons (*universitates personarum*) or of things (*universitates rerum*) ordered for a purpose which is in keeping with the mission of

coalesce around charismatic individuals or arise organically among people and groups in different contexts. They can be well funded and highly organized or less structured informal networks aimed at social change. They can be focused on one specific issue or have a broad social agenda. Generally, movements allow for "*degrees of participation,*" as members with varying levels of dedication and commitment to the cause surround a core group of militants.[30] In some cases, such as movements of religious life, members of this core group dedicate their entire lives to the cause of the movement.

To achieve their ends social movements often, but not always, create one or more social movement organizations. Christian social movement organizations take on different forms, including specific institutions, charities, NGOs, congregations, and societies. Social movement organizations emerging within a religious context are often called faith-based organizations. These movement organizations, in turn, may create umbrella organizations to link other groups with similar goals at local, national, or global levels in associations, federations, networks, or coalitions (for example, the Association of Catholic Colleges and Universities).[31] If there are multiple organizations created by the same social movement, they may create a movement-specific umbrella organization. For example, high schools in the United States established by the Jesuits form part of the Jesuit Secondary Education Association. For some Christian social movements there are complex layers of organizational life. Members of the Society of St. Vincent de Paul primarily participate in the movement at the local level through local conferences, which often are expressed in social and charitable organizations. These conferences are the basis of a layered structure comprising district councils, diocesan councils, national councils, and an international council.

Not all Christian social movements, as the case study of Plowshares illustrates, value centralized, organized structures. Some, in fact, reject the creation of any robust structure. While many do,

---

the Church and which transcends the purpose of the individuals." Code of Canon Law, no. 114 §1.

[30] Schneiders, *New Wineskins*, 29.

[31] Patricia Wittberg, "Faith-Based Umbrella Organizations: Implications for Religious Identity," *Nonprofit and Voluntary Sector Quarterly* 42, no. 3 (June 2013): 540–62.

movements need not create a formal organization to mobilize people or work for social change.

Implicit in the very concept of a Christian social movement and movement organization is that they are non-magisterial (not the official structure of their church), nongovernmental, and nonprofit. Social movements, like many NGOs, are defined partly by their independence from partisan, political, and economic forces. Those that get too close to governments or the corporate sector—pejoratively termed GONGOs (government-organized NGOs) and BINGOs (business-friendly international NGOs)—are largely perceived as illegitimate.

Given the broad and flexible understanding of movements used here, is there a better way to categorize the many types of Christian social movements? At a recent conference in Belgium, Johan Verstraeten put forth a fivefold typology of Catholic social movements: (1) "classical international Catholic movements," including the Young Christian Workers and those groups related to Catholic action and the church's justice and peace and charitable arms; (2) movements related to religious orders and congregations from the Franciscans to the Jesuits; (3) the new ecclesial movements that gained favor in the 1980s and 1990s; (4) radical Christian groups that have been linked with revolutionary movements; and (5) non-Christian movements in which Christians play an important role.[32]

In this study I focus on three examples of Christian social movements. One grouping that is well known, particularly in the Catholic tradition, comprises those movements of vowed religious that have formed around a specific spirituality or charism. These are most commonly expressed with the institutes of consecrated or religious life under their different forms, including congregations, societies, and orders. Though the vowed and ordained members make up the core of many of these movements, there are growing associations of lay people who seek to participate in the life of these efforts as collaborators in specific ministries or as members of groups of "associates" or "affiliates." These collectives have created many social movement organizations, including hospitals, schools, universities,

---

[32] Johan Verstraeten, "Catholic Social Thought and the Movements: Towards Social Discernment and a Transformative Presence in the World," ed. Cheryl Handel and Kathleen Shields, *Journal of Catholic Social Thought* 10, no. 2 (2013): 233–35.

research centers, and NGOs around the world. Chapter 2 looks at one of these movement organizations, Jesuit Refugee Service.

Lay movements of different kinds can be found in many Christian churches and across churches. A major category of lay social movements includes what Verstraeten describes as "classical international Catholic movements." These movements often form as a result of common social concerns or a desire for solidarity and mutual support for people among a specific milieu. They include movements based on age (for example, youth, adult, children), profession (for example, doctors, workers, farmers), and gender (for example, women's groups). One of the most classic movements of this category is the Young Christian Worker movement, which is examined in Chapter 3.

Not all movements, however, are as structured as religious congregations and the classical international lay movements. Some Christian social movements, such as the Plowshares movement, addressed in Chapter 4, have avoided any formalized structure.

A CHURCH IN TRANSITION

As with the Christian church as a whole, Christian social movements are experiencing several profound changes precipitated by a number of ecclesial, social, and demographic shifts. These dynamics present both new opportunities and pressures for Christian communities around the world. Consider, for instance, the major changes resulting from a decreasing number of vowed religious, particularly in North America and Western Europe.

By virtue of their commitments and communities, socially active religious women, brothers, and priests have been the backbone of countless social action movements and apostolates. Whole systems of education, healthcare, and charitable works depended upon the cheap labor, flexibility, experience, and leadership offered by vowed religious. As members of broader social movements they bring invaluable skills, networks, and financial assets that support social change.

Since the 1960s social institutions sponsored by religious congregations have continued to develop despite the decreasing numbers of vowed religious in certain areas. New "lay boards" created to manage different institutions sponsored by vowed religious communities and lay people, groups of lay affiliates, and associates have taken root, and lay people, including many non-Christians, have taken leadership roles in social movements connected with religious communities.[33]

While lay people have certainly risen to the occasion to fill the positions left by religious, these changes in personnel raise new questions. For instance, how should a group that identifies with a religious institution maintain that identity as the number of vowed religious in leadership decreases? How should different institutions (for example, hospitals, schools) sponsored by the same religious community relate to one another? For other efforts at social change, there is also the practical question of finding the funds necessary to hire professional lay staff members. Developing a deeper theological and ethical framework to understand the role of identity and mission within movement organizations, as this book aims to do, ought to help in managing the shift from religious to lay leadership in Christian social movements.

Perhaps the most powerful changes taking place in Christianity, however, are the massive demographic shifts that are taking place in the church. Christianity is growing in Africa, Asia, and Latin America at unprecedented rates. This is the most sweeping demographic shift that the Christian church has experienced in its two-thousand-year history. Writing shortly after the Second Vatican Council, Jesuit theologian Karl Rahner described the shift of the church away from Europe as the dawn of a third period in Christianity, a period he called the world church. Even Rahner could not have imagined the profound transformations and rate of change that are taking place at the present. It could be argued that with the election of Pope Francis, the first non-European pope for hundreds of years, and with the demographic shifts taking place, we are now in a fourth period of Christianity, which might be called the global church.

In *The Future Church* John Allen explores some of these dramatic demographic changes and their implications for Christianity and Catholicism in particular. While the majority of Catholics in 1900 were in Europe or North America, by 2025 it is projected that "only one Catholic in five will be a non-Hispanic Caucasian."[34] At the same

---

[33] Doris Gottemoeller, "History of Catholic Institutions in the United States," *New Theology Review* 14, no. 2 (2001): 16–27.

[34] John L. Allen, *The Future Church: How Ten Trends Are Revolutionizing the Catholic Church* (New York: Doubleday, 2009), 17.

time, the Christian church in Europe and North America is becoming increasingly diverse. Migrants are offering new sources of energy for Christian communities, and it is estimated that many churches in the United States will be predominantly of non-European descent in the coming decades.

These changes will have a tremendous impact on the social engagement of the Christian churches. How the global church will navigate these dynamics is unclear. What is certain, however, is that Christian social movements will be affected by these changes. For some groups these changes will be difficult. Some movements will not be able to respond fully to the new reality. Some are likely to disappear completely, while others will drift away from their Christian identity. These changes will be especially difficult for existing movements with long-established structures and traditions.

For example, when I was elected president of IMCS, I was the first American in many decades to hold that post. Our lay movement was one of the first international structures within Catholicism to have non-European presidents, even before the Second World War. My immediate predecessors were from Indonesia and Madagascar, and my successors came from India and South Sudan. I was on a team with a South African priest and another lay team member from Cameroon. Many, however, assumed that because our movement was based in France, that we must be a European movement with access to many resources. Actually, our European and North American movements were generally weak and disengaged, while our African, Asian, and Latin American members were quite engaged and our global directives and internal resources came largely from our non-European members. Unfortunately, this made relying only on membership dues from our members in the so-called global South, who were young students, very difficult.

Although change is seldom easy, the shifting dynamics are also bringing new life and new opportunities to the world of Christian social movements. New social movements and initiatives are taking root from the global South. At the same time the leadership structures of many, but not all, established movements are becoming increasingly diverse. The global ecclesial conversation will become more profound as the leaders of Christian movements reflect the actual composition of the global church, the people of God in the world.

Being church in global age is not easy. Like the church as a whole, Christian social movements must find ways to navigate a wide range of issues concerning identity, mission, and organization. In the coming years these questions will likely become more important and will demand greater discernment if we are to find a way to overcome the globalization of indifference.

LOOKING AHEAD

This chapter has sought to establish a framework to better appreciate the transformative role of Christian social movements and organizations. Four initial conclusions emerge that set the stage for the following chapters. First, *while imperfect and wide ranging in their actions, Christian social movements have tremendous potential to be sources of grace in a world of suffering and indifference.* At their best they are reshaping globalization with the gospel values of love and justice. At the same time they are transforming the social consciousness of the institutional church.

Second, *the potential of Christian social movements stems primarily from their intermediary role within the church, within society, and the ways in which they mediate between the two.* Their nonofficial and nongovernmental role gives them an organizational flexibility that is needed for the global age. As organized collectives distinct from the institutional structures of the church, Christian social movements are more free to play the role of innovators, laboratories, and prophetic voices within the church.

Third, *despite their transformative presence in the world and the church, Christian social movements remain underappreciated in many circles.* The nearly exclusive attention to "hard power" in both global politics and the church leads many, including some inside the movements themselves, to overlook their role. A deeper theological analysis is needed to better situate these ecclesial groups. Finding ways to speak of their role theologically can help overcome what Ronald Musto describes as a "moral amnesia" surrounding the contribution of communities within the church.[35]

Fourth, *the present global and ecclesial context in which movements operate is rapidly changing.* These changes are raising new

---

[35] Musto, *The Catholic Peace Tradition*, 1.

issues for movements, particularly around questions of identity, mission, and organization. A theological framework of "structural grace," as developed in subsequent chapters, I hope, can help movements address these and other questions.

But first, what are some examples of dynamic Christian social movements at work in the church and in the world today? How do these questions of identity, mission, and organization surface in specific case studies? The next chapter begins by examining the Jesuit Refugee Service, a humanitarian organization sponsored by one of the largest Christian social movements in the world today.

Chapter 2

Jesuit Refugee Service

A Movement at the Margins

It is important for the whole Church that welcoming the poor and promoting justice not be entrusted solely to "experts" but be a focus of all pastoral care, of the formation of future priests and religious, and of the ordinary work of all parishes, movements and ecclesial groups. In particular—this is important and I say it from my heart—I would also like to ask religious institutes to interpret seriously and with responsibility this sign of the times.

—POPE FRANCIS,
ADDRESS TO THE JESUIT REFUGEE SERVICE IN ROME

In 2011, Moshen and Aneesa, a young professional couple living near the Syrian capital of Damascus, announced their engagement. Rather than being one of the happiest times of their lives, their road to marriage was one of the most difficult. Within a few months the young couple's hopes and excitement about the future turned into despair, fear, and separation because of the Syrian Civil War.

An office manager with a degree in accounting, Moshen had taken to the streets in peaceful demonstrations against the Syrian regime. He, like so many others, was hopeful that positive change was on

This chapter is adapted in part from a chapter that appeared in Kevin Ahern, "Structures of Grace: Catholic Nongovernmental Organizations and the Mission of the Church," PhD thesis, Boston College, 2013.

the horizon. When the conflict began in March 2011, Moshen knew his life was in danger.

Like so many other Syrians, Moshen had few options. If he stayed, he risked interrogation, imprisonment, and possibly death at the hands of the governmental authorities. With no passport and few resources, where would he go? How would he leave? What about his family? What about Aneesa?

In December 2012 a human smuggler led twenty-six-year-old Moshen and other desperate Syrians across the border with Jordan. This was a risky journey. After some time in the overcrowded Zaatari refugee camp, Moshen ended up in Amman under the sponsorship of a Jordanian friend. Thankfully, Aneesa could obtain a passport, and the two were reunited in Jordan, where they married and obtained official status as refugees. Moshen recalls the desperation of the moment:

> It was very tough being away from loved ones. Although I was now with my fiance, my family was still in Damascus; this broke my heart. It was the first time I had left my beloved country. I was afraid of everything. Some people welcomed us; others were indifferent. I felt like a stranger in my land of exile.[1]

The tragic events experienced by Moshen and Aneesa are sadly not uncommon. The Syrian Civil War has created one of the worst humanitarian disasters in human history. Tens of thousands of people, many of them civilians, have been killed, and over nine million people—more than double the population of Ireland—have been compelled to leave their homes in search of security. As with other refugees and internally displaced people in the world, the Syrian experience of forced displacement is marked by a range of human emotions, including loss, fear, hope, hunger, and desperation.[2] How ought Christians respond to the tragedies of war and the drama of forced displacement in our global world?

---

[1] For the story of Moshen and Aneesa (not their real names), see "Jordan: An Arduous and Perilous Journey to Safety," *JRS USA*, October 16, 2013, www.jrsusa. org. The website seeks to give voice to the experiences of refugees.

[2] *Syrian Arab Republic: Humanitarian Bulletin* 45 (United Nations Office for the Coordination of Humanitarian Affairs, 2014), https://syria.humanitarianresponse. info.

Christian social movements and churches have been at the forefront of the humanitarian response to the Syrian catastrophe.[3] Among these, the Jesuit Refugee Service (JRS) is particularly noteworthy. Since the onset of the crisis, JRS teams in Jordan, Lebanon, and Turkey have provided emergency aid to thousands of individuals and families, including Moshen and Aneesa. JRS's existing presence in Syria and Jordan, originally set up to serve Iraqi refugees, enabled it to offer a rapid response to the critical humanitarian, psychosocial, and educational needs of thousands of Syrians.

Founded in 1980 as an official work of the Society of Jesus (Jesuits), JRS has responded to the plight of millions of refugees in some of the most dangerous and desperate places in the world. Inspired and guided by the Ignatian charism and Jesuit mission to serve faith and promote justice, JRS aims to address both the symptoms and root causes of forced displacement.

As the first of three case studies, this chapter highlights the role played by JRS and its mission of accompanying, serving, and defending refugees around the world. The experience of this Jesuit movement organization highlights several questions of ethical and theological import to other Christian social movements and movement organizations engaged in the struggle for social transformation. But first, how did the Jesuits, a Christian movement most known for its work in education, get involved in caring for the needs of refugees?

CONCERN FOR THE MARGINALIZED
AND THE JESUIT MISSION

Concern for human beings at the margins, in particular those displaced from their homes, is not a recent development within the Jesuit movement. Since the foundation of the Society of Jesus in the sixteenth century, Jesuits have understood service to people who are poor as a part of their mission. For example, St. Ignatius of Loyola (1491–1556) and his companions who founded the Society of Jesus

---

[3] See, for example, the official list of partners of the UN's Syria Regional Refugee Response. The list includes several Christian movements, including AVSI, Caritas, Catholic Relief Services, International Catholic Migration Commission, International Orthodox Christian Charities, JRS, Lutheran World Federation, Operation Mercy, Samaritan's Purse, World Vision, and YMCA. "Complete List of Partners," *UNHCR: Syria Regional Refugee Response*, 2014, www.unhcr.org.

organized several impressive social projects early in the movement. These included relief efforts for thousands displaced by a famine in 1537, the creation of the Casa Santa Marta for women seeking to leave prostitution, and service to those in prison.[4]

The whole notion of engaging in service beyond one's local community is intrinsic to the Jesuit mission. It is embodied by the fourth vow of service to the mission of the universal church that many Jesuits take and is clearly evident in the *Spiritual Exercises of St. Ignatius*, the foundational text for all who see themselves in the Ignatian tradition. For those involved in the Jesuit movement, the *Exercises* are not simply a guiding text written by their founder. On the contrary, they frame a journey that Jesuits and close collaborators experience in annual retreats and regular moments of prayer and reflection. As part of the process of living the *Exercises*, one is invited to become more aware of God's gracious actions in one's life. This deeply Ignatian awareness, as Wilkie Au explains, should evoke both gratitude toward God and loving service in the world.[5] Service, in other words, is not something secondary or auxiliary to Ignatian spirituality. Rather, service is "a critical element as one seeks to respond to God's grace."[6] To be a companion of Jesus, to be a Jesuit, one must become a person of service, or what would later be described as being a "man or woman for others."[7]

The Service of Faith and the Promotion of Justice

In the nearly five hundred years since the foundation of the Society, the Jesuit commitment to service has been expressed in a wide range of

---

[4] These early efforts are detailed in John W. O'Malley, *The First Jesuits* (Cambridge, MA: Harvard University Press, 1993).

[5] Wilkie Au, "Ignatian Service, Gratitude and Love in Action," *Studies in the Spirituality of Jesuits* 40, no. 2 (Summer 2008): 14.

[6] Ibid., 10. The awareness of God's gracious actions in the world should evoke both gratitude toward God and loving service in the world. As Au points out, Ignatius's hope was that "people might be filled with gratitude and love for God and moved to express that love in acts of service."

[7] The goal of forming "men for others" was first articulated by Arrupe in 1973; the wording was later expanded to be more inclusive. Pedro Arrupe, "Men for Others," presented at the Tenth International Congress of Jesuit Alumni of Europe, Valencia (Creighton University Online Ministries, 1973), www.creighton.edu.

what one Jesuit describes as "ministries of consolation," in particular education.[8] By the mid-twentieth century the Jesuit mission began to be framed by a strong commitment to social justice—something that would be an important factor in the establishment of JRS. As with other Christian social movements, the Jesuits were deeply shaped by the holistic vision of mission put forth by the Second Vatican Council. The council's call for congregations and societies of vowed religious to engage in their own process of renewal inspired the Jesuits to redefine their mission in the world and to see action for justice as a constitutive element of the Jesuit movement. For the Jesuits, this process began in 1965 with the Thirty-First General Congregation (1965–66), organized following the death of the Jesuit Father General Jean-Baptiste Janssens, SJ. In the Society of Jesus, general congregations (GCs) are convened to enable delegates to take major decisions in the life of the movement and, in particular, to elect new leadership. GC 31 elected Pedro Arrupe, SJ (1907–91), to succeed Janssens and began the arduous process of renewing one the largest congregations of vowed religious in the world in light of the council's teachings.

The reception of the council continued with GC 32 (1974–75), called by Arrupe to respond more fully to the challenge of Vatican II. Utilizing an inductive process that consulted Jesuits around the world, GC 32 offers a new definition of the Jesuit mission as articulated in its highly influential "Decree 4": "The mission of the Society of Jesus today is the service of faith, of which the promotion of justice is an absolute requirement. For reconciliation with God demands the reconciliation of people with one another."[9]

Echoing the final statement of the 1971 Synod of Bishops, in which Arrupe took part, "Decree 4" argues that the promotion of justice is "an integral part of evangelization."[10] This concern, GC 32

---

[8] Kevin O'Brien, "Consolation in Action: The Jesuit Refugee Service and the Ministry of Accompaniment," *Studies in the Spirituality of Jesuits* 37, no. 4 (Winter 2005).

[9] General Congregation 32, "Decree 4: Our Mission Today: The Service of Faith and the Promotion of Justice," in *Jesuit Life and Mission Today: The Decrees of the 31st–35th General Congregations of the Society of Jesus*, ed. John W. Padberg, Jesuit Primary Sources in English Translation 25 (St. Louis: Institute of Jesuit Sources, 2009), no. 2.

[10] Ibid., no. 30.

argues, is rooted in the broader mission of the church, the demands of the gospel, and the "priestly service of faith."[11] Justice therefore must be integrated into all ministries of the Society (theological reflection, social action, education, mass media) and not solely one sector among many.

"Decree 4's" definition of the Jesuit mission had a tremendous impact on the life and work of Jesuits around the world. It transformed existing Jesuit institutions, encouraged individual Jesuits to undertake creative projects of social action and social analysis, and inspired the creation of JRS and many other social ministries. While it has not been without controversy, the wording of the decree, as Thomas Greene, SJ, reflects, "has become part and parcel of our Jesuit response when we are asked to define the contemporary mission of the Society."[12] The wide adoption of justice language by members of the Jesuit movement (including lay collaborators) represents a remarkable development and illustrates Vatican II's strong impact on movements of vowed religious.

Nuns on the Bus

In 2012, a group of women representing movements of Catholic religious life in the United States embarked on a bus tour of nine states to call for greater political action to address the needs of people who are poor. The Nuns on the Bus tour captured people's imagination, drew attention to the shortcomings of congressional budget proposals, and highlighted the prophetic role of vowed religious in the struggle for social justice.[13] The campaign was sponsored by NETWORK, a national social justice organization founded by American Catholic Sisters in 1971 during the post-conciliar turn to justice shared by other Christian social movements. Since then, NETWORK has been an active presence lobbying the US Congress and raising awareness to national and international social justice issues.

These concerns were amplified several months later when Simone Campbell, a Sister of Social Service and the executive director of NETWORK, explained the purpose of the tour on national television during

[11] Ibid., no. 18.
[12] Thomas Greene, "Observations of the Social Apostolate, Justice and the Decrees of General Congregations 31 to 35," *Promotio Justitiae*, no. 108 (2012): 1.
[13] Simone Campbell, *A Nun on the Bus: How All of Us Can Create Hope, Change, and Community* (New York: HarperOne, 2014).

her address at the Democratic National Convention: "This is what we nuns on the bus are all about: We care for the 100 percent, and that will secure the blessings of liberty for our nation. So join us as we nuns and all of us drive for faith, family and fairness."[14]

JRS: A NEW APOSTOLIC INITIATIVE

The Jesuit reception of the Second Vatican Council with GC 32 enabled the Society to see and respond to one of the major humanitarian crises of the twentieth century. The complex global reality of forced displacement in the 1970s, particularly those fleeing conflicts in Vietnam and Central America, demanded a concerted response on the part of the Jesuits given their renewed commitments to justice and social engagement. The key figure in facilitating the new articulation of the Jesuit mission was Pedro Arrupe, who led the Society from 1965 to 1983. A native of the Basque region, like St. Ignatius, Arrupe entered the Society after medical studies. As a missionary near Hiroshima during the Second World War he witnessed firsthand the suffering and horrors of war and forced displacement.

Although the tragedy of forced displacement had long existed in different parts of the world, the scale of the crisis that emerged in 1970s, particularly in South East Asia, called for new initiatives. Given the teachings of Vatican II and renewed understanding of the Jesuit mission articulated by GC 32, the Society could not ignore this situation. During an informal gathering of the Jesuit Curia in Rome in late 1979, the plight of the so-called boat people was discussed. The following day Arrupe sent telegrams to Jesuit superiors asking how the Society might respond to the crisis.[15] The response to this appeal, as Arrupe himself recalled, "was magnificent. Immediate offers of help were made in personnel, know-how and material."[16]

---

[14] Simone Campbell, "Transcript of Simone Campbell Remarks as Prepared for Delivery, Democratic National Convention," *Daily Kos*, September 5, 2012, www.dailykos.com.

[15] Michael Campbell-Johnston, "What Don Pedro Had in Mind When He Invited the Society to Work with Refugees," in *Everybody's Challenge: Essential Documents of Jesuit Refugee Service, 1980–2000*, ed. Danielle Vella (Rome: Jesuit Refugee Service, 2000), 40.

[16] Pedro Arrupe, "The Society of Jesus and the Refugee Problem: Letter to All Jesuit Major Superiors (14 November, 1980)," in *Everybody's Challenge: Essential*

After months of informal efforts it became clear that a more robust response was both possible and necessary. In September 1980
Arrupe organized a consultation in Rome to reflect on how the
Society might develop a coordinated effort to address the growing
numbers of refugees in line with the Ignatian charism and Jesuit
mission to serve faith. Following the consultation Arrupe announced
the establishment of the Jesuit Refugee Service as an international
project of the Jesuit Curia, organized (at first) by the Social Secretariat. Initially, the aim was simple. The Jesuit movement possessed a
tremendous amount of human, educational, and logistical resources
that could be placed in the service of refugees. As a coordinating
structure within the Jesuit leadership, JRS could mobilize and network these resources.

The establishment of JRS is perhaps the most creative response of
the Society to Vatican II and the new sense of mission outlined by
"Decree 4" of GC 32. Although the Jesuits have long operated glob-
ally with a universal sense of mission and availability, as illustrated
by the fourth vow, they, like most religious congregations, operated
primarily through provincial structures. Because of its global reality,
the plight of forced migrants demanded another type of response,
one that went beyond both local initiatives and charitable efforts
alone. Arrupe knew that the Jesuits, by virtue of their many institutions, available skilled personnel, and global presence, were in a
prime position to respond to both the immediate needs of refugees
(charity) as well as the root causes of their plight (justice). As a work
of the whole Society of Jesus, JRS was one of the first Jesuit movement organizations beyond the Jesuit Curia to span existing Jesuit
provincial and regional divisions.

From its foundation as "a switchboard," JRS has developed into
a global apostolic force for some of the most marginalized people
in the world. Though it remains directly accountable to the father
general as an official work of the whole Society, JRS developed its
own international leadership, programs, structures, guidelines, and
canonical status. In the 1990s it established nine regional structures.
This focused and coordinated structure enabled a rapid response to

Documents of Jesuit Refugee Service, 1980–2000, ed. Danielle Vella (Rome: Jesuit
Refugee Service, 2000), 28.

the social and political conflicts following the Rwanda crisis and the breakup of Yugoslavia. In 2000, the leadership of the organization drafted the *JRS Charter* and a new set of *JRS Guidelines*, which were approved by the Jesuit leadership and the Vatican. These documents outline the mission of the organization and its relationship to the broader Jesuit movement.

Today, JRS continues to develop in response to the reality of refugees around the world. The organization is challenged constantly to respond to new emergencies and governmental policies, such as the Syrian disaster. There are presently JRS programs in over fifty countries on six continents. Over half a million people, like Moshen, are served by its diverse staff of fourteen hundred, including seventy-eight Jesuits and sixty-six members of other religious congregations.[17] Additionally, several thousand refugees on stipends support JRS's work in the camps. Guiding all of this work is a threefold mission described by its charter: "to accompany, serve and defend the rights of refugees and forcibly displaced people."[18] What does this mission actually look like in practice? And how do these actions draw from the wider Jesuit mission and movement?

Accompaniment

More than anything, perhaps, JRS is characterized by the Ignatian principle of accompaniment, which its charter defines as the task of affirming with refugees "that God is present in human history, even it most tragic episodes" (no. 15). In many respects this is the organization's defining characteristic. In a world where many humanitarian organizations maintain a professional distance from the people they serve, even to the point of living in comfortable compounds with

---

[17] "Who We Are: About Us," *Jesuit Refugee Service*, http://www.jrs.net.

[18] Jesuit Refugee Service, "The Charter of Jesuit Refugee Service," March 19, 2000, no. 9, www.jrs.net. In its *Statutes*, approved in 2003, this threefold mission is described in Article 7: "The mission of JRS is to take care of the pastoral needs of the refugees and their religious and spiritual formation. JRS also attend to their human, spiritual, material and cultural needs and defends their human rights. "The Statutes of JRS as a Foundation of Canonical Rite" (Jesuit Refugee Service, 2003), Art.7, JRS Archive.

many amenities,[19] JRS's "style of presence," willingness to be with the displaced, and attention to the whole person makes it unique.[20]

With accompaniment, the apostolic work of JRS goes much deeper than simply providing urgently needed material relief. True to its etymological roots, accompaniment involves "breaking bread" with those in need. It means becoming a companion and friend to the other on a shared journey. It involves being attentive to the integrated nature of the people that they serve, including their social, physical, spiritual, and physiological needs.[21] In the face of the suffering, loneliness, and despair of the refugee camp, the presence of a compassionate companion, though difficult to measure, can engender hope and contribute to healing.[22]

As a principle and a practice, accompaniment is rooted in the biblical tradition and Ignatian mission. The gospel story of the road to Emmaus (Lk 24:1–35), where Jesus is encountered as his disciples break bread with a fellow traveler, is often cited as an example of what it means to accompany another.[23] Within the Ignatian theological tradition the principle is expressed in the teachings and spirituality of the first Jesuits. To be a "companion of Jesus," as Mark Raper points out, one must also be a companion to those "with whom he prefers to be associated, the poor and the outcast."[24]

---

[19] For an analysis on some of the ethical issues surrounding the relationship between humanitarian workers and the people they serve, see Michael N. Barnett and Thomas G. Weiss, eds., *Humanitarianism in Question: Politics, Power, Ethics* (Ithaca, NY: Cornell University, 2008).

[20] Daniel Villanueva, "The Jesuit Way of Going Global: Outlines for a Public Presence of the Society of Jesus in a Globalized World in the Light of Lessons Learned from the Jesuit Refugee Service," STL thesis (Weston Jesuit School of Theology, 2008), 79.

[21] Arrupe affirms this in his letter establishing the creation of JRS ("The Society of Jesus and the Refugee Problem"): "The help needed is not only material: in a special way the Society is being called to render a service that is human, pedagogical and spiritual. It is a difficult and complex challenge; the needs are dramatically urgent."

[22] Michael J. Schultheis, "Rebuilding the Bridges and Clearing the Footpaths: A Parable of JRS," in *The Wound of the Border: Twenty-five Years with the Refugees*, ed. Amaya Valcárcel (Rome: Jesuit Refugee Service, 2005), 146.

[23] See Anne Elizabeth de Vuyst, "Breaking Bread, Sharing Life," in *God in Exile: Towards a Shared Spirituality with Refugees*, ed. Pablo Alonso et al. (Rome: Jesuit Refugee Service, 2005), 43–45.

[24] Mark Raper, SJ, "Pastoral Accompaniment among Refugees: The Jesuit Refugee Service Experience," in *Everybody's Challenge: Essential Documents of Jesuit*

For JRS, the principle has a significant impact on both its humanitarian aid and advocacy work. Accompaniment encourages distinctive attitudes and practices, including psychological support, pastoral care, compassion, listening, solidarity, respect, capacity building, and empowerment.[25] In this approach the dignity of refugees is stressed; they are seen as agents and participants in the common task of social transformation and healing. In the words of Arrupe, "it is the oppressed who must be the principal agents of change."[26]

Service

A second core dimension of JRS's mission is service. Like accompaniment, this task is deeply rooted in the Christian tradition. In the Bible service to the poor and those in need is described as a constitutive element of Christian discipleship.[27] The forcibly displaced, in particular, demand attention.[28] Memories of forced displacement and of the Jewish people in Egypt and Babylon and the emigration of the Holy Family to Egypt deeply shape the Christian commitment to serve the poor. Refugees and aliens, the Bible instructs, are to be welcomed and treated with respect because "you too were once aliens in the land of Egypt" (Lv 19:33; Ex 22:20; 23:9).

This mission of service is expressed in an impressive series of programs aimed at directly aiding forcibly displaced people in refugee camps, detention centers, conflict zones, and increasingly in cities with urban refugee populations. In 2012, JRS served over 600,000

Refugee Service, 1980–2000, ed. Danielle Vella (Rome: Jesuit Refugee Service, 2000), 85.

[25] See Joe Hampson, "JRS Accompaniment: A New Way of Being Present?" December 2, 2009, www.jrsusa.org.

[26] Arrupe, "Men for Others."

[27] This concern is explicit throughout the New Testament. It can be seen in the beatitudes (Mt 5:3–12; Lk 6:20–26), the parable of the good Samaritan (Lk 10:29–30), the parable of the rich man and Lazarus (Lk 16:19–31), Jesus's description of the last judgment (Mt 25:31–46), the washing of the feet (Jn 13:1–17), and in the prophetic denunciations of St. James (Jas 2:14–26), to name only a few.

[28] A full treatment of the Christian ethical approach to migration and service to refugees is beyond the scope of this project. See the excellent articles on this by two Jesuits: Drew Christiansen, "Movement, Asylum, Borders: Christian Perspectives," *International Migration Review* 30, no. 1 (Spring 1996): 7–17; Agbonkhianmeghe E. Orobator, "Justice for the Displaced: The Challenge of a Christian Understanding," in *Driven from Home: Protecting the Rights of Forced Migrants,* ed. David Hollenbach (Washington, DC: Georgetown University Press, 2010), 37–54.

men, women, and children.[29] While emergency services and health-care are part of its work in some areas, JRS's primary operational presence is through educational and pastoral/psychosocial services.

It should not be surprising that the humanitarian organization of the Jesuit movement would focus much of its attention on education. In 2012, over 220,000 refugees participated in JRS educational projects—one of the few humanitarian groups to offer such servic-es.[30] For example, Moshen, the refugee mentioned at the beginning of this chapter, is among the many Syrians, Iraqis, and Palestinians who have benefited from the educational courses offered by JRS in Jordan.

Attention to education says much about the concerns of JRS to address the dignity of the whole person. As JRS's former director, Peter Balleis, SJ, points out, education is not a priority for most other major NGOs and agencies serving refugees, including the UN High Commissioner for Refugees (UNHCR). "Nonetheless," he writes, "it is very important for camp life itself and for the fu-ture of refugee children."[31] In the midst of humanitarian disasters, education becomes a justice issue. It not only brings the promise of a better economic future, but it helps to empower women and reduces the risk of being forced into service by armed groups, ex-tremists, and criminal networks who often prey on the despair of young people.[32]

More recently, JRS has partnered with Jesuit colleges and uni-versities in the United States in an innovative effort to offer higher educational opportunities to refugees through online distance learning. In its third year of operation, in 2012, Jesuit Commons: Higher Education at the Margins (JC-HEM) offered higher educa-tion courses to hundreds of refugees in Malawi, Kenya, and Jordan. JC-HEM draws upon faculty from Jesuit colleges and universities to offer a diploma in liberal studies awarded by Regis University in

---

[29] Danielle Vella, ed., *Jesuit Refugee Service Annual Report 2011* (Rome: Jesuit Refugee Service, 2011), www.jrs.net.

[30] Danielle Vella, ed., *Jesuit Refugee Service Annual Report 2012* (Rome: Jesuit Refugee Service, 2012), 7, www.jrs.net.

[31] Peter Balleis, "The Specific Jesuit Identity of JRS," in *Everybody's Challenge: Essential Documents of Jesuit Refugee Service, 1980–2000*, ed. Danielle Vella (Rome: Jesuit Refugee Service, 2000), 104–5.

[32] Amaya Valcárcel and Danielle Vella, eds., *Advocacy in Jesuit Refugee Service* (Rome: Jesuit Refugee Service, 2011), 24.

Colorado as well as certificates in specific community service learning tracks.[33]

From its foundation JRS has committed itself to providing spiritual and pastoral services to refugees and occasionally to other humanitarian workers. These services include the celebration of the Eucharist and other sacraments in refugee communities, animating prayer and reflection groups, pastoral visits to detention centers, training of other pastoral workers, psychosocial counseling and referral services, and community building.

In the United States, for example, JRS USA's Detention Chaplaincy Program offers religious and pastoral care to noncitizens of all faiths in government detention centers in Texas, Arizona, New Mexico, and New York. JRS chaplains and volunteers who are part of this program visit detention centers, celebrate mass, lead ecumenical prayer services, facilitate fellowship, and offer spiritual counseling. Through this service "JRS USA's chaplains and pastoral care workers give support to those who find themselves suffering and in crisis. They help individuals who are struggling to find purpose and meaning, value and direction, hope and love in their lives."[34]

In a very different context JRS Middle East serves urban refugee families through family visit teams. JRS staff who are on these teams visit the homes of displaced families to "assess their living conditions, spend time with them in a safe place, listen to their concerns and dispel any sense of isolation."[35] Through educational, pastoral, and psychological support, JRS draws attention to the fact that refugees are more than desperate people in need of a place to stay. Refugees are human beings endowed with dignity and rights. In order to serve them, all dimensions of the refugees need to be addressed.

Advocacy

The work of JRS with refugees does not stop at addressing their immediate emergency, educational, and psychological demands. Framed within the Jesuit justice mission, JRS is committed to advocate for and

---

[33] See *Jesuit Commons: Higher Education at the Margins*, 2014, www.jc-hem .org.

[34] "Serve: Our Programs," *Jesuit Refugee Service USA*, http://jrsusa.org/services.

[35] "Serve: Psychosocial Support," *Jesuit Refugee Service Middle East and North Africa*, www.jrsmena.org.

defend the rights of refugees. For JRS, advocacy includes but is much broader than the formal lobbying of intergovernmental institutions. Shaped by the Jesuit mission, it begins and finds its meaning with the refugees themselves. The experience of direct service gives rise to advocacy as JRS seeks to find durable solutions for today's refugees while also uncovering and addressing the root causes of forced displacement. Advocacy is an "integral part of the JRS mission" at different levels of work, from pleading the cause of an individual person to lobbying regional and global intergovernmental organizations on issues affecting whole communities.[36]

In the field, JRS's advocacy work often seeks to alleviate the sufferings of individuals and specific groups by taking up their cause with officials in the camp, UN agency, or host government. In many places, such as detention centers in the United States and Australia, JRS teams may be the only vehicles for refugees to communicate their concerns to those in positions of power and to the wider community.

At the international level JRS works with several UN entities and the European Union. It is one of only a handful of NGOs with observer status at the International Organization for Migration and is a key actor in the UNHCR's annual consultations with civil society.

Since 2002, the organization has also maintained active consultative status with ECOSOC, through which it has advocated on a wide range of issues, including the basic rights of refugees, children in armed conflict, and the obligation of states to provide quality education for forcibly displaced children.[37] While meetings in comfortable conference rooms in Geneva, Brussels, and New York may seem very far away from the realities of a UNHCR camp or the life of an urban refugee, the presence of JRS in these different forums enables it to bring the experiences of refugees to bear in decision-making processes that may have life or death consequences for vulnerable populations.

The transformative potential of JRS's advocacy work is evident in its leading role in what Mark Raper, SJ, describes as "one of the

---

[36] Valcárcel and Vella, *Advocacy in Jesuit Refugee Service*, 3.

[37] "Statement Submitted by Jesuit Refugee Service to the ECOSOC Substantive Session of 2011.," May 9, 2011, E/2011/NGO/10, United Nations Economic and Social Council.

most successful NGO campaigns anywhere."[38] Having witnessed the devastation caused by landmines among refugees, Denise Coghlan, RSM, the director of JRS Cambodia, helped to mobilize JRS country programs and regional offices around the world to exert pressure on governments. The JRS European office became a key agent in the International Campaign to Ban Landmines and pushed ratification of anti-landmine legislation throughout Europe. At the same time Coghlan and other members of JRS helped to bring the voices of refugees wounded by destructive weapons to global attention. Recalling the success of the campaign, Sr. Coghlan writes:

> Our interest in banning landmines began during work in refugee camps in the 80s, where we saw first hand the horrific consequences these weapons have on their victims. The Cambodia anti-landmine movement has been very influential in the International Campaign to Ban Landmines. It began with a letter from four soldiers in the JRS Centre of the Dove, a vocational training project that provides landmine survivors with skills... In 1997, one of these former soldiers, Tun Chunnereth, rode his wheelchair onto the stage in Oslo and received the Nobel Peace Prize on behalf of the campaign. He is working with JRS in Siam Reap, continuing his crusade against landmines. We have the Nobel Prize on display in our office.[39]

JRS's advocacy work is also distinctive in the ways in which it is rooted in serious research and reflection. As one of the original goals of the organization, research and analysis on policy issues helps to support both its operational and advocacy work. JRS is well suited for this task, given the Ignatian intellectual tradition and the global Jesuit network. To this end JRS has developed partnerships with several Jesuit and non-Jesuit research universities and institutions, including Boston College, the University of Deusto, and Georgetown University, to study and analyze issues associated with forced displacement. In the 1990s it partnered with the Refugee Study Centre

---

[38] Mark Raper, "Mercy and the National Interest," in *Everybody's Challenge: Essential Documents of Jesuit Refugee Service, 1980–2000*, ed. Danielle Vella (Rome: Jesuit Refugee Service, 2000), 65.

[39] In Valcárcel and Vella, *Advocacy in Jesuit Refugee Service*, 23.

(RSC) at the University of Oxford to create the Pedro Arrupe Tutorship. Recognizing the role played by JRS in humanitarian aid to refugees, Oxford created the tutorship to serve as "a bridge between the RSC and JRS and the operational world of humanitarian organisations, both non-governmental and inter-governmental."[40]

JRS IDENTITY, MISSION, AND ORGANIZATION

What does the experience of JRS say about the role of Christian social movements? As a movement organization committed to accompanying, serving, and defending people at the margins of society, JRS sheds light on the transformative potential of Christian communities in the alleviation of suffering caused by conflict, poverty, and environmental disaster. The experience of JRS, however, also raises several issues concerning identity, mission, and organization.

First, what is the role of movements of vowed religious in the promotion of justice? Not everyone in the church has embraced the post-conciliar turn to social justice in the same way. Is it appropriate and in line with their true vocation, some ask, for religious to be involved in working for justice? Does work for justice and social transformation distract religious from their more fundamental "spiritual" task? Church officials, political leaders, and even some in the religious communities themselves have raised these questions.

In the late 1980s Avery Dulles, SJ, for instance, expressed concern that the definition of the Jesuit mission put forth by GC 32 would overshadow and diminish the more fundamental mission of the Society and the role of Jesuits both as scholars and as priests.[41] In his 1994 book *Faith beyond Justice: Widening the Perspective*, Martin Tripole, SJ, offers one of the most extensive critiques of GC 32's formulation of the Jesuit mission. For him, the promotion of justice had been "raised by GC 32 to an inappropriate level of foundational

---

[40] Maryanne Loughry, "The Pedro Arrupe Tutorship in Oxford," in *The Wound of the Border: Twenty-five Years with the Refugees*, ed. Amaya Valcárcel (Rome: Jesuit Refugee Service, 2005), 248–49.

[41] Avery Dulles, "Faith, Justice, and the Jesuit Mission," in *Assembly 1989: Jesuit Ministry in Higher Education* (Washington, DC: Jesuit Conference, 1990), 19–25; David Hollenbach, "Faith, Justice, and the Jesuit Mission: A Response to Avery Dulles," in *Assembly 1989: Jesuit Ministry in Higher Education* (Washington, DC: Jesuit Conference, 1990), 26–29.

mission principle."[42] The promotion of justice, he argues, may be a legitimate response to the charism of St. Ignatius today, but it does not define the Jesuit mission and must not overshadow what he sees as the more fundamental task of serving faith. For Tripole, GC 32's turn toward justice is problematic for three reasons. First, it "too narrowly focused on human justice" and fails to take account of evangelization in its full sense. Second, it risks displacing traditional ministries that may not have a clear social focus such as teaching math and pastoral work. Finally, the concern for the promotion of justice may entail a "confusion" of the Jesuit priestly identity.[43]

These same concerns have been expressed by Vatican officials in relation to the Jesuits and other movements of vowed religious. For example, in an address to an ordination ceremony in Rio de Janeiro, a text he later cited when addressing Jesuit leadership, John Paul II stressed that the role of priests is different from that of the laity. Their primary function, he argued, is not social justice or charity, but spirituality and the care of souls.[44] John Paul II and other Vatican officials often expressed their concerns in warning about a temptation to a so-called "horizontalism." Without denying the importance of social concerns for the Christian faith, the Polish pope's missionary encyclical, *Redemptoris Missio* (1990), for instance, laments a trend among religious congregations that reduces salvation and the human person only to its "horizontal dimension" (RM, 2 and 59).

Following the theological approach of his predecessor, Pope Benedict XVI also downplayed the role of the church in the direct action for justice, particularly in his encyclical *Deus Caritas Est* and his 2011 *motu proprio* "On the Service of Charity."[45] In both texts, he emphasizes that the role of the church is in the service of charity and the conversion of hearts and not in the direct work for justice.

While admitting that there have been excesses in some interpretations of Jesuit mission as laid out by GC 32, Jesuit leaders have con-

---

[42] Martin R. Tripole, *Faith beyond Justice: Widening the Perspective* (Saint Louis: Institute of Jesuit Sources, 1994).

[43] Ibid., 31, 25, 76.

[44] John Paul II, "Who Is the Priest? Remarks of Pope John Paul II During Ordination Ceremonies in Rio de Janeiro," *Origins* 10, no. 9 (July 31, 1980); John Paul II, "Allocution to the Jesuit Provincials" (Vatican City: Libreria Editrice Vaticana, 1982), www.vatican.va.

[45] Benedict XVI, *"Motu Proprio" On the Service of Charity* (Vatican City: Libreria Editrice Vaticana, 2012), Art 1, www.vatican.va.

sistently reaffirmed a vision of mission that includes the promotion of justice as a constitutive element. This is clear in the final texts of GC 35 in 2008. GC 35's second decree, "A Fire that Kindles Other Fires: Rediscovering Our Charism," emphasizes the apostolic nature of the Jesuit charism and its desire to follow Christ by participating in the "Church's universal mission" in the world today. The decree explicitly affirms the Society's previous commitments to justice and situates this concern in Christian discipleship:

> In following this way, Jesuits today affirm all that has been specified regarding the Society's mission in the last three General Congregations. The service of faith and the promotion of justice, indissolubly united, remain at the heart of our mission. This option changed the face of the Society. We embrace it again and we remember with gratitude our martyrs and the poor who have nourished us evangelically in our own identity as followers of Jesus.[46]

A second question, related to the first, emerges from a different perspective. *Should humanitarian organizations, whether religious or secular, be involved in justice or advocacy work?* Not all those in the humanitarian field share the commitment of JRS to advocacy and justice. To some, the promotion of justice violates the traditional humanitarian principles of impartiality, neutrality, and independence first articulated by Jean Pictet, the founder of the International Committee of the Red Cross. Proponents of this approach, such as David Rieff, believe that a stance of impartiality and neutrality is the most effective way to create a protective "humanitarian space" to serve the immediate and urgent needs of refugees. Advocacy, long-term strategies for development, advanced educational projects, and attention to human rights are seen as political and thus in violation of humanitarianism's sacred principles.[47]

---

[46] GC 35, "Decree 2: A Fire That Kindles Other Fires: Rediscovering Our Charism," in Padberg, *Jesuit Life and Mission Today*, no. 15.

[47] David Rieff, *A Bed for the Night: Humanitarianism in Crisis* (New York: Simon and Schuster, 2002). For critiques of the principle of humanitarian neutrality, see Michael N. Barnett and Jack Synder, "The Grand Strategies of Humanitarianism," in *Humanitarianism in Question: Politics, Power, Ethics*, ed. Michael N. Barnett and Thomas G. Weiss (Ithaca, NY: Cornell University, 2008), 143–71; Mary B. Anderson, *Do No Harm: How Aid Can Support Peace—or War* (Boulder,

Adherence to a position of strict neutrality and independence became increasingly difficult to maintain following the end of the Cold War with an increasing number of "complex humanitarian emergencies" and intra-state conflicts, particularly in Eastern Europe and Africa. For some aid agencies, such as Médecins Sans Frontières, the apolitical delivery of relief was insufficient. One could not ignore the root causes of the conflict and the violations of basic human rights. Within this context of what has been described as "contested humanitarianism," JRS has adopted a rights-based approach that differs from classic humanitarianism as it seeks to "address not only symptoms but also causes."[48]

For JRS, as an apostolic work guided by the mission of the Jesuit movement, any approach to the humanitarian crisis that does not take into account the demands of justice and reconciliation is insufficient. Despite the questions raised about the legitimacy of action for justice, JRS, like the Society as a whole, has continued to insist on the integrated relationship between its mission and justice. Peter-Hans Kolvenbach, SJ, the former Father General of the Jesuits, summarizes the value of justice within the work of JRS well in a 2006 address:

The Church discovered only very slowly that charity is not sufficient if there is no justice. What has to be done by JRS is not just charity but also justice. If you really love, you will do justice. You will not do justice out of justice, but out of love... One can say charity just to do something but it is very clear all these people have their rights which need to be attended to. They have the right to go back to their country. They have the right to join in a just society. JRS is called to help do this, not out of legal or juridical motivations but out of Christian love.[49]

The experience of JRS also raises questions of identity that are shared with other religious social movements. *How should specific works or ministries relate to the broader sponsoring/founding religious order?* For many organizations, the answer to this question

---

CO: Lynne Rienner Publishers, 1999); Jean-Claude Favez, *The Red Cross and the Holocaust* (Cambridge: Cambridge University Press, 1999).

[48] Barnett and Synder, "The Grand Strategies of Humanitarianism," 150.

[49] Peter-Hans Kolvenbach, "Address" (presented at the Jesuit Refugee Service International Meeting, Santa Severa, Italy, 2006).

is far more complicated than it appears at first glance. Movements of vowed religious have established a multitude of movement organizations including schools, hospitals, and NGOs. The canonical, theological, and practical relationship between movements of vowed religious and their sponsored entities vary widely and are not always clear. Religious communities have sought to respond to this challenge in different ways. Some, for example, speak of a "family" of institutions and communities (e.g., the Lasallian Family or Vincentian Family) and have created umbrella organizations for entities sponsored by the founding movement. Requirements and expectations between sponsoring movements, their governing bodies, and movement organizations are not always clear, however. This is all the more complicated with decreasing numbers of vowed religious and an increasing religious pluralism in the staff and leadership of the sponsoring institution.

Concerned with this dynamic, the last General Congregation of the Society of Jesus sought to spell out what it means for an entity to use the Ignatian or Jesuit label. According to "Decree 6" of GC 35, an Ignatian work is one that is related to the spirituality and charism of St. Ignatius and the *Spiritual Exercises*. More concretely, a work can be considered Ignatian "when it intentionally *seeks God in all things*; when it practices Ignatian discernment; when it engages the world through a careful analysis of context, in dialogue with experience, evaluated through reflection for the sake of action."[50] Ignatian works can operate regardless of the participation of vowed Jesuits.

A Jesuit work, by contrast, is an Ignatian work that possesses "a clear and definitive relationship with the Society of Jesus." To be considered Jesuit, such works must also have a mission that aligns with that of the Society by "a commitment to a faith that does justice through interreligious dialogue and a creative engagement with culture."[51] Such works have close ties to the structures of the Society and are ultimately accountable to the father general.

According to both this definition and its own canonical statutes, JRS is squarely a Jesuit work. While there are fewer than eighty vowed Jesuits involved in the work of JRS, most of the key leadership roles are occupied by Jesuits. Internationally, the JRS international director

---

[50] GC 35, "Decree 6: Collaboration at the Heart of Mission," in Padberg, *Jesuit Life and Mission Today*, no. 9.
[51] Ibid., no. 10.

must be a Jesuit and is appointed directly by the father general. Even with this provision, the structural relationships between the Society and JRS have not always been clear. For example, some regional Jesuit superiors sought to have a greater voice in this process of choosing JRS regional and national directors. To address this concern the *JRS Guidelines* urged greater lines of communication and put forth two models for JRS's service operations. In some regions JRS projects are to be coordinated by the local Jesuit province and/or regional assistancies themselves. In other regions, where there are urgent humanitarian needs or where the local Jesuit structures currently lack the resources adequately to serve the forcibly displaced, JRS International will play the primary role in organizing the projects and appointing the regional director.

This dynamic, however, raises other questions of participation and inclusion. If the leadership of the organization is appointed by the Society, how is it accountable to the staff? What about accountability to refugees? Are there any drawbacks for a structure that privileges vowed men in leadership and gives autonomy to some regions of the world and not others?

Finally, a distinct, albeit related, question concerns the relationship between non-Jesuit staff and Jesuit identity. *What does participating in a social movement or work of vowed religious mean for non-vowed staff or members?* In other words, if JRS is an integral part of the Jesuit movement, what does that say for non-Jesuits, including lay men, lay women, sisters, non-Christians, and others who work or volunteer for JRS? Do they participate in the Jesuit movement? For example, can a Muslim staff member share in the Ignatian charism? Unlike some Christian humanitarian organizations, being a believer is not a requirement to work or volunteer with JRS. In some areas the majority of those involved in JRS program are not Catholic.

JRS is certainly not the only institution faced with such questions of identity and membership boundaries. Similar questions can be raised, for instance, with a Hindu doctor at a hospital sponsored by the Sisters of Mercy or an atheist philosophy professor at a Franciscan college. Finding answers to these theological and practical questions of movement identity is not always easy.[52]

---

[52] Charles E. Curran, "The Catholic Identity of Catholic Institutions," *Theological Studies* 58, no. 1 (1997): 108.

The Jesuits and other movements of vowed religious are not alone in their struggle to address questions of identity, mission, and organization. The case studies in the following two chapters offer other perspectives that will help to set the stage for a deeper theological analysis in later chapters.

Chapter 3

Young Christian Workers

A Movement from the Margins

During the third session of the Second Vatican Council in 1964 a surprising figure rose to address the council fathers. For the first time in history a lay person who was not a monarch or royal delegate was invited to address an ecumenical council. Commenting on the draft document on the nature of the church *(De Ecclesia)*, Patrick Keegan stressed the importance of Christian social movements and organizations:

> How are the vast majority of Catholics to be made aware of their apostolic responsibility to bear witness in their daily life, as members of a family, as members of the community of the Church and of the whole community? . . . It is here that we see the first role of our organisations. It is clear that associations provide the most favourable conditions for Christian formation and for sustaining the individual in the development of his creative potential and in the witness they must bear to

---

In the process of drafting this chapter I consulted with several members of the Young Christian Workers (YCW) movement. I am especially grateful for the discussions with Ludovicus Mardiyono, international president of the International Young Christian Workers (IYCW), and Amelie Peyrard, international president of the International Coordination of Young Christian Workers (CIJOC), as well as the feedback given to me by Stefan Gigacz, who coordinates several historical projects in relation to the YCW.

the world. The establishment and development of organised groupings should therefore be strongly encouraged.[1]

Patrick Keegan's address to the council was made on behalf of a small group of lay auditors appointed by Pope Paul VI to participate in Vatican II. Like most of the others, Keegan was actively engaged in several Christian social movements. This son of an Irish immigrant miner knew well the importance of organized groups in the church and in civil society. From his youth he had been instrumental in establishing the Young Christian Workers (YCW) in England. He had served as the president of the movement at the international level and, at the time of the council, was the president of the World Movement of Christian Workers, the YCW's adult counterpart.

Contrary to some accounts a culture of active social engagement on the part of the laity is not a new development in the life of the church. From medieval confraternities and sixteenth-century reform movements to contemporary Christian justice efforts those who are neither ordained nor vowed religious have been active agents for social change. The decades leading up to Vatican II were rich in creative initiatives directed by them. One of the most notable movements to emerge in this period was the YCW (JOC in French and Spanish).

Not to be confused with the Catholic Worker movement founded in New York by Dorothy Day and Peter Maurin, the YCW initially formed as a response to the social conditions of Europe following the industrial revolution and the two world wars.[2] It has since grown and developed into a global movement. For more than eighty years, the YCW and other movements in the tradition of "specialized Catholic action" have sought to combat social injustices locally and internationally through the formation and empowerment of the laity and the direct action for social and political change.

------

[1] "Address of Mr. Patrick Keegan, On Behalf of the Auditors, to the Fathers of the Second Vatican Council," *Pioneers of the Cardijn Movements*, http://pioneers. josephcardijn.com.

[2] Several international Christian social movements were founded following World War I or World War II. For many lay leaders the response to these horrible events took the form of national and international movements "spontaneously created on the free initiative of the faithful" to meet a real need for action in national and international life. Christian social movements were seen as one way to prevent future wars. See Ramon Sugranyes de Franch, *Le Christ Dans Le Monde: Les Organisations Internationales Catholiques* (Paris: Fayard, 1972), 21.

The story of the YCW and other movements of specialized Catholic action, it could be argued, is one of the most undertold stories of twentieth-century Christianity. The inductive social analysis methodology of see-judge-act popularized by these movements and their organization and empowerment of the laity foreshadowed and in many ways set the stage for the teachings of Vatican II and the subsequent emergence of liberation theology.

Today, thousands of young people participate in YCW groups in more than seventy countries around the world, with thousands more belonging to movements closely associated with the YCW vision. As a lay movement of young workers, YCW illuminates markedly different experiences of Christian social movements from the Jesuits and other movements of vowed religious.

With few exceptions the militants of the YCW are not priests, vowed religious, or lay ecclesial ministers employed by the church. While largely Catholic, members of the YCW include young people from many churches and religious traditions. In contrast to the Jesuit Refugee Service and other Christian humanitarian movements, the members, leaders, and even international representatives of the YCW are members of the target group. The YCW is not, in other words, a service of the church *for* young people in need. It is not a youth program or youth pastoral sponsored and run by a diocese or religious order with highly trained experts. It is a movement *of, for,* and *by* young workers themselves. This way of being church reflects a specific commitment for young people, especially for those at the margins of society. As one text describes the movement, "The YCW has a preferential option for the kind of young people who are not highly advantaged financially or educationally, for those who live in the less well to do areas and find it hard to make their voice heard."[3]

Despite the significant differences between the YCW and movements of vowed religious, there are similarities in their vision of the church's mission. Originating in a different historical context, the YCW, like the Jesuits, has come to understand action for social justice to be an important part of its mission as a movement. While a detailed history of this global movement of young workers is beyond the scope of this book, this chapter looks at the YCW, its development

---

[3] International Co-ordination of Young Christian Worker Movements, *ICYCW Declaration of Principles* (Rome: CIJOC-ICYCW, 2004), no. 4, www.cijoc.org.

as a global movement, and some of the questions raised as it has struggled to balance horizontal and vertical demands of mission.

THE YCW AND SPECIALIZED CATHOLIC ACTION

Joseph Cardijn and the Young Christian Workers

The YCW movement originated within the context of European social Catholicism and the attempts by the church to address the "worker question" during the second industrial revolution. In the midst of rapid technological changes the working conditions of young workers were deplorable, unhealthy, and unsafe. Industrial disasters such as the Triangle Shirtwaist Factory Fire (1911) in New York were not uncommon in the growing urban centers. Even in areas where child labor laws were in place, adolescence for most of those in cities meant factory work. The slow response to these rapidly changing realities on the part of the Christian community led many workers to leave the church, with many joining Marxist and communist groups.

Inspired by the teaching of Pope Leo XIII's groundbreaking encyclical *Rerum Novarum* (1891), a young Belgian priest named Joseph Cardijn (1882–1967) facilitated the creation of the YCW in 1912.[4] Born to "a poor working man" and a "domestic servant" in Hal, Belgium, Cardijn knew the dark side of industrialization and witnessed the disregard for the dignity of workers.[5] At his father's deathbed, in 1903, the young seminarian pledged to consecrate his priestly life to serving the working class.

Following his ordination Joseph Cardijn traveled outside Belgium to study religious and secular initiatives for young workers. In Germany he visited the groups of workingmen founded by Fr. Adolf Kloping. In France, Cardijn met with Marc Sangnier, the founder of Le Sillon, a Catholic worker-student movement, and Léon Harmel, founder of worker cooperatives. In England he discussed the best practices for organizing young people with two notable

---

[4] Marguerite Fievez, Jacques Meert, and Roger Aubert, *Life and Times of Joseph Cardijn*, trans. Edward Mitchinson (London: Young Christian Workers, 1974).

[5] Joseph Cardijn, quoted in Michael De La Bedoyere, *The Cardijn Story: A Study of the Life of Mgr. Joseph Cardijn and the Young Christian Workers' Movement Which He Founded* (Milwaukee: The Bruce Publishing Company, 1959), 13.

non-Catholics: Robert Baden-Powell, the founder of the Scouting movement, and Benjamin Tillett, a major trade union leader.[6]

Cardijn's 1912 appointment as a curate in the royal parish in Laeken, just outside Brussels, enabled him to put his passion for working-class youth into action. Among other duties the priest was put in charge of a group of young women in the parish. In cooperation with several women, including Victoire Cappe, a Belgian labor leader, they organized study circles and branches of the Needleworkers' Union. Reflecting the style that would later mark the YCW, the groups of poor and largely uneducated women were empowered to be "completely responsible for the finances, accounts and secretarial work of their organization."[7] This was a major step forward from the paternalistic styles that often marked the church's efforts for the young and for the poor.

The circles of young women inspired young workingmen to seek out similar experiences—efforts that were cut short by the First World War. Following the war three young workers, Fernand Tonnet, Paul Garcet, and Jacques Meert, sought out Cardijn's help to create a movement of study circles for men in 1919 under the name Jeunesse syndicaliste (Young Trade Unionists).[8] As the movement grew through Belgian parishes it came into conflict with the Belgian Catholic Youth Association and Cardinal Mercier, who believed all youth efforts should fall under the official organs of Catholic action set up by the hierarchy.[9] In contrast to the models of Catholic action, which sought to unite all lay Catholic activity under a unified

---

[6] The Cardijn Online community has published Cardijn's own account of his visit to England. Joseph Cardijn, "1911 Worker Organisation in England," Cardijn Online, 1911, www.josephcardijn.com.

[7] Cardijn recounts his experience with young women "coming from the worst streets in Laeken: laundrywomen, ironing-women, workers in the chocolate and cigarette factories, girls in the feather trade, the shoe-polish, the wood, the cardboard box, the jam, nurses, messengers and many others." Quoted in De La Bedoyere, *The Cardijn Story*, 44.

[8] Both Tonnet and Garcet died at the hands of the Nazis in the Dachau camps, leading Cardijn to describe them as JOC martyrs. "Canon Cardijn's Tribute to JOC Martyrs," *Catholic Herald*, July 20, 1945; Adrien Tonnet, *Fernand Tonnet, mort à Dachau: biographie* (Genval: L. de Lannoy, 1945).

[9] Pius XI famously defined Catholic action in 1928 as the "participation and cooperation of the laity in the hierarchical apostolate." Pius XI, "Letter of Pius XI to Cardinal Bertram," in *Clergy and Laity: Official Catholic Teachings*, ed. Odile M. Liebard (Wilmington, NC: McGrath, 1978), 30–34.

umbrella directed by the hierarchy, Cardijn sought to establish a specialized movement autonomous from the generalized Catholic action model. In 1925, the young priest made his first trip to Rome to make an appeal to Pope Pius XI directly. In an unscheduled private audience he secured permission from the pope for a specialized movement of young workers. In the following months the first national congress of the Jeunesse ouvrière chrétienne (JOC), or Young Christian Workers, was organized with Tonnet as president.

Soon, thousands of cell groups were created in Belgium under four different national movements: one for francophone men (JOC); one for francophone women (JOCF); one for Flemish-speaking men (KAJ); and one for Flemish-speaking women (VKAJ). Each branch had its own president and leadership consisting of young workers chosen by their peers. In 1927, the JOC spread to France with the assistance of Fr. Georges Guérin, where it was to become an important force in twentieth-century French Catholicism.[10] By 1939, YCW groups existed in fifty countries in Europe, America, Asia, Africa, and Oceania.[11]

INTERNATIONAL MOVEMENTS OF
SPECIALIZED CATHOLIC ACTION

After the Second World War an international bureau was set up in Brussels with Patrick Keegan of England as president. In 1957, a world assembly in Rome of 32,000 workers from eighty-five counties established the International Young Christian Workers (IYCW) with the approval of Pius XII.[12] At the international level the movement adopted a federated model with an inductive approach. National delegates, chosen by local cell groups, would meet in councils to elect the international leadership, with the candidates for president requiring a *nihil obstat* from the Vatican Secretariat of State. While he may rightly be considered the founder, chaplain, and champion of this movement, Joseph Cardijn strongly believed that young work-

---

[10] See Pierre Pierrard, *Georges Guérin: une vie pour la JOC* (Paris: l'Atelier/ Editions Ouvrières, 1997); Denis Pelletier and Jean-Louis Schlegel, *À la gauche du christ: Les chrétiens de gauche en France de 1945 à nos jours* (2012).

[11] Albert Hari, *IYCW: International Young Christian Workers, Seventy-five Years of Action*, ed. Fondation internationale Cardijn (Strasbourg: Signe, 2000), 23–25.

[12] Ibid., 58.

ers themselves should be the primary protagonists in a movement of young workers.

The "jocist" model of "specialized Catholic action" inspired the creation of similar groups in other milieus based on the YCW's participatory approach and inductive method of see-judge-act. These included adult workers, students, farmers, members of the independent or middle class, families and children (see text box). Originating independently from the jocist model, the movements of students and graduates associated with Pax Romana, including the International Movement of Catholic Students (IMCS), incorporated many of the methods and structures into their own ways of working and eventually identified themselves as movements of specialized Catholic action.[13]

THE INTERNATIONAL MOVEMENTS OF SPECIALIZED CATHOLIC ACTION AND DATES OF FOUNDATION

WORKERS
- International Young Christian Workers (JOCI) 1957
- International Coordination of Young Christian Workers (CIJOC) 1987
- World Movement of Christian Workers (MMTC) 1966

FARMERS
- International Movement of Catholic Agricultural and Rural Youth (MIJARC) 1954
- International Federation of Rural Adult Catholic Movements (FI-MARC) 1964

MIDDLE CLASS
- International Independent Christian Youth (JIIC) 1931
- International Movement of Apostolate in the Independent Social Milieus (MIAMSI) 1963

CHILDREN
- International Movement of Apostolate of Children (MIDADE) 1966

STUDENTS/INTELLECTUALS
- International Young Catholic Students (JECI) 1946
- International Movement of Catholic Students (MIEC-Pax Romana) 1921

---

[13] See Buenaventura Pelegri, *IMCS-IYCS: Their Option Their Pedagogy* (IMCS Asia Secretariat, 1979); Kevin Ahern, "Structures of Hope in a Fractured World: The Ministry of the International Catholic Youth Movements," ed. Susan Ross, Diego Irarrázaval, and Paul Murr, *Concilium*, no. 1 (2010): 76–84.

- International Catholic Movement for Intellectual and Cultural Affairs (MIIC-Pax Romana) 1947

OTHER

- International Confederation of Christian Family Movements (ICCFM) 1966
- Cardijn Community International (CCI) 2011

The YCW and the Church's Renewed Relationship with the World

The methods and vision of specialized Catholic action were influential in the mid-twentieth-century ecclesial renewal. For example, the see-judge-act method developed and practiced by the YCW movement was endorsed by Pope John XXIII in 1961 as the method of Catholic social doctrine in his encyclical *Mater et Magistra* and later developed by theologians and social activists into other methodological directives such as the pastoral circle or the action-reflection-action method.[14]

At Vatican II, key theologians, council fathers, and lay auditors were deeply informed by the jocist model.[15] Both Yves Congar, OP, and Marie-Dominique Chenu, OP, for example, worked closely with the JOC in France. Reflecting on his experience with the movement, Congar wrote: "I owe much to these young men. They revealed to me the sense of insertion of the Gospel in humanity."[16]

The specialized Catholic action movements also played an active role in directly shaping the deliberations of Vatican II. In the decades leading up to the council the IYCW, Pax Romana, and other jocist movements were the primary agents in organizing the World Congresses for the Lay Apostolate—an important laboratory that helped prepare the way for Vatican II's teaching.[17] And it was from

---

[14] See, for instance, Frans Jozef Servaas Wijsen, Peter J. Henriot, and Rodrigo Mejia, eds., *The Pastoral Circle Revisited: A Critical Quest for Truth and Transformation* (Maryknoll, NY: Orbis Books, 2005).

[15] For example, Stefan Gigacz, coordinator of Cardijn Online, has documented dozens of council fathers with direct ties to the YCW movement. See Stefan Gigacz, "Cardijn Bishops at Vatican II," *Cardijn Online*, 2014, http://priests.josephcardijn.com.

[16] Elizabeth Teresa Groppe, *Yves Congar's Theology of the Holy Spirit* (Oxford: Oxford University, 2004), 30.

[17] Rosemary Goldie, "Lay Participation in the Work of Vatican II," *Miscellanea Lateranense*, no. 40–41 (1974/75): 503–25; Bernard Minvielle, *L'Apostolat des laïcs*

these very organizations that Paul VI chose the lay auditors for the council, including Keegan. Cardijn was active in a number of conciliar commissions that drafted the documents that would become *Gaudium et Spes* and *Apostolicam Actuositatem*.[18] Just months before the final session, Pope Paul VI made a historic decision to honor Cardijn, and by extension the lay apostolic movements, by naming him a titular bishop and cardinal with the right to vote in the final session of the council.

Like the Jesuits and other religious orders, the movements of specialized Catholic action redefined their mission in the wake of Vatican II with strong commitments to justice and the marginalized. In its first major gathering following Vatican II, the death of Cardijn, and the youth revolutions of 1968, the IYCW's Beirut World Council (1969) started to outline new directives that called for greater action for justice, an openness to non-Catholic and non-Christian members, and a move away from the parish model.[19]

The new commitments to justice and liberation were particularly visible in Latin America, where the jocist youth movements helped to set the stage for what would be known as liberation theology. In Brazil, for instance, the Juventude Universitária Católica (JUC), an affiliate of the Cardijn-based student movement, encouraged the creation of Christian base communities through the efforts of Paulo Freire and other militants.[20] Meanwhile, in Peru, Gustavo Gutiérrez, the national chaplain of the Unión Nacional de Estudiantes Católicos (UNEC), the IMCS federation, drew inspiration from his work with students and the jocist method in outlining a theology of liberation in a lecture first published by the IMCS regional secretariat in Montevideo in 1969.[21]

à la veille du concile (1949–1959): histoire des congrès mondiaux de 1951 et 1957 (Fribourg, Switzerland: Editions Universitaires, 2001).

[18] See, for example, Achille Glorieux, "Histoire Du Décret," in *L'apostolat des Laïcs: Décret "Apostolicam Actuositatem,"* ed. Yves Congar, *Unam Sanctam 75* (Paris: Editions du Cerf, 1970), 91–140.

[19] Hari, *IYCW*, 80–82.

[20] "Brazilian Catholic Action was undoubtedly important in preparing the ground from which the base communities were later to spring." Faustino Luiz Couto Teixeira, "Base Church Communities in Brazil," in *The Church in Latin America, 1492–1992*, ed. Enrique D. Dussel, trans. Francis McDonagh, vol. 1, *A History of the Church in the Third World* (Maryknoll, NY: Orbis Books, 1992), 410.

[21] Gustavo Gutiérrez, *A Theology of Liberation: History, Politics, and Salvation* (Maryknoll, NY: Orbis Books, 1988), 175n1; Christian Smith, *The Emergence of Liberation Theology: Radical Religion and Social Movement Theory* (Chicago: University of Chicago, 1991), 54.

According to Ana Maria Bidegain, the shift in mission that took place within IYCW, IMCS, and the IYCS following the council situated them as "prophetic minorities" within the church. Their new integrated approach to mission enabled them "interpret the Latin American realities to the whole Church community. It is this context," she asserts, "that gave birth to Liberation Theology, Basic Christian Communities, [and] Medellín."[22] In his important work on the history of the church in Latin America, Enrique Dussel makes a similar point. According to Dussel, the jocist youth movements prepared the ground for the emergence of liberation theology: "It was from both the practice and theory of these groups that the most important theological break in Latin American history was to emerge."[23]

Similar social and political commitments were also expressed in Asia and Africa.[24] As with Brazil, Argentina, and Peru, the new options for justice and for the marginalized adopted by the youth movements often put them into direct conflict with oppressive governments—and their allies in the church—in Vietnam, India, Indonesia, Korea, and Singapore. In South Africa the YCW, YCS, and IMCS affiliates participated actively in the struggle against apartheid, a contribution recognized by Nelson Mandela in his address to the 1995 IYCW World Council, in which he also sums up the distinctive vision of the YCW movement:

> YCW was founded with the specific aim that the Church should respond to the needs of workers, but not as charity where the workers are passive recipients of aid. YCW's emphasis on active participation of its members in developing plans to change their

---

[22] Anna Maria Bidegaín, *From Catholic Action to Liberation Theology: The Historical Process of the Laity in Latin America in the Twentieth Century*, working paper 48 (Notre Dame, IN: Kellogg Institute, 1985), 22.

[23] Enrique D. Dussel, "Recent Latin American Theology," in *A History of the Church in the Third World*, 392; idem, *A History of the Church in Latin America: Colonialism to Liberation (1492–1979)*, trans. Alan Neely (Grand Rapids, MI: Eerdmans, 1981), 324.

[24] Bernard D'Sami, "The Impact of *Gaudium et Spes* on the Social Mission of the Church in Asia with Particular Reference to Catholic Students and Workers Movements," in *The Call to Justice: The Legacy of* Gaudium et Spes *Forty Years Later* (Rome, 2005), 4.

lives has proved to have great potential for capacity building among our youth. It is common knowledge that YCW has made a significant contribution to building the organs of civil society in South Africa, in particular worker organisations.[25]

THE COMMUNITY OF SANT'EGIDIO AND PEACE IN MOZAMBIQUE

On October 4, 1992, the feast of St. Francis of Assisi, representatives of the opposing factions of the Mozambican Civil War (1977–92) signed the Rome General Peace Accords, which led the way to a UN observer force to maintain the peace until national elections could be organized in 1994. The historic peace agreement put an end to decades of "systematic chaos" that had claimed the lives of more than a million people and resulted in the displacement of over five million.[26]

In the midst of war Archbishop Jaime Gonçalves requested help from the Community of Sant'Egidio, a new ecclesial movement founded in 1968 by Andrea Riccardi. Based in Rome, the movement gathers Christians from over seventy countries based in a common spirituality and the values of prayer, evangelization, friendship with the poor, ecumenism, and dialogue.

From 1990 to 1992 the community hosted eleven peace talks at its headquarters in Rome, eventually resulting in the accord. The role of Sant'Egidio in facilitating peace between governmental and rebel forces is an impressive example of the role of Christian social movements in what has been called multi-track or two-track diplomacy, a framework developed by Joseph Montville, to highlight the importance of non-state actors, including religious groups and social movements, in peacebuilding.[27]

---

[25] Nelson Mandela, opening speech presented at the IYCS World Council, Oukasie, South Africa, November 26, 1995, www.testimonies.josephcardijn.com.

[26] Andrea Bartoli, "Forgiveness and Reconciliation in the Mozambique Peace Process," in *Forgiveness and Reconciliation: Religion, Public Policy, and Conflict Transformation*, ed. Raymond G. Helmick and Rodney L. Petersen (Philadelphia: Templeton, 2001), 316–81.

[27] Louise Diamond and John McDonald, *Multi-Track Diplomacy: A Systems Approach to Peace*, 3rd ed. (West Hartford, CT: Kumarian Press, 1996); John McDonald, "Further Exploration of Track Two Diplomacy," in *Timing the De-Escalation of International Conflicts*, ed. Louis Kriesberg and Stuart J. Thorson (Syracuse, NY: Syracuse University Press, 1991), 201–20.

A MOVEMENT DIVIDED

Much like the 1971 Synod of Bishops, the 1974–75 General Congregation of the Jesuits, and the 1975 assembly of IMCS Pax Romana in Lima, Peru, the 1975 World Council of the IYCW in Linz, Austria, strongly affirmed the horizontal or social demands of the Christian mission. As with these other major meetings in the decade after Vatican II, the justice commitments of the IYCW were not entirely welcome by everyone in the church. The fifty-two national YCW movements present sought to renew "the worker character of the movement" and the option for workers of all faiths.[28] These commitments were expressed in a controversial "Declaration of Principles," a declaration not welcomed by all in the church.

In 1976, the Vatican raised concerns about the Christian character of the movement and launched an investigation concerning the declaration and its implementation throughout the world. Questions were posed to local bishops regarding the IYCW's religious identity.[29] The conflict with the Vatican was exacerbated by several organizational troubles, including the cancellation of a major meeting, the temporary dissolution of the international team, the organization of a world council in Madrid against the wishes of the Spanish Bishops' Conference, and the failure of the IYCW to obtain a *nihil obstat* from the Vatican for its president.

In 1986, the crisis came to a head as YCW movements from Italy, Portugal, England, Malta, and France formally withdrew from the IYCW to create a new structure, the International Coordination of YCWs (CIJOC). Unlike the IYCW, which was based in Belgium, the new organization is based in Rome, in an old convent secured for it by the Vatican. The creation of CIJOC was strongly supported by the Vatican's Pontifical Council for the Laity, which approved the new structure within three months. On August 4, 1986, the laity council sent messages to all bishops' conferences stating its support for the new structure and withdrawing recognition of the IYCW as a legitimate representative of the YCW movement. Interestingly, the new structure describes itself as a coordination and not a movement.

---

[28] Hari, *IYCW*, 85.

[29] Ibid., 88; Luc Roussel, "The YCW and the Vatican: From Confidence to Incomprehension and Rupture 1945–1985," in *The First Steps towards a History of the IYCW* (Brussels: IYCW, 1997).

The goal of the CIJOC is to coordinate YCW movements, not to act directly. These actions effectively meant the division of one of the largest and oldest international lay movements, with national YCW groups around the world forced to choose sides.

At the core of this division was a disagreement over how to balance commitments to justice and inclusiveness with ecclesial identity.[30] CIJOC sought to clarify its positions with the formulation of its own "Declaration of Principles." The two declarations highlight many commonalities between the IYCW and CIJOC. Both texts speak of the worker, youth, Christian, international, and autonomous characteristics of the movement—though the IYCW also has a section on the "mass characteristic." Both international bodies declare their concerns for young workers, the importance of the review of life method, and the need for organized structures to empower young workers to discover and claim their dignity in the face of injustice and oppression. The fundamental difference in the two texts is in the attention paid to and the interpretation of the movement's Christian identity.

For example, according to the CIJOC text:

> The main purpose of the YCW is to proclaim to young people that the life, death and resurrection of Jesus Christ and the gift of the Holy Spirit is decisive for their true happiness and freedom. This proclamation necessarily involves the YCW in action to strengthen the hope and secure the freedom of young people who suffer personally and collectively from all kinds of alienation, oppression and exploitation.[31]

The understanding of YCW as a movement tasked to evangelize young workers is integrated throughout the CIJOC declaration. The newer structure clearly states that the YCW is a "movement of the church" with a mission to "propose faith in Jesus Christ and live by it." Militants of the YCW, according to CIJOC, are called to be "conscious of the values of God's kingdom" and to know "Jesus Christ as friend and brother."[32]

---

[30] Hari, *IYCW*, 95.

[31] International Co-ordination of Young Christian Worker Movements, "ICYCW Declaration," nos. 6–7.

[32] Ibid., nos. 53, 3, 13.

In contrast, the IYCW declaration, which was revised in 1995, explicitly speaks of its Christian identity in only three paragraphs under the section of Christian characteristic. Even the section "The YCW in Brief" makes no explicit mention of faith, Jesus Christ, or the church. The fundamental objective of the YCW, according to the IYCW text, is to aid young workers to "discover the deepest meaning of their lives; live in accordance with their personal and collective dignity; and assume the responsibility for finding solutions to their situations at the local, national and international levels."[33] No mention is made of the religious identity of members or even member movements. The label Christian, for many groups of young workers, especially in places where the church has been seen as aligned with power structures and/or where non-Christians have joined the YCW, carries with it many secondary meanings that are often seen as baggage. Instead, for the IYCW, the Christian characteristic of the movement is most profoundly seen in the ways the movement follows the model of Jesus Christ by working to liberate young workers from their oppressive situations.

In "The Spirituality of Young Workers Today" the IYCW makes no explicit mention of Christianity to describe its religious identity. Instead it speaks of the importance of values present within "all major religions" including "love, unity, peace, brotherhood, truth and justice." Spirituality, it continues, helps to offer perspective to propel young workers to action in the face of the injustices faced by young workers today:

> Very often in our work place we do not have the feeling of "at home." We do not feel happy in our work place. We are not being valued and our worth is not being respected. . . . We start to reflect this situation with our spirituality. . . . We commit to do something to bring in change in the situation. We commit to respond to this situation. This is called action. This action comes from our own spirituality.[34]

Despite this more inclusive approach, many YCW national movements affiliated with IYCW continue to identify themselves

---

[33] Ninth International Council of the IYCW, "Declaration of Principles" (Brussels: International Young Christian Workers, 1995), no. 4.

[34] IYCW, "The Spirituality of Young Workers Today" (2014), www.joci.org.

as Christian and are recognized by their local church structures. However, some YCW national movements have chosen to move even further away from their original Christian identity. The Walloon JOC/JOCF Belgium, one of the first YCW national movements and a core member of IYCW, has recently changed its name from the Jeunesse Ouvrière Chrétienne to the Jeunes Organisés et Combatifs (Youth Organized and Competitive), keeping the acronym but dropping the explicit religious and worker connotation in the name.[35]

THE JOCIST MYSTIQUE

Despite the differences between IYCW and CIJOC declarations and understanding of Christian identity, it is possible to discern a common mission for the YCW in its work of serving, educating, and representing young workers. Since its foundation two main features have characterized the jocist vision or what some have called the YCW mystique.[36]

A Movement for and by Young Workers

First, the goal of the YCW is to create a movement where young lay workers take the lead in their own mobilization and the realization of their own dignity. This vision is non-paternalistic and participatory and contrasts with models of professional or institutionalized youth ministry or youth pastoral programs that offer young people services without providing them with opportunities for leadership.

Priests and other specialists may be present as chaplains or advisers, but the ideas and initiative ought to come from the lay members themselves. For Cardijn, the only effective way for young workers to "derive a true idea of their dignity and their worth" is through the formation of a "*special* organization, in which, *with them, by them* and *for them,* it is they themselves who work at their proper formation and little by little come to take the initiative in the practice of responsibility."[37] This same notion of empowerment and participation in the apostolate resonated not only with young workers and

---

[35] "Jeunesse Ouvrière Chrétienne 'Devient Jeunes Organisés et Combatifs,'" (2014), www.joc.be.

[36] Hari, *IYCW,* 15.

[37] De La Bedoyere, *The Cardijn Story,* 73.

students, but also with adult workers, farmers, and members of other professions. In the press release announcing its name change, JOC/ JOCF Belgium, for example, insisted on this fundamental mission: For and by youth: the JOC remains the JOC.

This notion of empowering those at the margins of society and the church to take the lead in their own milieus or social groups— what some called an apostolate of "like to like"—was affirmed by Vatican II's *Decree on the Apostolate of the Laity*, which made strong references to the jocist model. Citing an address of Pius XII to a YCW assembly in Montreal, the decree writes that "the young should become the first apostles of the young, in direct contact with them, exercising the apostolate by themselves among themselves, taking account of their social environment" (AA, no. 12).

Education and training is an essential component of this dimension of the YCW vision. Among YCW militants, the movement is often called a school for life.[38] At its best, it is a place where young people learn about themselves, broader social issues, the Christian ethical tradition, and other cultures. It is also a place where young people learn to cooperate with others and become leaders in organizing local meetings, national conferences, and international campaigns. The United Nations and many governments increasingly recognize this type of formation, which some have termed non-formal education, as playing a critical role in society. A recent paper from the European Union and Council of Europe on the role of youth organizations, for example, states:

> All learning in the youth field enables young people to acquire essential skills and competences and contributes to their personal development, to social inclusion and to active citizenship, thereby improving their employment prospects. Learning activities within the youth field—and youth work in general—provide a significant added value for society, the economy and young people themselves.[39]

---

[38] International Co-ordination of Young Christian Worker Movements, *ICYCW Declaration*, no. 16.

[39] *Pathways 2.0: Towards Recognition of Non-Formal Education and of Youth Work in Europe* (Strasbourg and Brussels: European Commission and the Council of Europe, 2011), 5, http://pjp-eu.coe.int.

A Movement Organized for Action

A second key feature of the jocist vision is the centrality placed on organized action, rooted in experience and discernment. The YCW is perhaps best known for its role in developing and popularizing the inductive method of see-judge-act or the review of life method. This approach has been tremendously important for Christian social movements around the world. Cardijn rooted his call for action in what he saw as a contradiction or tension between theological and historical realities. He framed the review of life method and his call to organized action in what he identified as three truths. The first truth for Cardijn is what he called the truth of faith, the conviction that each and every person is created with dignity, in the image and likeness of God, and is destined for communion in the reign of God. "Young workers," he insisted, "are not machines, or animals or slaves. They are the sons, the collaborators, the heirs of God." [40]

This first truth of faith finds a contradiction with the second truth, the truth of experience (or truth of life). This is the stark reality of not living in the fullness of the reign of God. Young workers today, as in the past, face injustice and suffering. According the IYCW "Declaration of Principles," young workers face a post–Cold War context with growing gaps between the rich and the poor, unequal distribution of technology and power, environmental exploitation, and the gradual erosion of rights of workers. [41]

In the face of these two truths Cardijn identifies a third, the truth of method (or truth of action). What is needed to confront this contradiction, he insisted, is organized action on the part of young workers at the local, national, and international levels:

Leaders and members learning to see, judge, and act; to see the problem of their temporal and eternal destiny; to judge the present situation, the problems, the contradiction, the demands of an eternal and temporal destiny; to act with a view to the conquest of their temporal and eternal destiny. To act individually and collectively, in a team, in a local section, in a regional

---

[40] Joseph Cardijn, "The Three Truths," presented at the First International Study Week of the YCW, Brussels, August 26, 1935, www.josephcardijn.com.

[41] Ninth International Council of the IYCW, "Declaration of Principles," no. 5.

federation, in a national movement, in meetings, in achievement, in life and in their environment, forming a single front, going forward to the conquest of the masses of their fellow-workers.[42]

According to the jocist method, movements and programs of support for specialized groups (such as workers, students, and farmers) are not enough. The Christian faith and the dignity of workers demand more than discussion, sharing, and prayer. Quoting the Epistle of St. James, Cardijn makes this point directly:

> The study circle does not exist for its own sake: its only meaning is in terms of action and organisation. The Apostle said: "Faith without works is dead." We must also declare that "the study circle without works is a dead study circle." The study circle is not just a teaching business. It communicates a faith, a faith enthusiastic for social, moral and religious action and organisation.[43]

At the local and national levels, actions take different forms. YCW Australia, for example, is engaged in a national campaign to address financial security and stability of young workers.[44] In 2014, YCW Philippines celebrated May Day with a week of actions presenting several demands, including "a 125–peso wage increase nationwide for workers in all sectors," an end to the "contractual work system," and an increase in quality education.[45] In India, the YCW recently organized a bicycle rally in rural areas of Tamil Nadu. As part of the action, thirty-two members of the YCW traveled the countryside with signs and organized street-corner meetings to demand increases in salaries and job security for young workers.[46]

At the global level the YCW movements take action through campaigns and international advocacy efforts. Both the IYCW and CIJOC have formal relationships as NGOs with the International

---

[42] Cardijn, "The Three Truths."

[43] Quoted in De La Bedoyere, *The Cardijn Story*, 77.

[44] "Campaigns," Young Christian Workers (2014), www.ycw.org.au.

[45] "May Day Celebration by the Philippines YCW: From Unemployment to Just Work," International Young Christian Workers (May 20, 2014), www.joci.org.

[46] "The Bicycle Rally of the India YCW," International Young Christian Workers (2014), www.joci.org.

Labour Organization (ILO) and the Council of Europe. Both are also members of the European Youth Forum, an important platform for youth NGOs. Since 1951, IYCW has been accredited as an NGO with ECOSOC. For its part, the CIJOC is recognized as an International Association of the Lay Faithful with the Pontifical Council for the Laity.

Through these different institutional relationships the two international YCW structures represent young workers in meetings with governments, church officials, and other NGOs. At times, they may be the only voices enabling young workers to speak directly on issues facing youth. For example, both CIJOC and IYCW were present with delegations at the recent International Labor Conferences of the ILO. At its 102nd session (2013), CIJOC and IYCW had two separate NGO delegations among only sixty NGOs present. At that session the IYCW presented a statement to the conference's Committee on Employment and Social Protection with a six-point plan to respond to the reality of young workers.

In a positive sign of cooperation between the two movement organizations of the YCW, both organizations also issued a joint twenty-one-page statement with five other Catholic NGOs entitled "Decent Work and the Post-2015 Development Agenda." Among other points, the statement calls upon "all governments, workers, and employers organizations . . . to work with youth movements and youth representatives to ensure a secure and meaningful future for the young generations."[47]

In 2014, CIJOC and IYCW again came together with other Catholic organizations to prepare for the 103rd session of the ILO Conference. Following a strategy meeting in Rome, ten movements reiterated key points from the 2013 statement and concluded by urging the participants in the conferences to recognize that

> decent work is essential to address the current challenges of inequalities and growing social injustice, while reinforcing human dignity and contributing to the common good. Human suffering resulting from unjust structures, from precarious and poorly remunerated forms of work, from human trafficking and

---

[47] "Statement of Catholic-Inspired Organizations on Decent Work and the Post-2015 Development Agenda" (2013), www.cijoc.org.

forced labor, from widespread forms of unemployment among youth and from involuntary migration cannot remain without response.[48]

YCW IDENTITY, MISSION, AND ORGANIZATION

The experience of the YCW raises several questions in relation to movement identity and mission that are also shared, to varying degrees, by the other Christian social movements, especially those close to the model of specialized Catholic action.

First, *how can movement organizations with federated structures maintain a common identity and cohesiveness across a global movement?* Both the IYCW and the CIJOC declarations of principles highlight the value of autonomy for their national movements, a freedom not enjoyed by the provincial structures of most congregations and societies of vowed religious. Unlike many congregations of vowed religious and other lay movements with centralized structures, the movements of specialized Catholic action are structured along the principle of subsidiarity, with each national movement having its own elected leadership, legal status, autonomy, and even descriptions of the YCW mission. This can be very advantageous as it enables young leaders to respond creatively to their own reality and context. It also makes more room for young people to take on leadership roles and define for themselves what it means to be a young worker.

However, this can also be problematic. The federated structure can make organizing international campaigns and engendering a sense of a common movement difficult. YCW national structures, in some respects, may compete with regional and international structures for the attention of local members. For example, rather than just one website, members of the YCW in Germany have access to at least three different movement websites: the national (CAJ), the European (JOC Europe), and the international levels (IYCW). Not to mention the website of CIJOC. Each site has its own style and pays attention to different social issues. One wonders how many members of the YCW regularly check all three levels.

---

[48] "Decent Work: The Best Way out of Poverty: Catholic-Inspired Organizations Reaffirm Their Commitment to Eliminate Poverty through Decent Work," International Labour Organization (May 9, 2014), www.ilo.org.

The autonomy of national movements can also lead to different interpretations of what it means to be YCW, making a split, as happened in the creation of CIJOC, more likely in a federated model, than in a more centralized model such as the Jesuits. Nothing, for instance, would stop several YCW groups from creating a third international YCW movement organization.

The split in the international YCW, between the IYCW and CIJOC, leads to a second question. *Do Christian social movements have any moral or ethical obligations to work toward unity within their movements?* Clearly, the YCW is not the only movement in the church that has experienced divisions. Consider, for instance, the many expressions of the Franciscan movement. The situation with the YCW, however, is slightly different given the movement's vision of uniting workers for common action.

There may be hope, albeit very slim, for reunification given the new atmosphere within the church under Pope Francis and the recent examples of cooperation at the ILO. Some efforts have been made in recent years to place the two international teams into dialogue with one another, and both the IYCW and the CIJOC have cooperated in networks with other international Catholic youth organizations and Catholic groups concerned with issues of work. The question remains, however, whether the international action of the YCW would be better served with one united movement organization.

The first two questions concern movement cohesion within a particular period of time. A third question concerns cohesion across time. *How can movements of young people with high levels of leadership transition maintain identity across time and ensure sustainability for the future?* One of the strengths of the YCW is that it is run by and for its target group—young workers. YCW groups are encouraged to enact age limits for leadership. This ensures that the voice of the movement remains young. Youth leadership in the YCW, however, does not necessarily mean that young leaders have the professional skills and resources necessary to run a national or international organization effectively.

Here is where chaplains, adult advisers, and support from the institutional church are invaluable in ensuring sustainability for youth-led movements. Chaplains play a particularly important role in advising young leaders, providing spiritual guidance, and maintaining links with the church and Christian tradition. Finding committed chaplains and the necessary institutional and financial support to maintain the YCW movement, however, are increasingly difficult. In many parts of the world bishops and religious superiors are increasingly reluctant to provide personnel to serve as full-time chaplains for the YCW and similar movements. Balancing the YCW commitment to youth-led structures with the need for sustainable infrastructure remains a challenge for the movement going forward, particularly where there are tensions with the institutional church.

Given its contribution to the church and society, the YCW movement sheds light on several important dimensions of the phenomenon of Christian social movements. As with the Jesuits, the YCW mission has been expressed through different movement organizations. For the YCW these structures include local cell groups, national movements, continental coordinations, and two global structures. Not all Christian social movements, however, express themselves through organized structures, as we will see in the following chapter.

Chapter 4

Plowshares

A Movement Crying Out from the Margins

They cut the fence and they started in about a half past two
They had no doubt when they thought about what they were called to do
The prophet said that hammers would make plowshares out of swords
And people turn their hearts to study peace instead of wars.

—RALPH HUTCHISON, "PLOWSHARES PLEASE"

In February 2014 a United States federal judge sentenced three Christian peace activists to prison sentences totaling more than thirteen years. The three—Michael Walli, a sixty-three-year-old member of the Dorothy Day Catholic Worker House in Washington; Greg Boertje-Obed, a fifty-seven-year-old Vietnam Veteran; and Megan Rice, SHCJ, an eighty-three-year-old Catholic religious sister—are an unlikely band of accused criminals. During her pre-sentencing statement Sr. Rice made an astonishing plea to the court: "We have to speak, and we're happy to die for that. To remain in prison for the rest of my life is the greatest honor that you could give to me. Please don't be lenient with me. It would be an honor for that to happen."[1]

---

[1] Patrick O'Neill, "Nuclear Weapons Facility Protest Sends Nun, Two Activists to Prison," *National Catholic Reporter*, February 19, 2014, www.ncronline.org.

What had these three peacemakers done? What would inspire an elderly nun to plead for a life sentence? Walli, Boertje-Obed, and Rice are members of the Plowshares movement, a diffuse collective of activists committed to peace, disarmament, and reconciliation. On July 28, 2012, they hiked through the woods and approached what many believed to be one of the most secure governmental facilities in the world, the Y-12 National Security Complex in Oak Ridge, Tennessee. Built as part of the Manhattan Project, the complex has been a source of uranium enrichment for nuclear weapons since the Second World War.

After cutting through three security fences, the trio approached the Highly-Enriched Uranium Manufacturing Facility for an action they named Transform Now Plowshares. They strung red crime tape at the site. They unveiled two banners, one stating: "Swords into Plowshares, Spears into Pruning Hooks —Isaiah." And they emptied eight baby bottles of blood on the building—blood donated by Thomas Lewis, a long-time Plowshare activist who died in 2008. When a security guard found them, they offered him bread, displayed flowers and a bible, and read a statement that began:

> Brothers and sisters, powers that be, we come to you today as friends, in love. We, like many of you, are people of faith, inspired by many who have gone before us, people like the prophets, Isaiah and Micah, Jesus as well as Gandhi, and the countless who call us "to beat swords into plowshares." May we now transform weapons into real, life-giving alternatives, to build true peace.[2]

For over thirty years the Plowshares movement has inspired hundreds of similar actions aimed at disarmament, peace, and reconciliation. Like the Jesuit Refugee Service and the Young Christian Workers, the Plowshares movement, inspired by the Christian tradition, has sought to respond to structural sin and injustice in a changing world.

In contrast to the other two movements in this project, Plowshares does not have a formalized structure. Rather, it is an unstructured

---

[2] Greg Boertje-Obed, Megan Rice, and Michael Walli, "A Statement for the Y-12 Facility," Transform Now Plowshares, http://transformnowplowshares.wordpress.com.

network of highly committed activists and communities that undertake actions aimed at transforming and abolishing war and instruments of war. Unlike the YCW or JRS, Plowshares (at least in its original form in the United States) is not recognized in any formal way by either the church or the state. In contrast to both the centralized structure of JRS and the federated structures of IYCW or CIJOC, there are no officially elected or appointed leaders of Plowshares. Rather than uniting in any formal way, the movement has coalesced around key charismatic figures and a common theology and style of resistance. Members engage in high-risk, deeply symbolic acts of civil disobedience that often result in arrests, trials, and imprisonment.

While deeply rooted in Catholic Christianity, the movement has included members of other religious traditions or no tradition at all. In some places, such as Sweden or Great Britain, it has little or no relationship with any faith tradition and has adapted its tactics and identity to meet the secular culture. While only a few hundred people have formally participated in official Plowshares actions in the United States, Europe, and Australia, the movement has helped to reshape the Christian response to war. Moreover, the innovative and controversial techniques adopted by these activists have been highly influential in the peace movement and have been adopted by other non-Christian activists and efforts aimed at social change.

AN INNOVATIVE MOVEMENT

The Plowshares movement began on September 9, 1980, when eight leaders—Fr. Daniel Berrigan, SJ; Philip Berrigan; Dean Hammer; Fr. Carl Kabat, OMI; Elmer Maas; Sr. Anne Montgomery, RSCJ; Molly Rush; and John Schuchardt—sneaked into the General Electric Nuclear Missile Re-Entry Division in King of Prussia, Pennsylvania.[3] With false identification cards the "Plowshares Eight" approached the testing facility where the nose cones for the Mark 12A minuteman missile were manufactured. Upon entering, they hammered on two nose cones, destroyed documents, and poured their blood on the weapons of war. Daniel Berrigan later explained

---

[3] For a historical analysis of the Plowshares movement, see Arthur J. Laffin and Anne Montgomery, *Swords into Plowshares: Nonviolent Direct Action for Disarmament* (San Francisco: Perennial Library, 1987).

the goal of this witness by situating it within the Christian commitments to peace and people who are poor: "We committed civil disobedience at General Electric because this genocidal entity is the fifth-leading producer of weaponry in the U.S. To maintain this position, GE drains $3 million a day from the public treasury, an enormous larceny against the poor."[4]

This was not a spontaneous action. The decision to enter the GE facility arose after months of planning and years of vigils by the local Brandywine Peace Community. Participating in the vigils, John Schuchardt, a lawyer, veteran, and member of Jonah House—a peace community in Baltimore—saw the need for a radical action to impede the production of weapons and draw attention to the evils of war. "Here we are vigiling," Schuchardt recalled, "but is it possible that a group of us could go in and bring this production line to a halt? These warheads have all these electronic components that would be very vulnerable to a hammer blow."[5]

> Unsure if such an innovative action would be supported, Jonah House members privately consulted key leaders in the US peace community. The group undertook nine months of reflection, prayer, and discernment to determine if this was the best course of action. I remember facing my fears and doubts. . . . Everyone stood to lose—nearly everything except our lives. The biggest loss, the one that loomed most fearsomely, was the prospect of years in prison, consequent family ruptures. And other losses: our good name and, as we saw it, our good work in the world.[6]

After nine months of prayerful discernment, eight activists were prepared to join this action. The name Plowshares, and the link to the biblical reference, came late in this process.[7] According to Daniel Berrigan, it was Rush, a grandmother and founder of the Thomas

---

[4] Quoted in Fred A. Wilcox, *Uncommon Martyrs: The Plowshares Movement and the Catholic Left* (Bloomington, IN: iUniverse, 1991), xii–xiii.

[5] Quoted in Sharon Erickson Nepstad, *Religion and War Resistance in the Plowshares Movement* (New York: Cambridge University, 2008), 30.

[6] Daniel Berrigan, *To Dwell in Peace: An Autobiography* (San Francisco: Harper and Row, 1987), 291.

[7] See Daniel Berrigan, "Foreword," in *The Plowshares Disarmament Chronology, 1980–2003*, ed. Arthur J. Laffin (Marion, SD: Rose Hill Books, 2003), ix–x.

Merton Center in Pittsburgh, who made the link between what they were trying to do and the prophetic vision detailed in Isaiah 2:4:

> He shall judge between the nations,
> and set terms for many peoples.
> They shall beat their swords into plowshares
> and their spears into pruning hooks;
> One nation shall not raise the sword against another,
> nor shall they train for war again.

The Plowshares Eight were quickly detained and arrested for their action. Having all previously served time for anti–Vietnam War actions, they were prepared for this and in fact welcomed the public arrest and trial as part of their efforts to bring attention to the evils of war and weapons manufacturing. As with subsequent Plowshares activists, the Plowshares Eight justified their actions with a "necessity defense," which stipulates that they were obliged to act to stop the manufacturing of weapons that threaten mass destruction and the future of humanity. After the judge denied them the possibility to use such a defense, a jury found them guilty of burglary, conspiracy, and criminal mischief. They received prison sentences ranging from five to ten years, with some of the group released early on appeal. They were re-sentenced in 1990 to two years of parole and time served.[8]

The Plowshares Eight initially did not see the King of Prussia action as the start of a new movement. This changed three months later when Peter DeMott, a war veteran, former seminarian, and member of Jonah House, spontaneously organized a second action by repeatedly ramming a commandeered van into the rudder of a Trident submarine under construction at the General Dynamics Boatyard in Groton, Connecticut.

In October 1981 a third Plowshares witness took place when five activists entered the GE Re-Entry Division Headquarters in Philadelphia. The "GE 5" walked as far as they could into the facility until they reached a locked door. They then organized a prayer service in the facility and poured bottles of their blood under the door of the weapons research laboratory until apprehended by guards at

---

[8] Nepstad, *Religion and War Resistance in the Plowshares Movement*, 33.

gunpoint. The statement offered by the GE 5 explains the use of blood, an important symbol for many Plowshares actions:

> We bring our blood and hammers into this corporate house of death. Our blood speaks of the consequences of Mark 12A production—the slaughter of human life and spirit and the neglect of human needs in favor of weapons. . . . We act today in hope with the belief that Mark 12A's can be stopped, that disarmament can happen and that human beings can make peace.[9]

On July 4, 1982, the General Dynamics Boatyard in Groton was the site of a fourth action led by nine activists, including Sr. Anne Montgomery of the Plowshares Eight. Entering by canoe, four activists boarded a Trident submarine, hammered on the ship, renamed it *USS Auschwitz* with spray paint, and poured blood on the vessel. Simultaneously, five other activists approached by land to hammer and pour blood on submarine equipment in a storage yard. They too were arrested and sentenced to jail.[10]

Less than two years after the action at the King of Prussia facility, a movement was taking shape. By the mid-1980s Plowshares quickly became a dynamic force shaping both the form and content of Christian social action in the United States. This new and very controversial movement inspired other actions and eventually spread to Europe and Australia. In 1983, Carl Kabat of the first Plowshares action, along with three Germans, organized the first campaign outside the United States at a US Army Base in West Germany. The movement would later spread with actions in Australia (1987), Sweden (1988), the Netherlands (1989), Great Britain (1990), and Ireland (2003). In both its Swedish and British manifestations the movement lost much of its founding Christian identity and adopted new organized forms that allow for more low-risk actions.[11]

In the United States the Plowshares actions have continued unabated even as US governmental policy has shifted from the Cold War to the so-called war against terror. While the movement has not

---

[9] Quoted in Laffin, *The Plowshares Disarmament Chronology, 1980–2003*, 15.

[10] Ibid., 15–16.

[11] Sharon Erickson Nepstad and Stellan Vinthagen, "Strategic Changes and Cultural Adaptations: Explaining Differential Outcomes in the International Plowshares Movement," *International Journal of Peace Studies* 13, no. 1 (2008).

dramatically changed the US nuclear position, it has succeeded in drawing greater support for disarmament among many Christians in the United States, even influencing the teachings of the US Catholic bishops. While they do not outright reject the possibility of justified use of force, the bishops' 1983 pastoral letter, *The Challenge of Peace*, develops the Catholic peace tradition by officially endorsing pacifism as a legitimate option for Catholics and by offering a strong condemnation of nuclear weapons.[12]

A PROPHETIC MISSION OF DISARMAMENT

Articulating the mission and identity of a diffuse movement can be difficult. While it lacks statutes and a formally agreed upon mission statement, the fundamental objective of Plowshares is clear: nuclear disarmament and the construction of a peaceful world. For Plowshares activists, particularly in the United States, this task is closely associated with specific readings of the Jewish and Christian scriptures, as indicated in the sentencing statement of the Plowshares Eight:

> In taking to heart the words of the prophets Isaiah and Micah, we determined to "beat swords into plowshares." . . . We wanted our action to ring with the truth that everyone can take responsibility for the weapons produced in our name. Our act was, simply, a response to the Gospel injunction to love our enemies. . . . We had acted in accord with the Nuremberg precept that citizens must act to prevent crimes against humanity. To prepare for nuclear war is to prepare for genocide and ecocide.[13]

Symbolic and Real Disarmament

According to Philip Berrigan the movement has two main goals. The first is "symbolic yet real disarmament."[14] Plowshares actions are characterized by direct nonviolent action to confront the production

---

[12] National Conference of Catholic Bishops, *The Challenge of Peace: God's Promise and Our Response* (Washington, DC: USCCB, 1983), nos. 111–122, www.usccb.org.

[13] Statement reprinted in Wilcox, *Uncommon Martyrs*, 234–35.

[14] Quoted in Laffin, *The Plowshares Disarmament Chronology, 1980–2003*, 7.

and use of genocidal weapons. Movement actions typically involve entering governmental or corporate facilities where weapons are produced or stored after a period of reflection and planning. Activists then undertake deeply symbolic actions, such as the pouring of blood, liturgical celebrations, displaying messages to indicate the criminal or genocidal nature of the weapons, and the use of hammers (including jackhammers), to embody the biblical prophecy of Isaiah and Micah.

These acts are not merely symbolic, as Berrigan points out. They involve the real destruction of weapons. Members of the Plowshares movement have caused millions of dollars worth of damage to security fences, submarines, missiles, weapon production facilities, computer equipment, blueprints, runways, railroad tracks, and airplanes.

Participants ground these controversial tactics by appealing to scripture and international law. For those informed by their Christian faith, the destruction of weapons is not only a matter of living out the prophetic vision of the Hebrew prophets, but it also reflects a clear commitment to Christian discipleship and following the teachings of Christ. Plowshares members often appeal to the beatitudes as a source of their action and vocation as peace builders.[15] The actions of Jesus overturning the moneychangers in the Temple (Mt 21:12–17) is also frequently cited as a model of the type of disruptive nonviolent action that lies at the heart of the Plowshares mission. John Dear, a priest and Plowshares activist, explains:

> Jesus was a nonviolent resister; indeed, a steadfast practitioner of nonviolent civil disobedience—a troublemaker, par excellance. His entire life led up to the culminating confrontation with the powers of his day, symbolized in the oppressive cult of the Temple system. His civil disobedience in the Temple provoked the ruling authorities to arrest Jesus. . . . Why did Jesus make such a scene, such a decision? Why did he provoke such trouble? Why was Jesus civilly disobedient? . . . He would speak the truth, dramatically, symbolically, at the center of the culture of death. He would turn over the tables of that culture, if necessary, but he would speak. . . . He would be obedient

---

[15] See Philip Berrigan and Elizabeth McAlister, *The Time's Discipline: The Beatitudes and Nuclear Resistance* (Baltimore: Fortkamp, 1989).

to God's will. He would make himself available to all. He was willing to be rejected, willing to risk his life, but he would go and speak up for what was right.[16]

Here, Dear highlights a key element of the Plowshares approach. Fidelity to God's law of love is more important than effectiveness. Jesus himself, as Philip Berrigan writes, was tried, convicted, and sentenced to death for breaking the law while adhering to the nonviolent mission of the gospel.[17] For members of the movement there is no expectation that their actions will immediately stop the production of all nuclear weapons. They know that the structures of violence will not be so easily defeated. But this does not change their duty to be faithful to the gospel.[18] According to Anne Montgomery, rather than speaking of Plowshares actions as acts of "civil disobedience," they should be described more as acts of "divine obedience. . . . Both divine and international law tell us that weapons of mass destruction are a crime against humanity and it is the duty of the ordinary citizen to actively oppose them."[19]

Plowshares activists, particularly those who may not identify strongly with the Christian identity, frequently speak a moral obligation to prevent genocide. This moral imperative, they argue, is solidified in international law through the Nuremberg Principles, established during the trial of Nazi war criminals after World War II. According to these principles, complicity in "a war crime, or a crime against humanity, . . . is a crime under international law."[20] Citizens, in other words, are obliged to act to stop any and all policies of their governments that constitute crimes against humanity.

For many movement participants who engage acts of resistance, the Nuremberg Principles justify their claims of innocence in their opposition to nuclear weapons. This reasoning is supported by

---

[16] John Dear, "Jesus and Civil Disobedience" (1994), www.fatherjohndear.org; John Dear, *The Sacrament of Civil Disobedience* (Baltimore: Fortkamp, 1994).

[17] Philip Berrigan, *Fighting the Lamb's War: Skirmishes with the American Empire: The Autobiography of Philip Berrigan* (Monroe, ME: Common Courage Press, 1996), 202.

[18] Nepstad, *Religion and War Resistance in the Plowshares Movement*, 212.

[19] Ibid., 61.

[20] See United Nations International Law Commission, *Principles of International Law Recognized in the Charter of the Nürnberg Tribunal and in the Judgment of the Tribunal* (1950), http://legal.un.org.

a 1996 advisory opinion of the International Court of Justice on the legality of the threat or use of nuclear weapons.[21] For Plowshares activists the risk of a crime against humanity—even if only a threat—obliges them to act to stop the genocidal nature of nuclear weapons. This is the argument at the core of the necessity defense that most Plowshares activists seek to use in their trials. Recalling the first Plowshares action, Philip Berrigan explains the basis for such a defense:

> We explained that nuclear war could happen at any time. It was imminent because the government was designing, building, and deploying nuclear weapons. It was imminent because our air, water, and food supply were being poisoned with radioactive isotopes; because atomic testing had already killed millions of people worldwide.[22]

Unfortunately, US courts, including the court at the Transform Now Plowshares trial, have generally rejected the use of this defense and any appeal to international law.[23] Plowshares activists in countries where international law has more sway have been more successful in this approach. For example, in 1996, the four women involved in the Seeds of Hope Ploughshares action were acquitted by a British jury after breaking into the British Aerospace factory at Warton in Lancashire and smashing the electronics on a Hawk jet with hammers. The four—Andrea Needham, Joanna Wilson, Lotta Kronlid, and Angie Zelter—initiated the action to protest the sale of two dozen British Aerospace Hawk jets to the Indonesian government, which was at that moment committing war crimes in its brutal conflict in East Timor (Timor-Leste). During the trial Wilson explained their appeal to the necessity defense: "We are pleading not guilty on the basis that we had lawful excuse as we were acting to prevent British Aerospace and the British Government from

---

[21] International Court of Justice, *Legality of the Threat or Use of Nuclear Weapons* (The Hague: International Court of Justice, 1996), www.icj-cij.org.

[22] Philip Berrigan, *Fighting the Lamb's War*, 187.

[23] "Defendants' Memorandum in Support of Their Response to the United States' Motion to Limit Their Defenses" (United States District Court Eastern District of Tennessee at Knoxville, November 16, 2012), NO. 3:12–CR-00107, http://transformnowplowshares.files.wordpress.com.

aiding and abetting genocide."[24] This was the first time a group of activists was acquitted for its Plowshares action. In 2006, an Irish jury acquitted Deirdre Clancy, Nuin Dunlop, Karen Fallon, Ciaron O'Reilly, and Damien Moran for their 2003 Pitstop Ploughshares action at Shannon Airport in Ireland, where US planes stopped on their way to war with Iraq. In a statement following the verdict they reaffirmed their beliefs:

> The conscience of the community has spoken. The government has no popular mandate in providing the civilian Shannon airport to service the US war machine in it's [sic] illegal invasion and occupation of Iraq. . . . The decision of this jury should be a message to London, Washington DC and the Dail that Ireland wants no part in waging war on the people of Iraq.[25]

Sharing Disarmament

A second goal of Plowshares, according to Philip Berrigan, involves "sharing disarmament," the task of witnessing to the power and possibility of peace and nonviolence to transform.[26] In this regard Plowshares activists have been successful in raising awareness to the dangers of nuclear proliferation among many American Christians. The symbolic actions and public statements of passionate, committed Christians, especially elderly priests and nuns, who risk their lives for peace captures the imagination of many in the church. The actions, the trials, and even the prison witness are all used to raise awareness of the evils of nuclear weapons.

THE PROTEST CHAPLAIN MOVEMENT

In 2011 social activists, inspired by the Spanish *Indignados* movement and the World Social Forum, convened in Zuccotti Park in New York City to protest a wide array of issues related to economic inequality, social

---

[24] "Seeds of Hope—East Timor Ploughshares," Catholic Social Teaching (2014), www.catholicsocialteaching.org.uk.

[25] "Not Guilty. The Pitstop Ploughshares All Acquitted on All Charges," Indymedia Ireland, July 25, 2006.

[26] Laffin, *The Plowshares Disarmament Chronology, 1980–2003*, 7.

justice, and the impunity of large Wall Street companies. Soon this innovative movement spread to hundreds of cities around the world and
helped to change public discourse, if only temporarily, with the slogan
"we are the 99%."

Though they were not the lead actors in the protests, some Christian
social movements did play a role in the Occupy movement. For example, Christian groups organized an interfaith march with the biblical
image of the golden calf—a symbol of what they understood to be the
idolatry endemic to the present economic system.

Among the more creative responses by Christians to the Occupy
movement has been the creation of Protest Chaplains, launched by
students studying theology at Harvard Divinity School. Concerned
with the spiritual care of those protesting in the parks, these teams of
ministers from different denominations and churches organized prayer
spaces in tent communities and arranged for regular Christian services
"on the streets," including Catholic masses. The website for the Protest
Chaplains movement describes its mission, in part, this way:

> American Christians have been far too polite, too quiet, and too
> accommodating of both the injustice and the blasphemous use of
> Jesus' name in committing atrocities in our nation and our world.
> That's why we want to protest with all those who, like us, *know
> in the deepest places of our souls* that another world is indeed
> possible. . . . And yet: many of us have been involved in orga-
> nizing, social justice efforts, and various campaigns, and we've
> seen burnout time and time again. So we're bringing the spiritual
> practices and our sense of the world as sacred to Wall Street and
> we hope to be of use to everyone who's camping out.[27]

More recently, separate examples of Protest Chaplains have appeared in the Maiden protest movement in Ukraine in 2013 and the
Umbrella movement in Hong Kong in 2014. In Ukraine, Greek Catholic
and Orthodox priests were actively present to offer their support to
protestors. In Hong Kong, Catholic priests celebrated mass on the
streets with the protestors. As with the Protest Chaplains, the Occupy
camps, tent-chapels, and spaces of prayers were set up in Ukraine and
Hong Kong to offer spaces of peace. The Protest Chaplain movement
in the United States and the similar experiences in Ukraine and Hong
Kong challenge the church to find ways to accompany people in future
movements for social change, because, as Protest Chaplains points
out, "Protesters have souls too!"

---

[27] "About Us," The Protest Chaplains (2013), http://protestchaplains.blogspot.
com.

PLOWSHARES AND THE CATHOLIC PEACE MOVEMENT

Plowshares did not appear out of thin air; it is deeply embedded in the broader movements of the American Catholic Left, in particular the pacifism of the Catholic Worker movement founded by Dorothy Day and Peter Maurin in 1933—a movement distinct from the Young Christian Workers featured in the previous chapter. In her survey of US Plowshares activists, sociologist Sharon Erickson Nepstad found that the majority (83.3 percent) reported being strongly inspired by Dorothy Day, with most having lived in a Catholic Worker community at some point in their lives.[28]

During the Second World War, Day took the very unpopular position of opposing the US involvement in the conflict. In the 1950s she made national headlines by publicly resisting New York City's defense drills. Rather than complying with orders to go to fall-out shelters, Day and her followers risked fines and arrest with demonstrations in City Hall Park.[29]

Inspired by Day's witness of nonviolent direct action, young members of the Catholic Worker movement took the lead in opposing the Vietnam War.[30] In 1963, Thomas Cornell and Christopher Kearns organized the first public protest of US-Vietnam policy. The following year they drew national attention by burning their draft cards.[31] Following their lead, David Miller, another Catholic Worker and a former student of Daniel Berrigan, was sentenced to two years in prison for burning his card, a violation of a law passed in response to the earlier actions of Kearns and Cornell. Weeks later, in November 1965, Roger LaPorte, a twenty-two-year-old Catholic Worker, immolated himself in front of the United Nations in opposition to the war. LaPorte's drastic action, which he did on his own, was highly controversial. The Archdiocese of New York quickly and publicly condemned it as a suicide. In the following days Daniel Berrigan

---

[28] Nepstad, *Religion and War Resistance in the Plowshares Movement*, 91.

[29] Jim Forest, *All Is Grace: A Biography of Dorothy Day* (Maryknoll, NY: Orbis Books, 2011).

[30] For a history of the relationship between the Catholic Worker movement and the innovative approach of the Plowshares, see Anne Klejment, "War Resistance and Property Destruction: The Catonsville Nine Draft Board Raid and Catholic Worker Pacifism," in *A Revolution of the Heart: Essays on the Catholic Worker*, ed. Patrick G. Coy (Philadelphia: Temple University Press, 1988), 272–312.

[31] Nepstad, *Religion and War Resistance in the Plowshares Movement*, 44–45.

joined his friends in a liturgy at the Catholic Worker community for LaPorte. His presence and brief sharing was perceived as violating orders from his superiors to refrain from public statements on the event, and he was ordered to leave the country for Latin America "with all possible speed."[32] As he later points out, the imposed "exile" by his Jesuit superiors, which might have been designed to "break" him, only served to "toughen [his] resolve."[33]

On October 27, 1967, Philip Berrigan, then a Josephite priest involved with the Catholic Worker and the civil rights movement; Thomas Lewis, a Catholic artist; David Eberhardt, a writer; and Rev. James Mengel, a veteran and United Church of Christ pastor, took the destruction of draft cards to another level. The Baltimore Four entered the Selective Service office, where they poured their own blood on draft files and were soon arrested.

On May 17, 1968, Philip organized a second draft-board raid, this time joined by his brother, Daniel; David Darst, FSC; John Hogan; Tom Lewis; Marjorie Bradford Melville; Thomas Melville; George Mische; and Mary Moylan. The nine removed over three hundred cards from the draft board in Catonsville, Maryland, and burned them with homemade napalm in the parking lot. The Catonsville Nine action, arrest, and subsequent trial brought increased attention to Christian peace activism and sparked similar draft raids across the country.[34] More was needed, these passionate activists argued, than "polite reform."[35] The urgency of the conflict demanded a response that was both nonviolent and revolutionary.[36]

While sympathetic to the cause, many in the Catholic peace movements, including Dorothy Day and Thomas Merton, OCSO, were cautious of the innovative tactics developed by the Berrigans and others—tactics that would become central to Plowshares actions.

---

[32] Thomas Buckley, "Man, 22, Immolates Himself in Antiwar Protest at UN," *New York Times*, October 10, 1965. See also Dorothy Day, "Suicide or Sacrifice?" *The Catholic Worker*, November 1965; Daniel Berrigan, *To Dwell in Peace*, 182.

[33] Daniel Berrigan, *To Dwell in Peace*, 184.

[34] Shawn Francis Peters, *The Catonsville Nine: A Story of Faith and Resistance in the Vietnam Era* (New York: Oxford University Press, 2012).

[35] Berrigan quoted in Wilcox, *Uncommon Martyrs*, 32; George Mische, "Inattention to Accuracy about 'Catonsville Nine' Distorts History," *National Catholic Reporter*, May 19, 2013, http://ncronline.org.

[36] See Daniel Berrigan, *To Dwell in Peace*, 215–40; Philip Berrigan, *Fighting the Lamb's War*, chap. 5; Philip Berrigan, *Prison Journals of a Priest Revolutionary* (New York: Holt, Rinehart, and Winston, 1970).

Not everyone agreed, for example, that priests and nuns should be involved in direct political action. Some questioned whether the destruction of property could still be considered a nonviolent witness. Would destroying human beings be next?[37] Still others did not believe that this was the best means to achieve the desired end. Would not the time and energy, they asked, be better spent lobbying political leaders and educating the public?[38]

The anti–Vietnam War activities of the revolutionary Catholic Left set the stage for the Plowshares movement in forging relationships, developing strategies for action, and developing a theology of Catholic radicalism. It was in this context, for instance, that Philip Berrigan and Elizabeth McAlister—both of whom had left their religious orders to marry—and a group of other activists formed Jonah House in 1972. In his autobiography Philip recalls the reason for establishing the community:

> Resisters cannot persist and survive without community. Sooner or later they will be frustrated and crushed. That's why we invested so much time, effort, and money into starting Jonah House. We wanted a place were people could share meals and ideas, study scripture together, and support one another through the long haul.[39]

Though inspired by the Catholic Worker's commitments and model of intentional community, Jonah House is not, strictly speaking, a Catholic Worker community. From its foundation it has sought to build relationships with other peace activists in a number of ways, including through the formation of the Atlantic Life Community—a network of peace groups on the East Coast of the United States committed to justice and nonviolent action. This was followed by the creation of the Pacific Life Community for those on the West Coast.[40] These networks regularly organize meetings, including Faith and Resistance retreats for activists and allies. Through these events

---

[37] Philip Berrigan, *Fighting the Lamb's War*, 95.

[38] Anne Klejment, *American Catholic Pacifism: The Influence of Dorothy Day and the Catholic Worker Movement* (Westport, CT: Praeger, 1996), 11. See also Andrew M. Greely, "L'Affaire Berrigan," *New York Times*, February 19, 1971.

[39] Philip Berrigan, *Fighting the Lamb's War*, 167.

[40] Nepstad, *Religion and War Resistance in the Plowshares Movement*, 56.

Plowshares maintains strong relationships with other Catholic, ecumenical, and nonsectarian groups in the United States, and it has formed many important personal ties with influential activists, teachers, and religious leaders who have provided support and encouragement to movement activists. At the same time, the prophetic actions of the Plowshares movement has helped to galvanize and mobilize the wider peace movement in the United States.

PLOWSHARES IDENTITY, MISSION, AND ORGANIZATION

Like JRS and YCW, a review of Plowshares raises important questions in relation to the mission, identity, and organization of Christian social movements. In contrast to both the YCW and JRS, Plowshares has no clearly defined organizational structures or agreed-upon mission statements. This has been both a strength and a liability to the movement over the past three decades. Despite the absence of a mission statement and a universally agreed-upon leadership structure, the Plowshares movement in the United States has maintained a clear identity and style. The campaign of Transform Now Plowshares in 2012 is remarkably similar to the first Plowshares action in King of Prussia, Pennsylvania, in 1980. The majority of actors continue to self-identify as Catholic. The tactics employed are acts of civil disobedience and nonviolent resistance that lead to arrest, trial, and prison witness. And the symbols displayed include blood, bibles, and hammers. The consistency and clarity in purpose and mission are in many ways key strengths of this homogeneous and prophetic movement.

The same cannot be said for expressions of the Plowshares movement outside the United States. While they began following the US model, activists in other countries felt the need to adapt movement identity, symbolism, and tactics to achieve the goal of disarmament in different social contexts, as Sharon Erikson Nepstad explores in her study on the movement. In both Great Britain and Sweden, the two places where Plowshares has organized the most actions outside the United States, the movement, according to Nepstad, has adapted in three important ways.

First, both the British Trident Ploughshares and the Swedish group Svärd till Plogbillar (swords into plowshares) decided to establish more formalized membership-based structures. Trident Ploughshares, for example, maintains a website and bank account. The Swedish group likewise developed a formalized structure before it dissolved.[41] Rather than depending on the charismatic leadership of the Berrigans and others, both European movements constructed new formalized leadership structures. The US movement, by contrast, has intentionally rejected any formalized structure.

Second, both the British and Swedish groups have moved away from the movement's Christian identity. Almost from the start Swedish activists dropped explicitly Christian aspects of the Plowshares identity and mission to adapt the movement to the largely secular context of Sweden. Appeals to scriptures, prayer, and the symbolic action of pouring blood, which resonate strongly within a Catholic cultural context, do not have the same impact in Sweden's historically Protestant culture. In Sweden, participants renamed Faith and Resistance retreats to Hope and Resistance retreats. As one activist reported to Nepstad, "*faith* and resistance is [*sic*] not our base."[42]

While the first campaigns in Britain strongly followed the US model, most British Ploughshares activists also adapted the movement to a more secular model. The Trident Ploughshares website, for example, describes itself in the following way:

Ploughshares is an enactment of the Biblical prophecies to "beat swords into ploughshares" but is now no longer a Christian movement but one which embraces people from many different faiths or from none at all. The underlying appeal is the universal call to peace, to abolish all war and to find peaceful ways to resolve our conflicts. It recognises the abuse of power that war always is, and the deep immorality of threats to kill.[43]

Not all in Britain have accepted this move away from the Christian identity. A smaller movement of activists seeks to maintain both the Christian identity and the use of high-risk prophetic actions.[44] This group, which is centered in the London Catholic

---

[41] Ibid., 170.

[42] Ibid., 156. See also Nepstad and Vinthagen, "Strategic Changes and Cultural Adaptations," 23.

[43] "The Ploughshares Movement: What Is Ploughshares?," Trident Ploughshares (2014), http://tridentploughshares.org.

[44] Nepstad and Vinthagen, "Strategic Changes and Cultural Adaptations," 33–36.

Worker, describes itself as the "orthodox Plowshares" movement. On November 3, 2000, it organized the Jubilee 2000 action. Martin Newell, CP, a British Catholic priest, and Susan van der Hijden, a Catholic Worker from Amsterdam, disabled a Trident warhead carrier on a British air force base and painted the phrases "The kingdom of God is among you," "Drop the debt, not the bombs," and "Love is the fulfillment of the Law."[45] According to van der Hijden, the split between the Trident group and this orthodox group occurred in part because the active Catholics were more willing to take risks. Their Catholic identity, she recalled in an interview, made them "more accepting of sacrifices or the idea of suffering for your beliefs. It was normal for us. It was kind of horrifying to them."[46] It may seem counterintuitive, but the deeper one adheres to Catholic identity, at least as seen through the Plowshares theology of resistance, the more one is willing to take radical, high-risk actions.

Finally, in adapting the movement to secular, historically Protestant contexts with the formation of more robust membership structures, both the British and Swedish models allowed for more low-risk tactics to attract more members and support for the cause of disarmament. Not surprisingly, the economic, personal, and physical costs of serving prison time for Plowshares actions is not widely attractive, especially for people with family responsibilities. To meet this concern, the Trident Ploughshares movement allows participants to choose different forms of engagement, including protest actions that are done with advanced notification to police. "These minimum disarmament actions," as Nepstad explains, "provide people with a way to feel as though they are having a real effect without making costly personal sacrifices."[47]

These adaptations in the Plowshares movement raise three important questions about the Plowshares identity and mission. *What happens to a Christian social movement if parts of it begin to move away from or reject its founding Christian identity?* In other words, how essential are Christian identity and symbolism to the movement? Must Plowshares campaigns follow the radical tactics of Plowshares

---

[45] "Jubilee Ploughshares: Catholics Convert Convoy," London Catholic Worker (2000), www.londoncatholicworker.org.

[46] Interview quoted in Nepstad and Vinthagen, "Strategic Changes and Cultural Adaptations," 34.

[47] Nepstad, *Religion and War Resistance in the Plowshares Movement*, 192.

Eight? Are secular members of the Trident Ploughshares in Britain members of the same movement as those in the United States, who are deeply informed by religious convictions? This question is not unique to Plowshares. Similar adaptations took place with some YCW groups in Northern Europe.

A second question concerns the organization of the Plowshares movement. *How can a diffuse movement maintain identity and cohesion without a clearly defined organization or mission statement?* Influenced by Dorothy Day's "Christian anarchism," and fearful that a robust organizational structure might enable greater surveillance and control by the state, the Plowshares Movement in the United States has intentionally resisted the formation of an official movement organization. The diffused movement structure has a number of benefits. Centrally organized movements are vulnerable to becoming bureaucracies, often take fewer risks, and are in danger of losing their prophetic edge—what Max Weber famously describes as "the routinization of charisma."

However, social movements without a strong movement organizations risk fragmentation and division. Generally, the more diffuse a movement organization is, the more difficult it becomes to maintain a shared purpose.[48] Given this challenge, how does the Plowshares movement maintain any sense of cohesion and identity?

According to Nepstad, several factors help create movement unity among Plowshares in the United States. First, Plowshares activists continue to draw inspiration from the founding generation of charismatic leaders, in particular, the Berrigans and Elizabeth McAlister. Their willingness to risk arrest, imprisonment, and possibly even death gives them a certain moral authority throughout the Christian peace movement. However, how the movement will manage following the passing of all the founding members has yet to be seen.

Second, Plowshares in the United States maintains its dynamic movement identity because of the theology of resistance that has developed within the Catholic Left. This biblically informed prophetic theology offers a consistent vision to mobilize Christian action against war. As the movement becomes more religiously diverse and the generation of activists with strong theological training (priests,

---

[48] Mayer N. Zald and Roberta Ash, "Social Movement Organizations: Growth, Decay, and Change," *Social Forces* 44, no. 3 (March 1, 1966): 327–41.

former seminarians, nuns, and so on) passes away, maintaining this theology will be a challenge.

A final factor is that the US Plowshares movement remains deeply embedded in other communities of the Catholic Left. Jonah House, the Atlantic and Pacific Life Communities, Catholic Worker houses, and to a lesser degree, the religious orders of priests and nuns involved in Plowshares actions have been invaluable sources of support, both practical and moral. Relationships and partnerships with other movements appear essential for more diffuse movements. For instance, these associated social movements help to spread and reinforce radical theological commitments and the theology of resistance. They are important spaces to share the vision of the movement with others. People often learn about Plowshares actions and the issues involved through publications, websites, and meetings of these associated groups, including Pax Christi USA and Sojourners.

At a much more practical level communities such as Jonah House play a critical role for activists, especially lay members with families. They offer "assistance with the logistics of high risk activism," including the planning of actions; help during trials; and aid during imprisonment.[49] The last includes helping to take care of children when parents face long-term prison sentences.[50]

A third question to surface with the Plowshares movement concerns its relationship to the wider Christian community. *Must a Christian social movement be recognized in some formal way by official ecclesial structures in order to be considered Christian?* Unlike JRS, CIJOC, and many YCW groups, Plowshares has no formal relationship with any church. There are no chaplains or ecclesiastical assistants. It has no status under Canon Law, and the official church structures are generally hostile to the innovative and controversial tactics of the movement. What does this say about the legitimacy of the Plowshares' charism when Catholic tradition generally sees bishops as having a responsibility for discerning the ecclesial nature of a movement?

This chapter's study of the Plowshares movement highlights the distinctive ways in which Christian social movements seek to respond to the gospel mission in the world. The difference among

---

[49] Nepstad, *Religion and War Resistance in the Plowshares Movement*, 114.
[50] Ibid., 108.

Christian social movements, as the last three chapters have shown, is not only a question of distinctive missions. The tactics and organization of the Plowshares is considerably different from both JRS and YCW. Despite these very real differences, there are some clear commonalities among the three case studies of this project. What does all this mean theologically? How do these Christian social movements relate to the church? What do they say about how God may be at work in the world? The next section of this book seeks to provide some answers to these questions.

Part II

Theological Considerations— Mission, Charism, and Grace

Chapter 5

Christian Social Movements
and the Church's Justice Mission

On the surface the three case studies of this project appear to have very little in common. Jesuit Refugee Service is an apostolic work (movement organization) of a religious society involved in the accompaniment, service, and defense of refugees. The Young Christian Workers is a global lay movement of, for, and by young workers. Both JRS and YCW are engaged in public social engagement for the global common good through different institutionalized relationships with the UN system. The Plowshares, by contrast, is a diffuse movement, most active in the United States, consisting of lay and religious activists committed to resisting the culture and instruments of war though prophetic actions. In contrast to the other movements, Plowshares has opposed the creation of any formal organizational structure.

Upon closer investigation, however, the three groups have much in common. Inspired by the Christian faith, JRS, YCW, and Plowshares are actively involved in confronting suffering and indifference in the world. All three have been shaped by the church's turn toward justice and inclusion in 1960s and 1970s. Each one, in its own way, is challenging the notion that religious groups ought to be relegated to the private (nonpolitical) sphere. And all three movements understand collective social action in the pursuit of social justice to be a constitutive element of their movement identity and mission.

After looking at these three case studies, this section now examines the significance of Christian social movements through two related theological frameworks. In this chapter I outline several models of mission that have surfaced over the past fifty years. Each missiological framework situates the justice work of Christian social movements in distinct ways. After approaching movements through the lens of the church's mission (missiology), Chapter 6 employs a pneumatological lens (study of the Holy Spirit) to assess how Christian social movements might be consider structures of grace. But first, what is the relationship between Christian social movements and the mission of the church?

Socially engaged Christian social movement are not without their critics. Not everyone accepts a role for Christian communities engaged in justice actions. While sophisticated arguments against a public role for religion have been made for well over a century, the recent attacks on religion by the "new atheists" are emblematic of a more popular resistance to the public role of all religious actors and organizations. Religion, it continues to be argued, has no place in political life. It should either be privatized or suppressed altogether. For the champions of this position today, including Sam Harris, Richard Dawkins, and Christopher Hitchens, religion functions primarily as a source of conflict and oppression and thus should not be allowed to occupy a place in the public sphere.[1]

Others, while accepting a public role for some Christian social movements, take issue with those movements committed to social justice. In the United States a very popular radio host, Glenn Beck, for example, urged his listeners in his March 2, 2010, broadcast:

> I beg you, look for the words "social justice" or "economic justice" on your church Web site. If you find it, run as fast as you can. Social justice and economic justice, they are code words. Now, am I advising people to leave their church? Yes! If I'm going to Jeremiah's Wright's church? Yes! Leave your church. Social justice and economic justice. They are code words. If you have a priest that is pushing social justice, go find another parish. Go alert your bishop and tell them, "Excuse me are you down with this whole social justice thing?" I don't care what the church is. If it's my church, I'm alerting the church authorities: "Excuse me, what's this social justice thing?" And

---

[1] See Richard Dawkins, *The God Delusion* (Boston: Houghton Mifflin, 2006); Sam Harris, *The End of Faith: Religion, Terror, and the Future of Reason* (New York: W. W. Norton, 2004); Christopher Hitchens, *God Is Not Great: How Religion Poisons Everything* (New York: Twelve, 2007).

if they say, "Yeah, we're all in that social justice thing," I'm in the wrong place.

His broadcast prompted a storm of rebuttals.[2]

Christian social movements also face resistance within the church. For some, it is not the role of the church or church institutions to be involved directly in the supposedly worldly or profane struggles for political, social, and economic change. As such, Christian movements and ecclesial organizations, especially those of vowed religious, should not be involved directly in social justice. It is not the role of the church, for example, to directly seek solutions to the root causes of forced migration, to change international labor standards, to urge action on human rights abuses, or to challenge the nuclear weapons industry. Rather, they argue, the role of the church should be limited to worship, spirituality, prayer, and education about social issues.

These different areas of resistance to the social engagement of Christian movements and movement organizations raise an interesting theological, and more specifically missiological, question: what is the relationship between collective action for social justice and the church's evangelizing mission? Put in another way, do nonmagisterial Christian movements and movement organizations act *as church* in their public engagement for justice?

At first glance socially engaged Christians might be surprised with these questions. Shouldn't the answer be obvious? Christian organizations clearly act as church in their promotion of human rights, the defense of migrants, and involved in peacebuilding efforts. A closer examination of Roman Catholic Church teaching, however, reveals a more complex picture.

In the fifty years since the Second Vatican Council debates continue on how best to receive its model of mission, particularly the relationship between mission and justice. While *Ad Gentes* explicitly addresses the topic, the council's teachings on mission are not limited to this document alone. In isolation, the decree offers surprisingly little about the relationship between mission and action for justice in the world. This relationship only becomes clear when one takes into account the broader vision of what has been described as "a

---

[2] For example, see Laurie Goodstein, "Outraged by Glenn Beck's Salvo, Christians Fire Back," *New York Times*, March 11, 2010, www.nytimes.com.

missionary council."[3] The theme of mission and questions about the church's relationships to the world surface throughout the other texts of the council, most notably in *Lumen Gentium, Apostolicam Actuositatem, Dignitatis Humanae,* and *Gaudium et Spes.*

Due to the process by which the conciliar documents were formulated, aspects of Vatican II's vision of mission are somewhat ambiguous and open to interpretation. Of particular relevance is the question of who is to be understood as the agent of social transformation. At times the council speaks of the responsibility of the whole church, "the people of God," to be a "sign and instrument" in history (LG, no. 1). Social engagement is described as a task of everyone—laity, clerics, and religious. In other places, however, the council points to the "special vocation" of its lay members to transform the temporal sphere and to do so in their personal capacity.[4] This has led to the development of two very different approaches to the mission-justice question. Each one situates Christian social movements in a different way. This chapter explores the ecclesial and missiological significance of Christian social movements in light of these two distinct models of mission. Ultimately, how one comprehends the ecclesial identity of Christian social movements says much about how one understands the importance of social justice for the church's mission.

EDUCATORS NOT ACTORS:
THE DISTINCTION OF PLANES MODEL

Before turning to the two predominant post-conciliar approaches to mission, it is worth briefly considering how Christian social movements were understood in the decades leading up to the council. Confronted with the inadequacies of ultramontane Christendom, which rejected secularization and sought to place society under the control of the church, French Catholic thinkers developed a new framework, "the distinction of planes," to enable lay Christians to participate in secular civil society. This was particularly urgent after

---

[3] Stephen B. Bevans, "Decree on the Church's Missionary Activity: *Ad Gentes,*" in *Evangelization and Religious Freedom: Ad Gentes, Dignitatis Humanae,* ed. Stephen B. Bevans and Jeffrey Gros, Rediscovering Vatican II (New York: Paulist Press, 2009), 3.

[4] See Richard R. Gaillardetz, *The Church in the Making: Lumen Gentium, Christus Dominus, Orientalium Ecclesiarum,* Rediscovering Vatican II (New York: Paulist Press, 2006), 149.

World War II as Christians sought to rebuild Europe and prevent a future disaster. This model emphasized the social responsibility of the laity by advocating for "the *complete* autonomy and secularity of the temporal order with respect to the church."[5]

According to this model clear distinctions are made between the church and the temporal plane, between the responsibilities of the church and those of the laity, and between the *actions of a Christian* and the *actions of a Christian as such*. Drawing from the philosophical work of Étienne Gilson, Jacques Maritain identifies "three distinct planes."[6] The first is the spiritual, liturgical plane of the church (for example, mass, prayer groups). The second is that of the temporal, concerned with social, political, cultural and economic activity (for example, work, voting, media). Both are good and, in their own ways, ordered to God as their final end. But they should be separate in most cases. Occupying an intermediary space is a third plane, where Christians act temporally as formal members of the church *only* "in order to defend their religious interests."[7]

This proposes a further distinction between the actions of "a Christian" and the actions of "a Christian as such." According to Maritain, the lay person acts—and indeed has the responsibility to act—as *a Christian* in the second plane in seeking to transform the society under the inspiration of Christian teachings. This action, even when done in association with other Christians in Christian social movements, however, does not constitute an action of the church or a direct participation in the apostolic mission. Rather, it is the action of the Christian in a personal capacity. By contrast, the action of the *Christian as such*, in which the lay person participates in the mission of the church, takes place only within the ecclesial-liturgical (first) plane of action and, when necessary, to defend the church in the third plane.[8]

In short, this model limits the direct engagement of church action in society. The sphere of action for official church structures including priests and vowed religious is the spiritual plane. Accordingly,

---

[5] Dean Brackley, *Divine Revolution: Salvation and Liberation in Catholic Thought* (Maryknoll, NY: Orbis Books, 1996), 69.

[6] Jacques Maritain, *Integral Humanism: Temporal and Spiritual Problems of a New Christendom*, trans. Joseph W. Evans (New York: Scribner and Sons, 1968), 298.

[7] Ibid., 297–98.

[8] Ibid., 294. See also 268–70.

ecclesial movements are limited only to a pedagogical or indirect role in relation to questions of justice. Instead of being agents of social change, their role is to "*prepare* laymen to act *as Christians*" in the worldly plane.[9]

Speaking directly about YCW and the movements of specialized Catholic action, Yves Congar, OP, described their role as indirect. They have "the duty of inspiring society with the Christian spirit," but this must be done indirectly through means such as education. It is not the role of Catholic action movements, *as organizations*, he stressed, to take up "the task of the direct 'technical transformation of the political or economic structures.'"[10]

This model, as Gustavo Gutiérrez points out in *A Theology of Liberation*, was not fully accepted by the specialized Catholic action movements that saw themselves as called to act as church in the promotion of justice. Any group that challenged this model, like the French Young Christian Students movement, which spoke out on the rights of Algerians in the 1960s, soon found itself in conflict with its bishop and ultimately, in the words of Gutiérrez, such groups "burned themselves out."[11]

MISSION AS LIBERATING SERVICE OF THE REIGN OF GOD

The distinction of planes was certainly an improvement over earlier Catholic models that wanted to reconstruct a Europe under the control of the pope. Ultimately, however, it proved ineffective for many Christian social movements.[12] In the decade following the council a dynamic justice consciousness took root among Christian social movements around the world. Catholic and Protestant movements began to perceive their role in relation to social questions in a new light. Following the Second Vatican Council the movements of vowed religious were invited to renew their own missions. Many, like the Jesuits in GC 32 (1974–75), rearticulated their own sense

---

[9] Ibid., 298.

[10] Yves Congar, *Lay People in the Church: A Study for a Theology of Laity*, trans. Donald Attwater (Westminster, MD: Newman, 1956), 269. See also 368.

[11] Gustavo Gutiérrez, *A Theology of Liberation: History, Politics, and Salvation* (Maryknoll, NY: Orbis Books, 1988), 49.

[12] Ibid., 48–49.

of mission with a strong commitment to justice and service to the poor. Similar shifts took place among the lay movements of specialized Catholic action, including the IYCW, whose controversial 1975 World Council articulated a "Declaration of Principles" with clear positions in favor of justice and liberation. It was also in this period that the Berrigan brothers and others in the American Catholic peace movement developed the provocative and innovative tactics that became central to the Plowshares movement.

This shift toward a justice consciousness is a result of many factors, including Vatican II's call for the church to engage the world; a return to the ethical teachings found in scripture; and the broader secular movements for liberation, women's rights, and civil rights that took place in the late 1960s and early 1970s. All of this reflects an emerging framework of mission that Stephen Bevans and Roger Schroeder describe as "liberating service of the reign of God."[13]

The new, more integrated approach is clearly evident in Paul VI's *Populorum Progressio* (1967) and *Octogesima Adveniens* (1971). In *Populorum Progressio,* Pope Paul follows *Gaudium et Spes* by rooting the church's concern for social justice and human development in the person of Jesus Christ, "who cited the preaching of the Gospel to the poor as a sign of his mission" (PP, no. 12). Building upon the work of the French theologian Louis-Joseph Lebret, OP, Pope Paul offers a holistic vision that calls the church to take action for the whole person and all people (PP, no. 14). The earlier divisions between the realities of the spiritual plane and the temporal world seem to disappear with this text, which links action for justice and development with authentic "spiritual progress" (PP, no. 76).

In its second section the encyclical commends the previous work of missionaries in their response to the social and cultural needs of people. While important, however, these "local and individual undertakings are no longer enough." Recognizing the increasing complexity and interconnection of social issues, Paul VI calls for "concerted action" that includes but goes beyond the local charitable efforts that marked mission in the past (PP, no. 13).[14]

---

[13] See Stephen B. Bevans and Roger Schroeder, *Constants in Context: A Theology of Mission for Today* (Maryknoll, NY: Orbis Books, 2004), chap. 10.

[14] Philip Land, "*Populorum Progressio,* Mission and Development," *International Review of Mission* 58, no. 232 (October 1, 1969): 400–407.

The church, he writes in *Octogesima Adveniens*, has "a double function" in the public sphere. First, it has a role of forming, educating, and inspiring Christian individuals with moral and ethical visions. Beyond the task of enlightening minds, it is also called to apostolic action. "It is not enough" merely to speak out against "injustices." Such words are meaningless "unless they are accompanied for each individual by a livelier awareness of personal responsibility and by effective action" (OA, no. 48). In both of these tasks ecclesial movements play an important role, something explicitly recognized toward the end of the encyclical when it speaks to the role of Christian organizations in transforming society (OA, no. 51).

This same point is repeated in a 1971 document by the Pontifical Council for the Laity to classify the IYCW and other lay movements who were members of the Conference of International Catholic Organizations (ICOs). The conference, originally created in 1927 by lay organizations seeking to participate in the League of Nations, reconstituted itself after the creation of the United Nations.[15] By the 1960s ICO became a juridical category for the more than thirty international lay organizations that were actively engaged with the UN system.

Building off *Gaudium et Spes,* the *Guidelines for the Definition of Catholic International Organizations* (1971) identifies the public engagement Catholic movements in United Nations advocacy with the mission of the church.[16] These movements, according to the *Guidelines*, are "a form of presence" of the church in international life. The recognition as an ICO by the Holy See "authenticates its

---

[15] For more history on the Conference of ICOs, see Rosemary Goldie, *From a Roman Window: Five Decades of the World, the Church, and the Laity* (Melbourne: HarperCollins Melbourne, 1998); François Blin, *Repères Pour L'histoire de La Conférence des Organisations Internationales Catholiques (1927–2008)* (Paris: Editions Eclectica, 2008).

[16] *Gaudium et spes* urges support for ICOs in their global advocacy work: "Different Catholic international bodies can assist the community of nations on the way to peace and brotherhood; these bodies should be strengthened by enlarging their number of well-trained members, by increasing the subsidies they need so badly, and by suitable coordination of their forces. Nowadays efficiency of action and the need for dialogue call for concerted effort. Organizations of this kind, moreover, contribute more than a little to the instilling of a feeling of universality, which is certainly appropriate for Catholics, and to the formation of truly worldwide solidarity and responsibility" (GS, no. 90).

participation in the mission of the Church."[17] Like *Octogesima Adveniens,* the *Guidelines* situate Catholic movements, at least those with recognition, as participating in the church's mission, even in their global advocacy for justice. Pope Paul VI reaffirmed this point in several addresses to the Conference of ICOs in the 1970s. In a 1975 address, for example, he spoke of the responsibility of Catholic organizations to "act in the world to transform it into a more just and humane society" based on "the spiritual and transcendent mission of the Church."[18]

The most influential statement on social justice appears later in 1971. In *Justitia in Mundo (Justice in the World)* the World Synod of Bishops roots the church's vocation to act for justice in God's reign and the gospel demands to love one's neighbor.[19] The Synod's most influential and controversial sentence appears in its introductory section with the claim that "action on behalf of justice and participation in the transformation of the world is a constitutive dimension" of the "Church's mission" (JM).

As Charles Murphy writes, this was a point of contention at the subsequent 1974 Synod of Bishops, meeting on the theme of evangelization.[20] In particular, questions were raised concerning the most appropriate way to interpret *constitutive.* Should *constitutive* be understood as "essential" or "integral"? Is action for justice so central to Christianity that there can be no evangelization without it?

---

[17] "International Catholic organizations are a form of presence. At the international level the recognition of an organization as Catholic implies the approval of it by the Holy See, which authenticates its participation in the mission of the church" (translation mine). Pontifical Council for the Laity, "Respiciens Normas Quibus Instituta Internationalia Catholica Definiuntur," *Acta Apostolicae Sedis* 63, no. 1 (1971): 952.

[18] See Paul VI, "Discours Aux Membres Des Organisations Internationales Catholiques," December 6, 1975, http://www.vatican.va.

[19] For a perspective on the 1971 Synod from the point of view of Philip Berrigan, who was in prison for his peace actions at that time, see his letter to Bishop William Baum Berrigan, in Philip Berrigan, *Fighting the Lamb's War: Skirmishes with the American Empire: The Autobiography of Philip Berrigan* (Monroe, ME: Common Courage Press, 1996), 139–45.

[20] Charles M. Murphy, "Action for Justice as Constitutive of the Preaching of the Gospel: What Did the 1971 Synod Mean?" in *Readings in Moral Theology No. 5: Official Catholic Social Teaching,* ed. Charles E. Curran and Richard A. McCormick (New York: Paulist Press, 1986), 160.

Adopting a different tone from the 1971 Synod, Pope Paul's 1975 apostolic exhortation *Evangelii Nuntiandi* points to evangelization—not action for justice and social transformation—as the constitutive element of the church's mission (EN, no. 14). This does not mean, however, that action for justice is foreign to mission and evangelization. On the contrary, Paul VI envisions mission as "a complex process" that, among other aspects, includes and demands efforts aimed at liberation and the creation of a more just social order. Mindful of the critiques of the 1971 Synod and the dangers of reducing "mission to the dimensions of a simply temporal project"—what has been called horizontalism—Paul prioritizes Christ's message of liberation "from everything that oppresses man" (EN, no. 24). Evangelization would "not be complete," he argues, if it fails to consider "the unceasing interplay of the Gospel and of man's concrete life, both personal and social" (EN, no. 29).

MISSION, JUSTICE, AND THE NEW EVANGELIZATION

Partly as a response to perceived excesses in the shift to justice, a different missiological framework took shape under the pontificates of John Paul II and Benedict XVI. While social concerns appear in their writings, both popes express concern that the direct engagement of lay movements, religious orders, and priests in public life might overshadow or even compromise the church's true spiritual mission of proclaiming Christ. In this period, the social engagement of the IYCW, the Jesuits, and priests/religious who were directly involved in politics were of particular concern to Vatican officials.

For instance, in his 1982 "Allocution to Jesuit Provincials," John Paul II critiqued the recent Jesuit turn to justice by stressing that the role of priests is different from that of the laity. Priests are not social workers, he insisted. The primary function of the priest, and by extension movements of priests, is not the promotion of justice but of spirituality and the care of souls.[21]

Though it strongly highlights the responsibility of Christians to work for solidarity in a world divided by sin and injustice, *Sollicitudo*

---

[21] John Paul II, "Allocution to the Jesuit Provincials" (Vatican City: Libreria Editrice Vaticana, 1982), www.vatican.va.

Rei Socialis (1987) describes the church's role in terms of "guiding people's behavior" and giving rise to personal "commitment to justice" (SRS, no. 41). This indirect approach, as Mary Elsbernd points out, amounts to a reinterpretation of *Octogesima Adveniens*'s vision for collective social action.[22] Much like the distinction of planes model, the church's role according to John Paul II, ought to be limited. Christians ought to act for solidarity and justice, but this is not a direct ecclesial function.

In *Redemptoris Missio* (1990) John Paul II cites his earlier text *Redemptor Hominis* (1979) to define the church's primary mission as the proclamation of Jesus Christ (RM, no. 4). At the beginning of the text he laments that this has suffered from a misinterpretation of conciliar teaching on dialogue, social engagement, and the possibility of salvation outside the church. In short, the task of proclaiming Christ cannot be put aside by those involved in social action or dialogue. A decade later the Congregation for the Doctrine of the Faith (CDF), under the leadership of Joseph Ratzinger, argued this point in *Dominus Iesus* (2000).

Not surprisingly, Pope Benedict XVI largely followed the line of his predecessor. In *Deus Caritas Est* (2005) he speaks of charity, and not justice, as the constitutive element in the church's mission (DCE, nos. 20–25).[23] True to his Augustinian outlook, he highlights the distinct roles of the church and the state, charity and justice, the laity and the church. It is the role of the state, not the church, he writes, to safeguard and promote justice. The church does not seek a direct engagement in political questions but instead aims to "purify reason" through its social doctrine (DCE, no. 28). In rather sharp contrast to both *Justice in the World* and *Evangelii Nuntiandi*, *Deus Caritas Est* leaves little room for direct action for justice as a role of the church. Much like the distinction of planes model, Benedict stresses that lay faithful "are called to take part in public life in a personal capacity" (DCE, no. 29). In his 2007 address to the leadership of more than eighty Catholic NGOs, Benedict cites this section of *Deus Caritas Est* when describing the role played by what the Vatican describes as Catholic-*inspired*

---

[22] Mary Elsbernd, "What Ever Happened to *Octogesima Adveniens*?" *Theological Studies* 56, no. 1 (March 1995): 39–60.

[23] Charles M. Murphy, "Charity, Not Justice, as Constitutive of the Church's Mission," *Theological Studies* 68, no. 2 (2007): 274–86.

NGOs rather than the previous language of international Catholic organizations.[24]

"The unavoidable connotation" with this line of thought, as Lisa Sowle Cahill points out, "is that the Church's 'real' identity inheres in the ordained and in ecclesial structures supervised by the episcopacy."[25] For many ecclesial movements this distinction between direct and in-direct social action is problematic because it opposes their collective actions for justice with their ecclesial identity. The final sections of *Deus Caritas Est*, in fact, warns the church's charitable and humani-tarian organizations against being "inspired by ideologies aimed at improving the world" (DCE, no. 33). But what would this mean for JRS and its efforts to seek durable solutions to forced displacement?

Concern over horizontalism among ecclesial movements is strongly developed a few months later with the CDF's 2007 *Doc-trinal Note on Some Aspects of Evangelization*. Citing *Redemptoris Missio* and *Deus Caritas Est*, the note raises concerns with what it perceives as relativistic or reductionist forms of evangelization, es-pecially in the areas of social action and dialogue—critiques made of both the Jesuits and the IYCW.[26] Nowhere in the note do we see the teaching of Pope Paul VI that action for justice is an integral part of evangelization.

With *Caritas in Veritate* (2009) there are hints of what Cahill describes as a "political reorientation" in Benedict's understanding of justice.[27] The church's role, he writes, is not limited only to "her charitable and educational activities." On the contrary, he points to the "public role" of the church and its duty to respond to issues that threaten human dignity (CV, no. 11). Citing Paul VI's *Evangelii Nuntiandi*, Benedict reiterates the linkages between evangelization and liberation. While he still prioritizes the role of social doctrine in the formation of conscience, he acknowledges that "*testimony to*

[24] Benedict XVI, "Address of His Holiness Benedict XVI to Representatives of the Holy See; to International Organizations and to Participants in the Forum of Catholic-Inspired Non-Governmental Organizations," *The Holy See*, December 1, 2007, www.vatican.va.

[25] Lisa Sowle Cahill, "*Caritas in Veritate*: Benedict's Global Reorientation," *Theological Studies* 71, no. 2 (June 1, 2010): 297.

[26] Congregation for the Doctrine of the Faith, *Doctrinal Note on Some Aspects of Evangelization* (Vatican City: Libreria Editrice Vaticana, 2007), no. 3, www.vatican.va.

[27] Cahill, "*Caritas in Veritate*," 304.

Christ's charity, through works of justice, peace, and development, is part and parcel of evangelization" (CV, no. 15). This is an important movement in Benedict's thought that clearly supports the public engagement of Christian social movements.

This shift in understanding is largely lost in the subsequent post-synodal apostolic exhortation *Africae Munus* (2011), the *Motu Proprio: On the Service of Charity* (2011), and the preparation documents leading up to the Synod on the New Evangelization in 2012. Collective action for justice and the role of Christian social movements, in fact, factors very little in the official texts of the 2012 Synod. This was noted by a few of the participants, including one bishop who critiqued the synod's document for the being "rather weak" in its treatment of justice.[28]

MISSION AS PROPHETIC DIALOGUE

The vision of mission and evangelization developed during the Second Vatican Council and in the immediate post-conciliar period inspired Christian social movements—both lay and religious—to understand action for justice as an integral dimension to their own specific missions and the mission of the church as a whole. These developments, however, have not been welcome by all in the church. Both Pope John Paul II and Pope Benedict XVI expressed concerns that some of the renewed understanding of justice had gone too far. Certainly, in the immediate wake of Vatican II there were excesses in the reception of the council. But this was not the norm. Following Vatican II, Christian social movements sought to respond to the council's integral vision of mission in balancing *both* the horizontal and vertical demands of faith. Such concerns are evident, for example, in the efforts by the leadership of the major missionary congregations to offer a holistic definition of mission. In 1981, SEDOS—the international forum of Catholic missionary congregations—drew heavily from *Evangelii Nuntiandi* in identifying four interrelated elements of mission: proclamation, dialogue, inculturation, and the liberation of the poor.[29]

---

[28] "Intervention of H. Exc. Rev. Mons. François Lapierre, PME, Bishop of Saint-Hyacinthe (Canada)," *Synodus Episcoporum Bollettino*, no. 12 (October 13, 2012), www.vatican.va.

[29] Bevans and Schroeder, *Constants in Context*, 254.

In *Constants in Context*, Stephen Bevans and Roger Schroeder have proposed a constructive synthesis of these distinct approaches to mission. Drawing from Vatican II, *Evangelii Nuntiandi, Redemptoris Missio*, and other ecumenical texts on mission, the two missiologists propose an integral framework that they term "mission as prophetic dialogue."[30] Such an approach, they believe, enables the church to faithfully participate in God's mission in light of the multifaceted realities of the contemporary world.

This approach is dialogical in the way it takes seriously the experiences, cultures, and contexts of people both inside and outside the visible church. A missionary church, as the council teaches, cannot ignore the pressing needs of people and the dynamic activity of God in history and culture. At the same time, the mission of the church must also be prophetic. Mission, as Pope John Paul II often stressed, cannot ignore the call to proclaim and witness to Jesus Christ and the reign of God. The mission of the church, therefore, must be challenging and rooted in Christian belief and practice. It is prophetic in the ways it "calls people beyond; it calls people to conversion; it calls people to deeper and fuller truth that can only be found in communion with dialogue's trinitarian ground."[31]

According to this model of prophetic dialogue the mission of the church in the world cannot be reduced to proclamation, action for liberation, or any single element. Mission as prophetic dialogue seeks to navigate between two extremes. On the one hand, this model cautions against a narrow view of mission that looks only at its role in social transformation—horizontalism. On the other, it reminds the church that it cannot reduce mission and evangelization to spiritual proclamation detached from the social realities of the world—what might be called verticalism. By looking at the council as a whole, it is evident that the mission of the church is more holistic and integral than any one task. Mission is complex as Pope Paul VI taught. Nevertheless it remains a single reality: "there is *one* mission: the mission of God that is shared, by God's grace, by the church. It has *two* directions—to the church itself *(ad intra)* and to the world *(ad extra)*."[32]

---

[30] Ibid.
[31] Ibid., 285.
[32] Ibid., 394.

More concretely, according to Bevans and Schroeder, mission as prophetic dialogue encompasses six interrelated elements: (1) witness and proclamation; (2) liturgy, prayer, and contemplation; (3) action for justice, peace, and the integrity of creation; (4) the practice of inter-religious dialogue; (5) efforts at inculturation; and (6) the ministry of reconciliation.[33] This list constructively situates Christian movements in the mission of the church. Most Christian movements are involved in more than one of these elements. Few, however, are in all six.

In many ways Pope Francis appears to embody this vision of mission. As with *Evangelii Nuntiandi*, and the model proposed by Bevans and Schroeder, Francis squarely situates the justice work of Christian social movements in the church's mission. Justice, reconciliation, concerns for the poor, and social transformation on the part of the church are major themes in his teachings, including *Evangelii Gaudium* (2013), written as a follow-up to the 2012 Synod—though not an official post-synodal text. Departing from a sharp division between action for justice and action for mission, Francis insists that "Christian preaching and life" is "meant to have an impact on society" (EG, no. 180). "No one," he writes, "can demand that religion should be relegated to the inner sanctum of personal life, without influence on societal and national life, without concern for the soundness of civil institutions" (EG, no. 181). Both as individuals and as communities, Christians are "called to be . . . instrument[s] of God for the liberation and promotion of the poor, and for enabling them to be fully a part of society" (EG, no. 187). The Christian mission must include awareness and action to "resolves the structural causes of poverty" (EG, 202).

He offers his own answer to the mission-justice question by insisting that all people, even those in "ecclesial circles," have an obligation to work for justice. "While it is quite true," he admits, "that the essential vocation and mission of the lay faithful is to strive that earthly realities and all human activity may be transformed by the Gospel, none of us can think we are exempt from concern for the poor and for social justice" (no. 201).

---

[33] Ibid., 351. These six elements were originally articulated by Bevans and Eleanor Doidge. See Stephen B. Bevans and Eleanor Doidge, "Theological Reflection," in *Reflection and Dialogue: What Mission Confronts Religious Life Today?*, ed. Barbara Kraemer (Chicago: Center for the Study of Religious Life, 2000), 48.

STRUCTURES OF THE CHURCH IN PURSUIT OF JUSTICE

To affirm that Christian social movements participate in the church's mission is not to claim that everything they do is perfect or that the positions they take are infallible. Nor is it to say that all Christians must adapt the same perspective on social issues. There are many examples in history where Christian social movements have adopted some very unchristian and unjust positions and tactics in defense of the faith.

Rather, to assert that these collectives partake in the church's mission is constructive for several reasons. First, it is important and necessary to affirm the ecclesial identity of these movements and the important role they play as part of the Christian community. This affirmation can bolster the moral, logistical, and even financial support that these movements receive. As a lay youth movement, the YCW, for example, depends upon the financial support of church structures, the logistical help of meeting spaces, and the guidance of chaplains, often priests or nuns appointed by the local church structures.

Second, clearly recognizing that Christian social movements such as JRS, YCW, and Plowshares are part of the church can help to raise awareness among the broader Christian community of the social issues they seek to address. Imagine, for instance, the impact if Plowshare activists or JRS workers were given spaces to share their stories in local parishes or Catholic schools in the United States.

Finally, the affirmation of the ecclesial identity of Christian social movements can help to illuminate issues and questions that ought to aid organizations best pursue that mission, including the challenge of balancing the horizontal and vertical demands of the evangelization. Before examining some of these ethical questions, the next chapter will consider these movements through another lens of theological inquiry, pneumatology, to examine how Christian social movements potentially embody God's grace in the world.

Chapter 6

Structures of Grace

On St. Patrick's Day, 2014, I received a panicked email. Ruki Fernando, a Sri Lankan activist friend of mine, had been arrested under charges of terrorism. We had good reason to believe that he might be mistreated, if not tortured, and there was a serious possibility that he might "disappear," that is to say, be killed.

Fernando, a young lay activist, along with Fr. Praveen Mahesan, OMI, had been investigating the arbitrary arrest of Balendran Jeyakumari and the detention of her thirteen-year-old daughter, Vipoosika, on suspicion of harboring a criminal. Months earlier the woman and her daughter publicly embarrassed the Sri Lankan government during the visit of British Prime Minister David Cameron. Not unlike the Madres de Plaza de Mayo in Argentina, the two women were part of a group of mothers and girls pleading with Cameron to investigate the disappearances of Tamil men, women, and children in the final phase of the war, including Jeyakumari's teenage son.[1]

Following Jeyakumari's arrest, Fernando and Fr. Praveen engaged in a fact-finding mission on her case. On March 16 they too were arrested under the Prevention of Terrorism Act. According to the government of Sri Lanka the two men are terrorists bent on inciting violence following the civil war. By contrast, according to NGOs and church groups they are human rights defenders investigating involuntary disappearances and arbitrary detentions.

---

[1] See the report issued by the UN High Commissioner on Human Rights "on promoting reconciliation, accountability and human rights in Sri Lanka" deleivered at the UN Human Rights Council on September 22, 2014. "Sri Lanka Needs a More Fundamental, Far-Reaching Accountability Process—Zeid," *Sri Lanka Guardian*, September 23, 2014, www.srilankaguardian.org. See also "Tamil Activist Detained in Sri Lanka," *BBC News*, March 14, 2014, www.bbc.com.

Both men have long been active in international Christian human rights movements. Fernando is a well-known leader in the movements of specialized Catholic action. For years he had served as the Asian coordinator of the International Young Catholic Students and worked with student groups across the continent. At the time of his arrest Fernando was working as human rights adviser to the INFORM Human Rights Documentation Centre and was closely associated with other human rights organizations.

Fr. Praveen, a Catholic priest and member of the Missionary Oblates of Mary Immaculate (OMI), was, at the time of his arrest, the director of the Centre for Peace and Reconciliation based in Jaffna. The center was created as a joint venture of the OMIs and Pax Christi Germany with the goal of creating a violence-free and just society in Sri Lanka through peace education, networking, and social action. Both men have also participated in delegations of the International Catholic Movement for Intellectual and Cultural Affairs (ICMICA Pax Romana) to the UN Human Rights Council, where they sought to draw attention to the injustices occurring in Sri Lanka.

Following their arrest the human rights community, led by many Christian social movements, called for their immediate release. ICMICA organized a World Day of Prayer, Thanksgiving, and Action for Human Rights Defenders and Peacebuilders on April 21, and a number Christian NGOs asked the United Nations to intervene. Members of different Christian movements in Europe and North America lobbied their own governments to take action. Thanks in large part to the political advocacy of Christian movement organizations, the two Catholic activists were eventually released.

What insights might a theological analysis bring to this and other similar experiences of collective Christian action for justice? A missiological lens, as the last chapter proposed, squarely situates the actions of Fernando, Fr. Praveen, and the multiple Christian movements involved in the defense of human rights within the mission of the church. This, however, is not the only theological insight to emerge from a study of Christian social movements. Beyond the ecclesiological and missiological considerations, the experiences of socially engaged Christian movements also raise questions of a pneumatological significance; that is, do the experiences of these movements reveal anything about the Holy Spirit's action in the world or God's relationship with humanity? Put in another way, can the work of Christian social movements in working to counteract structures of sin and oppression—without denying the dangers of collective egoism—be considered potential structures of grace? And if so, what might that mean for the organizations themselves and how they approach their social engagement?

Christian social movements, as the last chapter examined, reveal much about the nature of the church and its relationship to the wider world. While imperfect, these diverse communities of people participate in the mission of the church as they seek to witness to the gospel by working for social justice.

This chapter considers the potential ways that social movements and movement organizations, including Jesuit Refugee Service, the Young Christian Workers, and Plowshares, reflect or embody God's grace. As with the previous chapter, official Roman Catholic teaching helps guide the exploration of this topic. After laying out how Christian social movements reflect "structural grace," the chapter examines how this theological lens might shape the ways movements perceive and live out their own mission.

GOD'S GRACE AND SOCIAL TRANSFORMATION

Before exploring its possible social dimensions, it might be helpful to review briefly what is meant by the term *grace,* which is one of the most important words in the Christian lexicon. It has a long history that is impossible to detail fully here. The word has been used in different ways to describe a central aspect of the Christian understanding of God. At its core, grace speaks to God's gracious and powerful love for human beings. Grace is the force of love present in all the major events of salvation history, including creation, the incarnation, the resurrection, and Pentecost. While there are disagreements among Christians about the exact role and nature of grace, "all Christians," as the Jesuit theologian Roger Haight, SJ, points out, "agree on this: Grace is God's love for us."[2]

Traditionally, Christian theology emphasizes three key aspects of grace. First, grace is gratuitous. As its name suggests, it is a gift of God, freely given. Because of the limitations of human nature, one

---

[2] Roger Haight, *The Experience and Language of Grace* (New York: Paulist Press, 1979), 8.

cannot earn or merit grace. Even the preparation to receive God's grace is in itself a grace, called prevenient grace. In other words, everything depends upon God, the primary mover and agent of God's love. In *Evangelii Gaudium,* Pope Francis puts it this way: "No human efforts, however good they may be, can enable us to merit so great a gift. . . . This principle of the primacy of grace must be a beacon which constantly illuminates our reflections on evangelization" (EG, no. 112).

A second characteristic of grace is that it heals our sinful human nature. According to the Christian tradition sin distorts people's worldview and causes them to turn away from God and turn in on themselves. God's grace, which flows from the redemptive action of Christ, helps to heal this disordered view of reality and restore the divisions caused by sin. It is only through grace that people are liberated from the oppressive forces of sin present in their personal and social lives.

Finally, God's grace helps to raise or elevate people's nature to a new reality that enables them to participate in God's trinitarian love. The experience of God's gracious love radically transforms the recipient. No one who receives the gifts of God can remain passive. Christians often describe this as a process of divinization. Through this elevating power of grace people are empowered in their lives of Christian discipleship—including works of charity and justice. It is only through the gift of grace that human beings can perform truly good works in the world.

From the point of view of Christian social ethics, God's grace is absolutely essential for the church's mission of social transformation. Confusion on this point was a source of conflict during the Pelagian controversy in the fifth century when Pelagius reportedly rejected the necessity of grace to overcome original sin. According to this position, which was later ruled heretical, the power of free will was sufficient to do good and fulfill the law.

In response to Pelagianism the church asserted that grace was necessary to do good and overcome the visible and invisible scars of original sin. Genuine good works, from the orthodox-mainstream Christian point of view, in other words, only have meaning in light of grace. This debate again surfaced during the sixteenth century as Reformation leaders reminded the church that it is God's grace and not our liturgical, ecclesial, or social actions that will save us. The temptation to ignore the necessity for grace, especially in relation to good works, remains a danger for Christians today. In an individualistic culture it is easy to forget that one cannot do it all on one's own.

For contemporary Christians there is a temptation to think of grace as existing only on an invisible level. Grace, however, is not confined to nonmaterial plane. It is not some magical force separated from human experience, as the Belgian-Brazilian theologian José Comblin emphasizes. Since human beings are material and embodied beings, God's love for us, he argues, must also be material in some way: "If grace does not produce material and bodily modifications, it does not exist for the human being, it does not penetrate human life, it remains alien to humanity."[3] Roger Haight makes a similar point. In order "for grace to be real," he writes, "it must be experienced in some way."[4]

One of the ways in which grace is experienced in the world is through the actions of Christians and Christian communities that attempt to bring about positive social transformation aimed at healing broken relationships. Mindful of the risks of Pelagianism, the Christian tradition recognizes God as the source of the church's good works. Drawing from St. Augustine, St. Thomas Aquinas offers a constructive account of the relationship between grace and our free action for social change. In his *Summa Theologica* Thomas distinguishes between operating and cooperating grace. God, the principal mover, initiates goodness in us through *operating grace,* but it is up to human beings, to whom God has bestowed the gift of free will, to decide if they will respond to this initial movement by *cooperating* with God. Quoting Augustine, Thomas highlights this distinction: "He operates that we may will and when we will, he cooperates with us that we may perfect."[5]

As such, it is possible to discern God's grace present in the positive actions of human beings aimed for social change. Roger Haight explains this dynamic well:

---

[3] José Comblin, "Grace," in *Mysterium Liberationis: Fundamental Concepts of Liberation Theology*, ed. Ignacio Ellacuría and Jon Sobrino (Maryknoll, NY: Orbis Books, 1993), 522.

[4] Haight, *The Experience and Language of Grace*, 146.

[5] Thomas Aquinas, *Summa Theologica*, trans. Fathers of the English Dominican Province, Complete English (Westminster, MD: Christian Classics, 1981), II–II, 111, 2.

God and his grace are at the root of all love in this world; wherever there is authentic love in this world there God is acting. . . . God's grace, God's effective presence, is the driving and sustaining force of all human goodness and love, and this is the ultimate basis of every form of authentic human community, no matter how basic and natural any particular communitarian form may be.[6]

If what Haight says is true, then God's grace must be present in some way through the prophetic work of Christian social movements heroically working to serve those on the margins of society and calling for a new world where peace and love triumph over war and hate. To deny the presence of God's grace in the good work of Christian communities comes close to a "social Pelagianism." The truly good works of Christian movements, in other words, are not only a result of the heroic actions and decisions of individual leaders and members. Rather, they can be seen as being infused with God's motivating love.

This is not to say that Christian communities have souls and are the object of salvation. Rather, it is to draw attention to the presence of God in good work being done by communities and social movements, such as the work of church movements for human rights in Sri Lanka. But how does grace work through movements? I would like to suggest that there are at least three ways in which grace can be seen as operating in and through Christian social movements: structures of grace in opposition to structures of sin, structures of charity and solidarity, and structural embodiments of charisms.

STRUCTURES OF GRACE
IN OPPOSITION TO STRUCTURES OF SIN

First, Christian communities might be seen as collective embodiments, or structures of grace, in the ways in which their theological and spiritual commitments inspire them to fight against injustice, indifference, and what the Christian tradition has described as structural or social sin. Although the tradition has long recognized the social dimensions of sin, explicit attention to sin's structural aspects

---

[6] Haight, *The Experience and Language of Grace*, 169.

emerged in Catholicism after the Second Vatican Council. This new structural consciousness took place alongside the church's renewed attention to justice (as detailed in the previous chapter). Prior to Vatican II, Catholic moral theology, with its strong focus on the sacrament of penance, operated largely in a personal and individualistic framework. This, as Dermot Lane observes, led to an impression that the "Christian faith was a highly private affair."[7] Sin was perceived as a matter for the privacy of the confessional.

The renewed justice lens adopted by the church after Vatican II, along with developments in sacramental theology and ecclesiology, challenged the excessively personal and act-centered approach to sin.[8] The inductive social analysis (see-judge-act) methodology developed by the Young Christian Workers and adopted by Pope John XXIII (MM, no. 236) and liberation theology helped to engender an awareness of the root causes of suffering. Dialogue with sociological, psychological, and some Marxist theories deepened this awareness and drew attention to the broader social forces that sustain personal acts of sin. By the end of the 1960s theologians and many Christian communities—from the peace activism of American priests to the liberation movements of young workers—were considering the destructive effects of social structures in perpetuating, sustaining, and supporting situations of injustice and oppression. This was most explicitly articulated by liberation theology. In his groundbreaking work *A Theology of Liberation* (1971), Peruvian theologian Gustavo Gutiérrez described the presence of sin "in oppressive structures, in the exploitation of humans by humans, in the domination and slavery of peoples, races and social classes. Sin," he continues, "appears, as the fundamental alienation, the root of a situation of injustice and exploitation."[9]

The final text of the 1971 Synod of Bishops develops this point as it situates the evangelical role of action for justice in the face of "networks of domination, oppression, and abuse which stifle freedom

---

[7] Dermot A. Lane, *Foundations for a Social Theology: Praxis, Process, and Salvation* (New York: Paulist Press, 1984), 1. See Mark O'Keefe, *What Are They Saying about Social Sin?* (New York: Paulist Press, 1990), 5.

[8] See James F. Keenan, *A History of Catholic Moral Theology in the Twentieth Century: From Confessing Sins to Liberating Consciences* (New York: Continuum, 2010).

[9] Gustavo Gutiérrez, *A Theology of Liberation: History, Politics, and Salvation*, rev. ed. (Maryknoll, NY: Orbis Books, 1988), 103.

and which keep the greater part of humanity from sharing in the building up and enjoyment of a more just and more loving world" (JM, no. 3).[10] The consciousness of sin's social dimensions and the structural causes of poverty and oppression can be seen throughout the statements emerging from the major meetings of Christian social movements in the early 1970s, including the controversial IYCW International Council in 1975 and GC 32 of the Society of Jesus.

In 1984, John Paul II offered the most explicit treatment of social/ structural sin by a pope in his apostolic exhortation *Reconciliatio et Paenitentia*. While maintaining a degree of caution in relation to certain interpretations, the text draws upon liberation theology to call for action to overcome the structural causes of sin. In the exhortation, later echoed in *Sollicitudo Rei Socialis*, the pope warns against applications of social sin that ascribe moral agency to structures. Social sin, he argues, can only be applied to communities and structures *analogically*. In other words, only persons can have moral agency in the strictest sense. Structures may be considered sinful, but the agency and responsibility remain in persons. To place blame "on some vague entity or anonymous collectivity such as the situation, the system, society, structures or institutions" is dangerous because it risks overlooking the moral responsibility for the individual acts of omission or commission (RP, no. 16). In short, personal responsibility cannot be abrogated when denouncing complex institutions or systems (for example, apartheid or the nuclear weapons industry) as sinful. We cannot excuse our actions with the claim that "racism made me treat the other in a disrespectful way" or "it was the fault of the culture of corporate greed, not mine, that employees were mistreated."

On the contrary, a structural awareness of sin should help to draw attention to one's personal responsibility and culpability in relation to these structures. This, for instance, is a key point made by Plowshares activists who feel a certain sense of personal responsibility for the systems of war and oppression. While rejecting a nonpersonal interpretation of structural sin, John Paul II outlines three legitimate meanings of social sin.[11]

---

[10] Peter J. Henriot, "Social Sin and Conversion: A Theology of the Church's Involvement," *Chicago Studies* 11 (1972): 120–21.

[11] Albert Nolan, *God in South Africa: The Challenge of the Gospel* (Cape Town: D. Philip, 1988), 44.

First, every sin, even the most private and personal act, can "undoubtedly be considered as a social sin" (RP, no. 16).[12] Human beings, according to the Catholic tradition, are inherently social. As such, there can be no purely individual or personal sin. Our actions and the ways in which we live affect others.

Second, social sin may also legitimately refer to those sins that are more clearly social by nature. Examples include violations of human rights by those in positions of power, corruption on the part of political officials, and the imposition of unsafe working conditions by business executives. For John Paul II, this not only includes acts of "commission" but also includes acts of "omission," that is, when those in positions of power fail to "work diligently and wisely for the improvement and transformation of society" (RP, no. 16).

The final legitimate meaning of social sin, according to John Paul II, are those sins present in the relationships that exist among different communities, groups, or nations that "are not always in accordance with the plan of God, who intends that there be justice in the world and freedom and peace between individuals, groups and peoples" (RP, no. 16). From this perspective class warfare, racism, xenophobia, gross economic inequalities, and other obstinate confrontations between nations or groups would be considered socially sinful. This type of social sin is particularly dangerous because it can lead to the dehumanization of entire groups of people. And once a group is dehumanized, indiscriminate killing in warfare and economic exploitation are more easily seen as legitimate means to ends (SRS, no. 36).

Ethical Formation and Consciousness Building

In their efforts to witness to the gospel, Christian social movements struggle to combat each of these manifestations of social sin in their own distinctive ways. Christian social movements counteract the first meaning of social sin as they help individuals open up to the social demands of the gospel in the face of sin and injustice. The Brazilian Christian activist and educational theorist, Paulo Freire,

---

[12] See also Pontificium Consilium de Iustitia et Pace, *Compendium of the Social Doctrine of the Church* (Washington, DC: USCCB, 2004), no. 117.

described this the task of developing a critical consciousness as "conscientization." Such a transformative process can only effectively happen in the context of a community or movement.[13]

In *Christifideles Laici* (1988), Pope John Paul II speaks of the important role of Christian movements and associations "in the formation of the lay faithful," especially in regards to social questions (CL, no. 62). This was later affirmed by the *Compendium of the Social Doctrine of the Church*. Experience, as the *Compendium* recognizes, shows us that it is often through communities and movements within the church that Christians appropriate the skills and habits that enable them to respond to God's grace in the world.[14] In such communities people encounter and learn to imitate love, mutuality, service, and justice.

The pedagogical role played by the YCW, for example, highlights the potential of movements to shape the personal and ethical formation of leaders through cell groups, study sessions, publications, and campaigns. A central facet of YCW's mission is to empower and form critically engaged leaders during an important stage of human development. Its success can be seen in the many former YCW members who hold leadership positions in inter-governmental and nongovernmental agencies. This type of moral and ethical formation can have considerable efficacy in counteracting the roots of social sin at the personal level. The role of ethical transformation is also visible in JRS's pastoral and educational services, which often include elements of social and ethical formation aimed at empowering refugees to be agents of justice and reconciliation. The recent initiatives of JRS in the fields of reconciliation and higher education are especially noteworthy in this regard. JRS also helps to form the Christian conscience of its staff, donors, and collaborators around the world by raising awareness of the plight of refugees and the demands of the gospel in light of forced displacement. In a similar way the witness of Plowshares is designed, in part, to call others to conversion and to educate them about evils of the weapons industry.

---

[13] Paulo Freire, *Pedagogy of the Oppressed* (New York: Herder and Herder, 1970).

[14] Pontificium Consilium de Iustitia et Pace, *Compendium*, 549–50.

Accountability Politics

Christian social movements also work to counteract *Reconciliatio et Paenitentia*'s second meaning of social sin through advocacy and analysis aimed at holding political leaders and institutions accountable to the demands of the common good. This work is most often done in the "boomerang pattern of influence," whereby non-state actors challenge structures and office holders, normally seen as sovereign, to change their practices by bringing the voices of people on the ground to international institutions.[15] The "soft power" exercised by social movements and movement organizations in "naming and shaming" governments can often lead to more effective implementations of development programs and human rights policies. Consider the example of Fernando and Fr. Praveen in seeking to draw attention to the violations of human rights committed by the Sri Lankan government at the UN Human Rights Council.

Along with other movements, JRS, YCW, and Plowshares are involved in holding social and political leaders accountable. Both JRS and YCW—through CIJOC and IYCW—are actively involved as NGOs with the UN system. The voice of JRS at the international level, for example, helps to ensure that political leaders and institutions fulfill their promises to the forcibly displaced and their duties to the common good. Lacking both a formal organizational structure and any official recognition with governmental bodies, Plowshares adopts different tactics to hold social leaders accountable. Its prophetic acts of nonviolent resistance are often framed as public indictments of the sinful and criminal behavior of political leaders and institutions.

Transforming Social Relationships

Finally, these actors counteract the third legitimate meaning of social sin as they seek to transform social, political, and economic relationships to be more in line with the demands of the gospel. For most Christian social movements this is clearly evident in their actions to bridge the gaps caused by inequalities, nationalism, and

---

[15] Margaret E. Keck and Kathryn Sikkink, *Activists beyond Borders: Advocacy Networks in International Politics* (Ithaca, NY: Cornell University Press, 1998), 12.

racism. Many transnational Christian movements were formed following the two world wars precisely with this goal. All three case
studies in this project, for instance, highlight strong commitments
to peace and reconciliation.

For JRS, social transformation includes efforts aimed at building
solidarity and healing relationships between communities torn apart
by conflict. In many countries, particularly in Europe and North
America, JRS has become a leading voice for the social integration of
refugees and other migrants into their host countries. More recently,
such efforts are understood by JRS through the lens of reconciliation—a key theme addressed by the Jesuit's GC 35.

At the heart of the YCW mission is a desire to integrate into
society the realities of young workers, who are often marginalized
and excluded. The YCW hopes that the unity of young workers in
a movement will help to overcome the structural roots of the con-
tradictions between faith and life. By forming socially engaged ethical leaders, holding governments to account for their actions, and
transforming social relationships to be more in line with the gospel,
Christian social movements function as counterforces to structures
of sin and oppression in the world. But this is not the only way in
which Christian collectives potentially embody grace.

STRUCTURES OF CHARITY AND SOLIDARITY

Christian social movements might also be understood as structures
of grace in the ways in which they inspire and communicate the virtues of charity and solidarity. Though they do not explicitly speak of
structural grace in their official teachings, the idea is implicit in the
writings of both John Paul II and Benedict XVI. In *Sollicitudo Rei
Socialis,* for example, John Paul II affirms the necessity of grace for
transforming unjust relationships. In order to overcome the structural
sins that divide the human family, he argues, Christians will need "the
help of divine grace" to work for solidarity and a true development
that is informed by a moral and ethical perspective (SRS, no. 35). He
insists that structures of sin will only be "conquered" by an attitude
and virtue of solidarity that is aided by grace (SRS, no. 38). The *Compendium of the Social Doctrine of the Church* follows and develops
this point as it argues that the moral principle of solidarity must guide
and transform social institutions. Oppressive and unjust structures and

institutions, it asserts, "must be purified and transformed into *structures of solidarity* through the creation or appropriate modification of laws, market regulations, and juridical systems."[16]

In many ways Christian social movements arguably function as structures or agents of solidarity both in their internal efforts to foster this virtue among their members and in their external actions aimed at transforming institutions and social relationships. In *Christifideles Laici,* John Paul II applies his teaching on solidarity to the specific vocation of the laity in the church and in the world. Writing a year after the publication of *Sollicitudo Rei Socialis,* the pope speaks of charity as "the soul and sustenance of solidarity." All the faithful, he writes, are called to put charity into practice through acts of solidarity both in their personal capacity and "in a joint way by groups and communities" (CL, no. 41).

In *Caritas in Veritate,* Pope Benedict XVI develops the integrated relationship between charity and solidarity. In this encyclical he comes close to identifying organizations working for the common good as structures of grace by speaking of "networks of charity." Toward the beginning of the text Benedict considers the relationships among charity, grace, truth, and the church's response to suffering and injustice in the world. Here, the pope highlights the role of charity and grace at the center of personal and collective social action:

> Charity is love received and given. It is "grace" *(cháris)*. Its source is the wellspring of the Father's love for the Son, in the Holy Spirit. Love comes down to us from the Son. It is creative love, through which we have our being; it is redemptive love, through which we are recreated. Love is revealed and made present by Christ (cf. Jn 13:1) and "poured into our hearts

---

[16] Pontificium Consilium de Iustitia et Pace, *Compendium*, no. 193.The wording of "structures of solidarity" in the *Compendium* is not used in any papal encyclical and appears only a few other times in other official texts. The bishops of the United States of America, for example, call for the creation of "structures of solidarity" to address the divisions between the rich and the poor in their 1993 letter on peace. Later, in their joint letter on immigration with the bishops of Mexico, they celebrate the work of God in converting people and bringing about "structures of solidarity to accompany the migrant." National Conference of Catholic Bishops, *The Harvest of Justice Is Sown in Peace* (Washington, DC: USCCB, 1993), Introduction, www.usccb.org; United States Conference of Catholic Bishops and Conferencia del Episcopado Mexicano, *Strangers No Longer: Together on the Journey of Hope* (Washington, DC: USCCB, 2003), no. 40, www.usccb.org.

through the Holy Spirit" (Rom 5:5). As the objects of God's love, men and women become subjects of charity, they are called to make themselves instruments of grace, so as to pour forth God's charity and to weave *networks of charity.* (CV, no. 5)

With God's grace and love as a foundation and driving force, Benedict argues, people are individually and collectively enabled to offer a moral response to the negative realities of globalization in two specific areas: justice and the common good. As detailed in the previous chapter, charity and justice, according to *Caritas in Veritate,* are inseparable. While authentic charity "transcends justice" in its call for forgiveness, communion, and gratuitousness, it nevertheless "demands justice" and social transformation in the world. The special grace of charity, Benedict XVI argues, is not something detached from the world. Rather, it "always manifests God's love in human relationships as well, it gives theological and salvific value to all commitment for justice in the world" (CV, no. 6).

Writing in *Caritas in Veritate,* Benedict explains that charity and grace give rise to action for the common good—which, as he writes, is taking on an increasingly global dimension. "To desire the *common good* and strive towards it," he argues, is in fact "*a requirement of justice and charity.*" Action for the common good, however, will be all the more effective if it is "animated by charity." Using Augustinian language, the pope argues that such action, when guided by charity, contributes not only to the "earthly city" but also, and more important, to "the universal *city of God,* which is the goal of the history of the human family" (CV, no. 7). This treatment by Pope Benedict constructively grounds the work of Christian social movements in the virtue of charity, which for the Christian tradition is itself a grace, a gift of God.[17]

STRUCTURAL EMBODIMENTS OF CHARISMS

From a different perspective Christian social movements may also be considered structures of grace in the ways in which they embody or seek to institutionalize specific charisms or special graces. The

---

[17] See also M. Therese Lysaught, *Caritas in Communion: Theological Foundations of Catholic Health Care* (Washington, DC: Catholic Health Association, 2013), 8, www.chausa.org.

renewed theology of the Second Vatican Council helped to push past the christomonism (the tendency to focus exclusively on Christ) of earlier periods. Beyond recognizing the sacramental presence of the church in the world, the council reclaimed an appreciation for the role of charisms as animating forces within the church and church communities.[18] *Lumen Gentium*, in particular, recovers the Pauline notion of charisms while emphasizing the participation of all the people of God in the threefold office of Christ (priest, prophet, and king) (no. 12). God freely distributes such special graces, the constitution teaches, which may be ordinary or extraordinary, to the faithful of every rank *for the common good*. These charisms can express themselves anywhere among the people of God. Nevertheless, those in ecclesial office have a special responsibility to discern their authenticity since not all claims to charisms may be legitimate. Though a robust treatment of the council's recovery of the charism exceeds the scope of this book, two aspects are worth addressing.

First, Vatican II's treatment of the role of charisms in Christian life highlights the social and ethical dimensions of these gifts. The special graces or gifts of the Spirit that are charisms are not given solely for the benefit of the individual. Rather, they look outward toward the wider church and society. John Paul II speaks to this in *Christifideles Laici*: "Charisms are *graces of the Holy Spirit that have,* directly or indirectly, *a usefulness for the ecclesial community,* ordered as they are to the building up of the Church, to the well-being of humanity and to the needs of the world" (CL, no. 24).[19]

---

[18] The council's recovery of the language of charism surprised many since charisms were dismissed by Pope Gregory the Great as ceasing to exist after the "Golden Age of the apostolic era of the Church." Brendan Leahy, *Ecclesial Movements and Communities: Origins, Significance, and Issues* (Hyde Park, NY: New City Press, 2011), 83. See also Christian Duquoc and Casiano Floristán Floristán Samanes, eds., *Charisms in the Church*, Concilium (New York: Seabury, 1978); Karl Rahner, *The Dynamic Element in the Church*, trans. W. J. O'Hara (New York: Herder and Herder, 1964); Hans Küng, "The Charismatic Structure of the Church," in *The Church and Ecumenism* (New York: Paulist Press, 1965), 41–61; William Koupal, "Charism: A Relational Concept," *Worship* 42, no. 9 (1968): 539–45.

[19] Pope Francis makes a similar point: "The Holy Spirit also enriches the entire evangelizing Church with different charisms. They are not an inheritance, safely secured and entrusted to a small group for safekeeping; rather they are gifts of the Spirit integrated into the body of the Church, drawn to the centre which is Christ and then channelled into an evangelizing impulse. A sure sign of the authenticity of a charism is its ecclesial character, its ability to be integrated harmoniously into the life of God's holy and faithful people for the good of all" (EG, no. 130).

Here, John Paul II highlights not only the internal ecclesial dimensions of these gifts, but also their social dimensions that extend beyond the church and the local community. Charisms, in other words, cannot be detached from the realities and needs of the world. On the contrary, they are gifts given by God to build up the church, promote the common good, and address the needs of people both near and far. This is an important mark of discernment in determining the theological significance of Christian social movements. The presence of special graces can be determined, at least in part, by how Christian social movements contribute to the building up of the church and to the common good of society.

Second, Vatican II's recovery of the notion of charism, especially in its teaching on religious life, does not envision it only in a personal sense. Charisms can, as *Christifideles Laici* teaches, "even be shared by others in such ways as to continue in time a precious and effective heritage" (CL, no. 24). While some, like Joseph Ratzinger, have sought to define the charism of a community or movement in terms of its relationship to one individual founder or charismatic leader, experience shows that not all movements or communities in the church have individual founders.[20] Furthermore, even among those groups with individual founders, it is clear that the Holy Spirit is active in more than the one person credited with the movement's establishment.

In other words charisms may be seen to operate beyond a purely personal sense; they may be taking dynamic forms as corporate bodies adapt to meet the "changing circumstances of place and time" (ET, no. 11–12). The actions of the Holy Spirit within a community cannot be contained only in the life of the founder or even group of founders; nor does the spirit cease to be a dynamic presence in the community when its founders die. On the contrary, Christian communities continue to be guided by their charisms as they continually seek to be placed in the service of the common good. To limit

---

[20] Addressing the 1998 World Congress of the Ecclesial Movements, Joseph Ratzinger distinguished among what he sees as movements, currents, and actions in the church. For him, a genuine movement is one that derives its "origin from a charismatic leader" whose life serves as a model for the organization and its members. Joseph Cardinal Ratzinger, "The Ecclesial Movements: A Theological Reflection on Their Place in the Church," in *Movements in the Church: Proceedings of the World Congress of the Ecclesial Movements, Rome, 27–29 May 1998*, Laity Today 2 (Vatican City: Pontificium Consilium pro Laicis, 1999), 47–48.

charisms only to the insights and witness of the individual founder risks turning these special graces into museum pieces that are incapable of responding to new dynamic realities in the world. This also poses problems if the founder is later seen to be less than saintly, as was the case with the founder of the Legionaries of Christ. The charisms that animate social movements are much larger than any one recipient. The Jesuit renewal after Vatican II, which enabled the creation of JRS, is a prime example of the evolving dynamic and continued presence of communal charisms.

The presence of charisms or "special graces" in the life of Christian social movements is most clearly evident in the movements of vowed religious and the new ecclesial movements that have clear, self-identified charisms associated with their founders. As a Jesuit apostolic work, JRS personifies the Ignatian charism in its threefold mission of accompaniment, advocacy, and service with the forcibly displaced.

The YCW and Plowshares, by contrast, generally do not speak of possessing a specific charism. Does this mean that they are fundamentally different from movements of vowed religious and lay movements that speak of charisms? Or should the understanding of charism be broadened to include the guiding missions of other movements that contribute to life of the church and the common good but lack a single founder in the traditional sense? The YCW, for instance, clearly has a specific mission and style in the youth apostolate. In a similar way the mission of Plowshares in resisting war is clear. From the perspective of Christian faith, it is hard to ignore the fact that something of God is at work in these movements, even those that do not have one single founder.[21]

TOWARD A THEOLOGY OF SOCIAL/STRUCTURAL GRACE

From these three perspectives alone Christian social movements, if only in an analogous way, can be described as structures of grace.

---

[21] Brendan Leahy comments on the social dimension of charism: "The concept of charism, in other words, was viewed in the Council not only in an individual sense . . . but also in a communitarian sense, attaching to a community or institution and lasting over time. Leahy, *Ecclesial Movements and Communities*, 90. Tony Hanna writes of new ecclesial movements as 'collective charisms,' or founding charisms." Tony Hanna, *New Ecclesial Movements* (New York: Alba House, 2006), 187.

Clearly, more theological reflection is needed to unpack this concept of social or structural grace and its implications to the wider Christian community. Thankfully, some theologians—particularly liberation theologians—have already gestured toward the development of such a theology. Juan Luis Segundo, SJ, for example, imagines God's dynamic grace, as a "great wind" at work in history—empowering not only individuals but also relationships and social structures.[22] Leonardo Boff points to the role of the Holy Spirit in shaping basic Christian communities and reminds his readers of the priority of the charismatic over the institutional element of all church structures.[23] From a different theological perspective Daniel Daly has used the language of virtue ethics to propose categories of "structures of vice" and "structures of virtue."[24]

The most detailed efforts to date to explore the social dimensions of grace come from the Belgian-Brazilian missionary José Comblin. According to Comblin, God's grace manifests itself in history in concrete ways in both persons and in communities. Grace, he insists, is not some vague, invisible, and ineffective theory. Rather, it is a gratuitous presence of God that manifests itself in movements of people fighting against sin and oppression. It is, he writes, "the force that awakens, animates, and maintains the struggle of the oppressed, who are victims of injustice and evil."[25]

A framework of structural grace offers a theological lens through which Christian social movements can better understand their significance and the presence of God in the world. Applying this lens offers movements and the wider church resources to better discern how to respond to the ethical and theological questions that emerge in relation to Christian social movements. But how exactly can the presence or absence of grace be discerned in the life of a social movement? And what does this theological concept mean for the mission, identity, and organization of Christian social movements? The next two chapters seek to respond to these questions.

---

[22] Juan Luis Segundo, SJ, *A Theology for Artisans of a New Humanity,* vol. 2, *Grace and the Human Condition* (Maryknoll, NY: Orbis Books, 1973), 169.

[23] Leonardo Boff, *Church: Charism and Power: Liberation Theology and the Institutional Church*, trans. John W. Dierchsmeier (New York: Crossroad, 1985).

[24] Daniel J. Daly, "Structures of Virtue and Vice," *New Blackfriars* 92, no. 1039 (2011): 341–57.

[25] Comblin, "Grace," 530.

Part III

<hr>

Discerning God's Spirit
in Action—Identity, Mission,
and Organization

Chapter 7

Always in Need of Reform

The Need for Communal Discernment

*Christ summons the Church, as she goes her pilgrim way,
to that continual reformation of which she always has
need, insofar as she is an institution of men and women
here on earth.*

—UNITATIS REDINTEGRATIO (NO. 6)

*Ministry in a missionary key seeks to abandon the com-
placent attitude that says: "We have always done it this
way." I invite everyone to be bold and creative in this task
of rethinking the goals, structures, style and methods of
evangelization in their respective communities. A proposal
of goals without an adequate communal search for the
means of achieving them will inevitably prove illusory...
The important thing is to not walk alone, but to rely on
each other as brothers and sisters, and especially under the
leadership of the bishops, in a wise and realistic pastoral
discernment.*

—EVANGELII GAUDIUM (NO. 33)

For anyone seriously involved in the church's social action, the
limitations of Christian social movements should come as no surprise. For many young and idealistic activists it can be difficult to
realize that even the best movements and movement leadership have

flaws. I can think of several of young adults, for example, who when confronted by the failings of a movement, become completely disillusioned, burn out, and move on. There have also been many examples where the organizational structures and leadership do not quite live up to the values espoused by the movement. Sadly, Christian movements are not immune to uncharitable disputes between leaders, corruption, and failures to respond fully to the demands of the gospel.

But where does this leave us? How do we confront the limitations inherent in any human community? Do we just resign ourselves to their flaws? Do we give up on movements in general? Or should we seek to find ways to reform and renew movements and organizations to be more in line with their missions and gospel values?

To argue for the possibility of social or structural grace is certainly not to suggest that all aspects of Christian social movements are graced or that these organizations possess autonomous moral agency in the same way as a person. As human institutions, Christian social movements are inherently flawed and—as with other ecclesial structures—always in need of reform. This was clear in the examination of Jesuit Refugee Service, the Young Christian Workers, and Plowshares in the previous chapters. From the study of three very different entities a number of theoretical and practical questions surface in three broad areas: movement identity, movement mission, and movement organization.

Finding a way to navigate the difficult and often competing demands of identity, mission, and organization is not easy. The pilgrim journey of Christian social movements becomes increasingly difficult in a pluralistic world that is rapidly changing. As with all human institutions, Christian movements are always in danger of falling victim to the dark side of human collectives, including corruption, division, abuse of power, and what Reinhold Niebuhr described as "collective egoism." Regardless of their good intentions and noble missions, some movements may end up doing more harm than good. This is particularly dangerous in the operational work of movements concerned with development and humanitarian assistance, where the welfare and lives of vulnerable populations are at stake.

Like the broader movement, which is the church, Christian social movements are always in need of reform and communal discernment. The experience of the Second Vatican Council offers two broad principles for the renewal of any ecclesial structure. The first, which is described by the Italian word *aggiornamento,* seeks to bring the ecclesial structures up to date with the present reality and the changing needs of the common good. Here, Christians are called to read the "signs of the times" and apply the gospel mission in new ways that are relevant to contemporary cultures and experiences. *Aggiornamento,* however, would be incomplete without *ressourcement,* a French word meaning "return to the sources." In this regard attention must be paid to scripture, the experiences of the first Christians, and the development of the tradition throughout history. In its decree on religious life the Second Vatican Council urges movements of vowed religious to undertake this twofold process. On the one hand, religious movements should strive toward "a constant return" to the gospel and the animating charism of their community. At the same time, the renewal calls for the "adaptation" of religious life "to the changed conditions of our time" (PC, no. 2).[1]

How does the theological lens of structural grace inform church movements and organizations in their process of continual renewal? How can a deeper theological framework aid movements in discerning the best ways to embody their mission in a changing world? The acknowledgment that Christian social movements might share in the church's mission and reflect grace illuminates several markers for discernment that can aid them to respond more effectively to the ethical and organizational issues that surface in relation to their missions and the demands of the common good. This chapter briefly examines some of these markers and their relevancy for social movements today.

The task here is not to present clear-cut solutions to the very real challenges facing specific Christian social movements. That is the responsibility and role of the movements themselves. Each movement has its own specific resources and experiences. Rather, I hope that by highlighting a few points for discernment I can offer movements and movement organizations directional and cautionary road signs to navigate the sometimes difficult journey of living out their

---

[1] See also Maryanne Confoy, *Religious Life and Priesthood: Perfectae Caritatis, Optatam Totius, Presbyterorum Ordinis,* Rediscovering Vatican II (New York: Paulist Press, 2008).

mission in a changing global context. This will help set the stage for the concluding chapter, which identifies some possible practices for Christian social movements to utilize in discerning what roads to take in pursuit of their mission.

DISCERNMENT OF SPIRITS:
A CHALLENGE FOR CHRISTIAN SOCIAL MOVEMENTS

What is discernment? What does it mean for communities or movements to engage in a process of discernment together? In the Christian tradition there is a long appreciation for the importance of this task in the life of the church. In the Gospels, for example, Jesus calls his followers to read or interpret the "signs of the times" (Mt 16:3) and to make judgments on the legitimacy of prophets by considering their fruits (Mt 7:16). The First Letter of John calls readers to "test the spirits to see whether they belong to God, because many false prophets have gone out into the world" (1 Jn 4:1). Similarly, in the First Letter of St. Paul to the Thessalonians, the author urges his readers to "test everything; retain what is good" (1 Thess 5:21).

Etymologically, the word *discernment* comes from the Latin *discernere*, meaning "to distinguish" or "to separate." The goal in any process of *Christian* discernment, then, is to seek out what is good; to distinguish between what is of God and what is not; and to determine what actions, structures, and relationships are in accordance with God's will. This is not a simple process. Human beings are finite and fallible. It is not always easy to have a sense of what is and what is not of God. Nevertheless, discernment is an important tool and task in the Christian life of discipleship.

Discernment is not a task limited to persons at an individual level. Throughout the history of the church, beginning with the Council of Jerusalem (Acts 15:1–35), Christian communities have gathered together in councils, synods, and assemblies to deliberate with one another and seek out God's guidance on practical and theological questions. The results of communal discernment form the nucleus of the Christian faith. Without such discernment we would not have the creeds or the canon of scripture.

Communal discernment is not limited to major international meetings. Nor is it something only for bishops, priests, and religious. All Christian communities, movements, and churches are called to engage in a continual process of discernment. Practices of communal discernment offer a way forming consensus on important decisions. Ladislas Orsy, SJ, describes communal discernment as a prayerful and participatory process of decision making "to which all the members of the community contribute." The result of this complex process, he continues, is

> more than the summary of individual judgments or decisions; it is the fruit of a communal enterprise. It includes the sharing of all available data, the articulation of many insights into the known facts, the formulation of definite judgments, and the making of decisions. It includes even more an alertness to the movements of grace in each throughout the whole process.[2]

Such a process of seeking out God's will for a community is fundamental for any Christian social movement, especially as it seeks to address the "big picture" or macro questions of movement identity, mission, and organization. But how exactly should Christian social movements approach the discernment of these macro issues?

In his work on virtue ethics British philosopher Alasdair Macintyre offers three questions to guide personal moral discernment: Who am I? Who ought I to become? How ought I to get there?[3] These questions, in many ways, speak directly to the issues of identity, mission, and organization that are faced by most, if not all, Christian social movements. Applied to the communal level with a theological lens of structural grace, Macintyre's questions might be reframed and expanded as follows: Who are we as a movement (identity)? Where is grace or the Holy Spirit calling us to go (mission)? What do we need to do to get there (organization)?

---

[2] Ladislas M. Orsy, *Toward a Theological Evaluation of Communal Discernment* (St. Louis: American Assistancy Seminar on Jesuit Spirituality, 1973), 154.

[3] Alasdair C. MacIntyre, *After Virtue: A Study in Moral Theory*, 2nd ed. (Notre Dame, IN: University of Notre Dame Press, 1984).

SAMPLE QUESTIONS FOR COMMUNAL DISCERNMENT

Who are we as a movement (identity)?
- What is our mission? What is our charism?
- How and why were we founded?
- How has the movement developed or changed over time?
- Is our mission universally accepted by our members? If not, what are the points of difference?
- Do we see God or grace acting within our movement? If yes, how?
- How do we relate to other movements and movement organizations, especially to those movements with similar charisms and missions?
- What are the biggest strengths and weaknesses of our movement?
- Are there any movement members who feel marginalized from the movement? If yes, why?
- How do we relate to the wider church?
- Is our movement or movement organization still relevant? Or have we outlived our contribution?

Where is grace or the Holy Spirit calling us to go (mission)?
- What are the hopes and needs of our members and the people served?
- Where might we imagine Jesus Christ calling us to do?
- What are the current needs of the common good?
- What are the needs of the church?
- How does the gospel inform our specific mission?

What do we need to do to get there (organization)?
- What structures, relationships, or movement organizations, if any, are needed to serve the mission?
- What actions or tactics are necessary to serve the mission?
- Do our actions, tactics, and structures reflect the values of the mission and the gospel?
- Who are potential allies for our mission?
- What resources (human, financial, logistical, and so on) are needed?
- Who will do what and by when?
- What arrangements are needed to ensure participation and accountability in the life of the movement?
- How will we evaluate our progress?

Several factors need to be taken into account in any process of communal discernment, including the limitations and fallibility of human groups in perceiving God's will; the holistic or integral mission of the church; insights from scripture and church teaching; the stated mission of the movement or movement organization; the history and development of the movement over time; the perspective of different stakeholders related to the movement (members, target population, church partners, donors, and so on); the needs of the church; and the needs of the broader society. In order to be effective, communal discernment, especially concerning major issues, demands preparation on the part of the participants.

The process of communal discernment may not always be easy and may involve conflict and disagreement. By itself, disagreement is not a bad thing. Framed in a respectful tone, disagreement can be a healthy sign of a vibrant community. In the New Testament the apostles disagreed with one another and eventually found consensus on some, but not all, issues through a process of communal discernment. Discernment and disagreement are not always in opposition to one another.

It almost goes without saying that the success of communal discernment depends greatly on movement leadership; leaders can make or break a discernment process. Their challenging task, as Orsy reflects, "is to create one mind and one heart in the community, out of the multiplicity of ideas and desires, in harmony with the aspirations of the universal Church."[4] To this end, leaders ought to find a way to cultivate and support a culture of discernment throughout the movement. Above all, leaders themselves are called to be people of discernment with the skills and openness to listening to the hopes and experiences of members.

Clearly, a detailed analysis of the macro issues of identity, mission, and organization cannot be seriously considered by a movement every day or even every year. Such a serious analysis needs time, preparation, and prayerful reflection. To this end, the organization of major decision-making bodies every few years, such as the IYCW world councils and Jesuit general congregations, can help to evaluate the state of the movement, its mission, and the directions needed for the future. The discernment of macro issues at major moments in the life of a movement, however, is much more likely to be successful if leaders and members practice discernment on a daily basis on small questions. Here again, leaders can play an important role in forming

---

[4] Orsy, *Toward a Theological Evaluation of Communal Discernment*, 143.

a culture of discernment or a habitual way of approaching even the most basic daily questions though a theological lens.

Engendering such a culture of discernment can be challenging given the day-to-day demands faced by many social movements. Taking time to think, pray, and reflect can often seem an impossible luxury in the face of hungry refugees, the need to write a grant application, or the deadline to contribute to a UN process. Finding a common approach to discernment can also be difficult or awkward in movements and movement organizations with non-Christian members or staff. Nevertheless, there are ways of organizing communal discernment practices to involve non-Christians in the process. Movement leaders need to be sensitive to this dynamic and seek ways for non-Christian members and partners to share their own perceptions of movement identity, mission, and organization. Special attention must be paid to the concerns of any members who feel their voices are being marginalized from the discernment process.

MOVEMENT DISCERNMENT AND THE WIDER CHURCH

The members of a movement ought not be the only agents in a process of communal discernment. The claim that Christian social movements participate in the mission of the church implies that they have responsibilities toward the wider ecclesial community. No Christian movement or community can exist in isolation. According to the Christian tradition, any special gift or charism given from God to a person or group is not granted to them in isolation. The missions, charisms, and graces of a movement need to be seen in light of the realities of the wider church and the common good. Consultation with the broader church offers members and leaders perspectives on how to best to live out their mission. For many Christian movements there is a real danger of becoming detached from the experiences and needs of the wider church, the people of God. This is tempting for both established movements, which may drift away from church structures over time, and newer movements, which can get lost in the excitement and enthusiasm for their vision.

Indeed, one of the main critiques of the so-called new ecclesial movements has been the temptation toward a perceived sectarianism. Jean-Marie-Roger Tillard, OP, for example, has lamented a "certain elitism, often severe and arrogant with regard to the classical life of the ecclesial community."[5] Rather than integrating themselves into the life of the church (e.g., parishes, dioceses), some movements form parallel structures with their own priests and liturgies. Christian who are not part of the movement can often be seen as "mediocre" or "sinful." In *Evangelii Gaudium*, Pope Francis speaks directly to this danger:

> Church institutions, basic communities and small communities, movements, and forms of association are a source of enrichment for the Church, raised up by the Spirit for evangelizing different areas and sectors. Frequently they bring a new evangelizing fervour and a new capacity for dialogue with the world whereby the Church is renewed. But it will prove beneficial for them not to lose contact with the rich reality of the local parish and to participate readily in the overall pastoral activity of the particular Church. This kind of integration will prevent them from concentrating only on part of the Gospel or the Church, or becoming nomads without roots. (EG, no. 29)

Engaging members of the wider church in the process of a movement's communal discernment can go a long way to help its members avoid "becoming nomads without roots." But how effectively can the concerns and experiences of the faithful be integrated into a movement's prayerful decision making on questions of identity, mission, and organization? In many churches, ecclesial leadership is understood as having an important responsibility in spiritual and ecclesial discernment. In the Roman Catholic tradition, for example, bishops are tasked to discern and test the validity of church movements and to ensure their integration into both the local community and universal church (LG, no. 13). Church authority, of course, need not be a bishop. Other ecclesial structures, including official councils and assemblies, can play this role.

In an ideal situation the presence and participation of church leadership in the life of a movement ensures four things. First, bishops

---

[5] J.-M.-R. Tillard, *Flesh of the Church, Flesh of Christ: At the Source of the Ecclesiology of Communion* (Collegeville, MN: Liturgical Press, 2001), viii. See also Luca Diotallevi, "Catholicism by Way of Sectarianism? An Old Hypothesis for New Problems," in *"Movements" in the Church*, ed. Alberto Melloni, Concilium 2003/3 (London: SCM, 2003), 107–21.

and other church leaders can promote ecclesial unity and prevent the type of factionalism and division that concerned St. Paul. External voices that have responsibility for the whole church can aid movements to avoid the traps of collective pride, sectarian withdrawal, and destructive attitudes of superiority to others in the church. Second, church leaders should be able to assist movements at a much more practical level to access financial and human resources, connect with potential allies, and avoid unnecessary duplication. This practical assistance, including through the official appointment of chaplains, can be particularly helpful for those that gather young people, and movements of people who are poor.

Third, as movements seek to discern how to be true to their own specific missions, ecclesial leadership can help them to remain faithful to the universal mission of the church and to the sense of the faith of the people of God (the *sensus fidelium*). Finally, church officials, as external partners, can provide a much needed voice of constructive criticism. Jean Vanier, the founder of the L'Arche community, identifies the need for such external voices to help movements identify and face their limitations:

> Movements and communities will normally need help from outside in order to face their shadow side, to perceive and evaluate how authority has been exercised, how power is used and abused. They will also need to listen and accept criticism, to have the courage to question themselves, the honesty to admit shortcomings and the energy to change. They will have to rid themselves of certain aspects that were necessary at the beginning of the foundation but which have become outmoded, even a sign of death.[6]

This, of course, is the ideal situation. Like the leadership within specific Christian movements, the broader human leadership of the church is imperfect. For many movements throughout history the relationship with church leaders has been less than ideal. Movements have been rejected or accepted based on external political pressures and ungrounded biases. The suppression of the Jesuits in the eighteenth century, for example, reflected more of a political bias than a

---

[6] Jean Vanier, "The Rise of Catholic Movements," *The Tablet*, March 15, 1997.

theological debate.[7] Rather than offering constructive criticism when movements go too far, some authoritarian and punitive responses by church leadership have occasionally pushed movements further away from the church. At the same time, some movements have sought undue influence over church leadership to the detriment of other groups by encouraging favoritism, factionalism, rivalry, and the marginalization of critical voices. Shortcomings in the relationship between church authority and Christian movements, it must be admitted, have gone both ways.

Unfortunately, too much of the relationship between movements and ecclesial officials surround legal questions of official recognition, reform of statutes, and situations when the movement or a movement member violates church teaching. For example, in my four years as president of an international Catholic lay movement, the majority of our relationship with the Pontifical Council for the Laity surrounded legal questions. Rarely, if ever, did conversations center on the experiences and needs of our members or our mission.

If and when issues or tensions do arise between movements and church officals, the presence of what Pope Francis describes as "participatory processes" can go a long way to prevent conflict and division (EG, no. 31). Rather than seeing ecclesial authority through the lens of feudal power politics, juridical authority, or the corporate business model, perhaps the role of ecclesial leadership in movement discernment would be more constructively viewed by thinking in terms of a mission model or by appealing to the many gospel images that speak to a concern for seeking out and bringing back the lost (for example, the good shepherd, the woman searching for a coin). The pastoral style of Pope Francis can certainly be a model for the relationship between movements and their pastors.[8]

DISCERNING THE DANGERS OF
IDENTITY, MISSION, AND ORGANIZATION

How does a framework of structural grace inform Christian social movements in their discernment process? A more robust theological

---

[7] John W. O'Malley, *The Jesuits: A History from Ignatius to the Present* (Lanham, MD: Rowman and Littlefield, 2014).

[8] See also the reflections by Cardinal Bernardin on the relationship between Catholic institutions and the local bishop. Joseph Bernardin, "Catholic Institutions and Their Identity," *Origins* 21, no. 2 (1991): 33–36.

reading of the issues of movement identity, mission, and organization illuminates four sets of polar tensions that are faced by most, if not all, socially engaged Christian movements and communities. These pairs of opposing dangers or "social movement vices" do not tell a movement where to go. Rather, like the lines on a highway, they can indicate if a movement is diverging from course. Finding the middle way between these different pairs of extremes is essential for these groups as they seek to navigate their path in the world.

Disembodiment and Institutionalization

First, in their social engagement for the common good, Christian social movements are challenged to find a balance between the demands of mission and the need to organize some form of institutional structure. As the case studies in the previous chapters have shown, not every Christian social movement develops the same type of structured social arrangements. Some reject outright the creation of any formalized institutions or a structured movement organization. Even anarchist groups like Plowshares, however, have some form of organized relationships and established traditions.[9]

The tension between mission and institution carries with it a twofold danger for all movements and movement organizations. On one side, careful attention must be paid to avoid the ever-present danger of falling into the sinful, selfish, and destructive patterns of collectivism and institutionalization against which Reinhold Niebuhr warns.[10] All groups, even those without definite movement organizations, are in danger of gravitating toward a stifling institutionalization that can suppress the dynamic workings of the Spirit. As social movements grow, charisms become routinized, traditions develop, and organizational structures are established. Programs and actions are undertaken not in what Pope Francis describes as "a missionary key" but in "the complacent attitude that says: 'we have always done it this way'" (EG, no. 33).

In this process creative ways are needed to ensure that structures and patterns of relating do not, as Roger Haight warns, hamper the

---

[9] José Comblin, *The Holy Spirit and Liberation*, trans. Paul Burns, Theology and Liberation (Maryknoll, NY: Orbis Books, 1989), 85.

[10] Reinhold Niebuhr, *Moral Man and Immoral Society: A Study in Ethics and Politics* (Louisville, KY: Westminster John Knox, 2001).

"spontaneity and self-actualized intention of self-transcending love that is the fruit of grace."[11] This risk can be seen, to some extent, in the creation of the multiple organizational structures that serve the YCW movement (local, national, continental, global). The proliferation of movement structures, especially if they conflict and compete with one another—as is the case with IYCW and CIJOC—can hinder rather than advance mission.

At the other extreme there is a danger for Christian social movements to neglect any form of organizational structure. While sometimes necessary in service of the mission, this disembodiment carries serious risks for the movement. In the absence of structures of accountability and participation, leaders perceived as charismatic are more likely to abuse power. Furthermore, without clear structures, movement effectiveness, cohesion, and sustainability remain difficult over time. Different communities within the movement, as has been the case with the Catholic Worker movement and Plowshares, risk drifting apart and even losing connection with the founding mission. How the Plowshares movement in the United States will weather the passing of the founding generation of activists is yet to be seen.

Within the Catholic tradition the church has always maintained that charism and mission are not in opposition to institutional structures.[12] Christian social movements, not unlike the church as a whole, are therefore charged to ensure that the structures and institutions that are developed are placed in the service of mission and the common good and not the other way around. This means that in order to carry out effectively their specific missions, Christian social movements must be flexible enough to adapt to the needs of an ever-changing world. But they also must develop and attend to participatory structures to guarantee that movement's actions are based on mission, the directives of its members, and the needs of the common good.

---

[11] Roger Haight, *The Experience and Language of Grace* (New York: Paulist Press, 1979), 180.

[12] In speaking of organizational charisms, Pope John Paul II notes, "The institutional and charismatic aspects are co-essential as it were to the Church's constitution. They contribute, although differently, to the life, renewal and sanctification of God's People." John Paul II, "Address of His Holiness Pope John Paul II on the Occasion of the Meeting with the Ecclesial Movements and the New Communities, Rome, 30 May 1998," in *Movements in the Church: Proceedings of the World Congress of the Ecclesial Movements, Rome, 27–29 May 1998*, Laity Today 2 (Vatican City: Pontificium Consilium pro Laicis, 1999), 221.

Maintaining structures that are both mission based and participatory can be a mark of legitimacy for movements involved in advocacy efforts. For example, the participatory structures of both the IYCW and CIJOC enable them to be credible voices for young workers at the United Nations, the International Labour Organization, and in front of church officials. Young workers choose national leaders who elect the international teams and set the directives for the international structures for the coming years. As a humanitarian organization sponsored by a religious congregation, the structure of JRS is quite different. The professional leadership of JRS is not elected in the same way as in membership-based organizations like the YCW. The Society of Jesus maintains direct oversight over JRS. The refugees served by the organization are not in a position to choose directly who will represent JRS internationally and what issues they will focus on. Thus, JRS cannot speak in the name of refugees in the same way that IYCW or CIJOC can speak in the name of young workers. Nevertheless, JRS maintains legitimacy and respect for its work because of its mission to empower and accompany the refugees themselves. Perhaps more than anything else, the mission and practice of accompaniment helps to ensure that the organization is focused on the real needs of the forcibly displaced and not the trends of the humanitarian professionals. It can also be argued that the institutional relationship of JRS to the Society of Jesus, which ultimately has oversight over the work of JRS, helps to maintain a strong focus on the mission of the organization to accompany, defend, and serve refugees around the world.

A theological framework of structural grace can help movements to navigate these dangers in two ways. An awareness of the theological role of social movements affirms the primacy of grace, mission, and charism in the work of the movement. Movement structures, traditions, and organizations must always be placed at the service of mission and charisms. At the same time, a theological lens can counter a temptation to detach or disembody grace-filled charism from the patterned human relationships and structures that are often necessary to address the complex issues facing humanity.

Horizontalism and Verticalism

By their very nature Christian social movements mediate between faith and life. As detailed in Chapter 5, they are not always successful in navigating between the demands of the gospel and the changing needs of the common good. Over the past thirty years some church officials have expressed concerns over the dangers of what they call horizontalism, whereby the church's mission is reduced to working only for justice and peace. Since his first homily as pope, Francis has frequently warned about the danger of neglecting the spiritual or vertical dimensions of faith. Without the proclamation of Christ, he warns, the church "will become a pitiful NGO."

Admittedly, these concerns are not without some basis in truth. Misinterpretations of the Christian social vision and excitement about urgent causes have led some to disconnect their actions for social transformation from their spiritual core and, by extension, the founding mission of the movement. In certain cases attention to social concern has resulted in or accompanied a "de-christianization" of organizations founded with clear ecclesial missions. Once the majority of movement or organizational members no longer identify with the Christian mission of the movement, it becomes difficult, if not impossible, to return to a more robust Christian identity. This has been the case with a number of educational, social, and healthcare institutions in Europe and North America. Consider, for instance, the loss of explicitly Christian identity in the Young Men's Christian Association (YMCA) in the United States (now known as the Y) or the loss of ecclesial identity of colleges started by churches and religious congregations, including Harvard University, Yale University, Marist College, and Manhattanville College.

Among Christian movements there is also a temptation to another extreme—verticalism—whereby the social implications of the Christian faith are neglected or ignored in favor of a detached spiritualism. Clearly, it is not the role of every church organization to be involved in social transformation in the same way. Diversity in what John Paul II described as the "single but complex reality" that is mission is valuable and necessary for the church to respond adequately to its evangelical vocation in the world (RM, no. 41; EN, no. 24). Nevertheless, there remain organizations and structures within the church community for whom the social dimensions of the church's mission as highlighted by Vatican II and more recently by Pope Francis seem irrelevant compared to some supposedly "real" evangelization that is detached from the needs of the world.

In the face of these dangers Christian social movements are challenged to embrace both the horizontal and vertical dimensions of the Christian mission. The framework of mission as "prophetic dialogue," proposed by Bevans and Schroeder and detailed at the end of Chapter 5, can help retain the holistic vision of mission put forth by Vatican II—what Kristin Heyer calls the "fullness of the tradition."[13] Attending to this integral vision will help organizations avoid the temptation to separate the gospel mission from the demands of justice either through a horizontalism or a sectarian withdrawal from the world. In an address to a meeting of new ecclesial movements, Pope Benedict XVI speaks to this challenge as he reminds them of the social implications of mission, charism, and genuine charity:

> Missionary zeal is proof of a radical experience of ever-renewed fidelity to one's charism that surpasses any kind of weary or selfish withdrawal. . . . The extraordinary fusion between love of God and love of neighbor makes life beautiful and causes the desert in which we find ourselves living to blossom anew. Where love is expressed as a passion for the life and destiny of others, where love shines forth in affection and in work and becomes a force for the construction of a more just social order, there the civilization is built. . . . Become builders of a better world according to the order of love in which the beauty of human life is expressed.[14]

Uniformity and Fragmentation

A third set of polar tensions faced by Christian social movements concerns movement cohesion and identity. At one extreme, excessive focus on unity and uniformity leaves little room for diversity and difference. At the other extreme, the embrace of diversity can lead to a fragmentation that makes it impossible to agree on a common mission or shared social action plan.

This has been a difficult challenge for all three case studies in very different ways. All three allow non-Christians to join as members

---

[13] Kristin E. Heyer, *Prophetic and Public: The Social Witness of US Catholicism*, Moral Traditions Series (Washington, DC: Georgetown University Press, 2006), 187.

[14] Benedict XVI, "Message of His Holiness Benedict XVI," in *The Beauty of Being a Christian: Movements in the Church*, ed. Pontifical Council for the Laity, *Laity Today* 11 (Vatican City: Libreria Editrice Vaticana, 2007), 7.

or staff—something that would have been nearly unimaginable fifty years ago. All have also encountered challenges as they adapted to meet the needs of new cultures and social conditions. The experinces of these movements leads one to question the limits of adaptation and inclusiveness. How can identity be maintained amid difference? These are not simple questions. Nor are they issues faced only by Christian social movements.

Here it is possible to see some of the real differences among movements with more centralized organizational structures (for example, the Jesuits), those with decentralized or federated structures (for example, the YCW), and those who resist any formal movement organization (for example, Plowshares). Each approach has its own strengths and weaknesses in terms of forming movement cohesion. For example, YCW national movements have far greater autonomy than Jesuit provinces. They are free to choose their own priorities, membership criteria, and even change their name. While it is more united, the risk for the Jesuit model is that a centralized structure might impose a uniformity that inhibits effective responses that draw from local knowledge. In recent years local Jesuit leaders expressed concern that they had no say in how JRS was being directed in their regions by the Rome office. JRS has sought to address this by adapting its model to allow for greater input and decision making by local Jesuit leaders and by refugees in its work.

JRS faces additional challenges in relation to unity and diversity around its mission as a Jesuit apostolic work. With an increasing number of non-Jesuit and non-Christian staff members, it can sometimes be difficult for JRS to maintain its Jesuit and Ignatian identity in the service of the forcibly displaced. Training new staff about St. Ignatius or the *Spiritual Exercises* may not seem to be a priority when thousands of people are fleeing conflict. In recent years the organization has sought to be more intentional about sharing and deepening its Jesuit identity while also welcoming others to join in that mission. As with other organizations and institutions sponsored by religious congregations (for example, universities, hospitals), this task consumes time, energy, and resources. New efforts, such as the identification of core values in the strategic plan and the publication of theological reflections on the work of JRS, may serve as a model for other faith-based organizations seeking to deepen their identity while also welcoming pluralism.

For YCW, the federated structure enables greater freedom and creativity at the local level. The risk, of course, is the splintering and division of the movement into different groups across ideological lines, as can be seen with the creation of CIJOC. For some of the other movements of specialized Catholic action, such as the International Movement of Catholic Students (IMCS-Pax Romana), the issue is even more complicated, given that many national movements and local groups have their own names and identities (for example, Canadian Catholic Students' Association, All Indian Federation of Catholic Students, Federazione Universitaria Cattolica Italiana).

This is not to say that there have not been breakaway groups among movements of vowed religious with centralized structures. The Franciscans, for example, have multiple branches of lay and ordained Franciscan men and women around the world. Many of these were splinter groups from the older structures. There are even groups of Franciscans in Protestant denominations. The differences among some of the groups are so vast that one may wonder how they all claim to be part of the same family. As the punch line of an old joke goes, only God knows how many different Franciscan communities exist in the world.

Maintaining unity amid diversity is not simply a matter of structure, however. Plowshares activists in the United States have been surprisingly successful in maintaining cohesion and a shared sense of purpose despite their diffuse structure. This, as Chapter 4 shows, is largely a result of the presence of charismatic leaders; strong traditions of nonviolent direct actions; and support from aligned movements and communities, notably Jonah House. As the movement spread to Sweden and Britain, the Christian symbols and identity of the movement were dropped; more confrontational and risky actions were replaced with traditional forms of protests; and the links with intentional communities all but disappeared. All of this raises another question: At what point does a different embodiment of a mission constitute a separate movement?

Finding a way to balance the "catholicity" (small "c") of any group—that is, to balance the values of unity and diversity—is critical. A theological framework of structural grace offers perspective to this challenging task. The Holy Spirit, as Comblin reflects, is indeed a uniting force within a community, but this is done "in freedom, without coercion, pressure, or persuasion. Thus, true Christian unity cannot be uniformity, since this can be brought about only by imposition."[15] In *Evangelii Gaudium*, Pope Francis makes a similar point. For the pope, the Holy Spirit is both the source of genuine diversity and unity in the church. If we value diversity without a view toward unity, he warns, we risk "becom[ing] self-enclosed, exclusive and divisive." At the same time, "whenever we attempt to create unity on the basis of our human calculations, we end up imposing a monolithic uniformity" (EG, no. 131).

The tension of finding unity amid diversity is not just an issue within movements. It also applies at a broader level among movements. Despite their best intentions and common faith, jealousy and competition can often surface in the relations among Christian social movements. This is clearly in tension with traditional teaching on charism. The Christian community has long recognized the need for multiple charisms or special graces to meet different social and ecclesial needs. These charisms, as St. Paul warned, ought not to be seen as competing with one another. There is room, and in fact a need, for different gifts. At the same time, genuine charisms are fundamentally united.

The distinctive charisms that animate different Christian movements share a common source and end with God. In fact, the authenticity of any charism, according to Pope Francis, can be judged by "its ability to be integrated harmoniously into the life of God's holy and faithful people for the good of all. Something truly new brought about by the Spirit need not overshadow other gifts and spiritualities in making itself felt" (EG, no. 130). Confusion over this and competition among groups in the church is not a new issue facing Christian communities. Addressing movements of consecrated life, John Paul II recalls the frustration of St. Bernard of Clairvaux (1090–1153) on this question:

Those who are united by a common commitment to the following of Christ and are inspired by the same Spirit cannot fail

---

[15] José Comblin, *The Holy Spirit and Liberation*, trans. Paul Burns, Theology and Liberation (Maryknoll, NY: Orbis Books, 1989), 96.

to manifest visibly, as branches of the one Vine, the fullness of the Gospel of love. . . . Saint Bernard's words about the various Religious Orders remain ever timely: "I admire them all. I belong to one of them by observance, but to all of them by charity. We all need one another: the spiritual good which I do not own and possess, I receive from others. . . . In this exile, the Church is still on pilgrimage and is, in a certain sense, plural: she is a single plurality and a plural unity. All our diversities, which make manifest the richness of God's gifts, will continue to exist in the one house of the Father, which has many rooms. Now there is a division of graces; then there will be distinctions of glory. Unity, both here and there, consists in one and the same charity." (VC, no. 52)

Avoiding undue tensions and fragmentation takes on a special urgency given the complexities of the world's problems. While cooperation among movements is sometimes difficult and not always desirable, division and competition will impede the mission of specific movements and their efforts at overcoming structures of sin. A more robust theological perspective can help Christian social movements negotiate these dangers. If these organizations do indeed participate in the same mission of the same church, and if they reflect charisms rooted in the same divine source, then Christian social movements should be open to exploring ways for cooperating with one another in a way that respects the specific mission and identity of each party involved. At times, this may also mean merging two different structures or organizations that have increasingly similar missions and goals. Striking the right balance between unity and diversity can often involve painful decisions. A theology of structural grace can help those involved to remain focused on the demands of the common good and the grace-filled mission needed to address those demands.

Collective Despair and Collective Pride

Finally, a framework of social or structural grace helps Christian social movements avoid two dangers that stem from how they understand themselves theologically. One danger faced by Christian social movements is the denial of God's presence or potential presence in the good works of a movement or movement organization. This takes on many forms. For some, it is a social Pelagianism, the good works that we do are a result of our human skills and leadership alone. God's help is not seen as needed to overcome sin and its effects in the world. Others, including many committed Christians, simply never consider the possibility that God might be working in some way through their social movement. This can contribute to the dangers of the horizontalism mentioned earlier. The spiritual dimension of the movement gets lost in the face of social and institutional tasks. In a certain sense this reflects a form of collective despair whereby the potential presence of God's grace is ignored or seen as beyond the realm of possibility.

A second danger goes to the other extreme. Rather than denying the presence of God at work in the movement, there is the opposing temptation to equate everything a movement does to the fullness of God's will. There has always been, as Brendan Leahy reflects in his study of the new ecclesial movements, a danger for all charismatic groups in the church to demonstrate "a certain arrogance by presenting themselves as the perfect Church." This, he argues, "neglects the insight that God the Father's house has more rooms, many ways of living the same faith."[16]

All human collectives, including the church, are at risk of this form of collective pride, or what might be described as a self-deification of the community.[17] Excitement and passion for the movement can lead members and supporters to become blind to its faults and shortcomings. This attitude can make collaborating with other movements and groups difficult and organizational adaptation nearly impossible.

DISCERNING THE EFFECTS OF GRACE

Bringing attention to these four pairs of tensions that surface from a framework of structural grace can go a long way to aid movements as they seek to discern how to respond to the macro issues of identity, mission, and organization. But it does not necessarily give

---

[16] Brendan Leahy, *Ecclesial Movements and Communities: Origins, Significance, and Issues* (Hyde Park, NY: New City Press, 2011), 134.

[17] Reinhold Niebuhr, *The Nature and Destiny of Man? A Christian Interpretation*, vol. 1 (Louisville, KY: Westminster John Knox, 1996), 218.

direction for a movement going forward. Clearly, it is not possible to claim that grace is always and everywhere present in all Christian movements. How, then, can the church discern the presence or absence of grace in a movement or movement action? Here, St. Paul offers some helpful wisdom in his Letter to the Galatians. As in his other writings, the apostle expresses concerns about divisions within early church communities.[18] Paul calls the Christian community to a process of discernment to find a way to maintain unity amid the diversity of graces. In response to disagreements over community practices he argues that authentic faith ought to be judged by the visible effects or fruits of the Spirit. The Holy Spirit is absent in practices that lead to discord, sin, and conflict—what he describes as "works of the flesh." He then details more than a dozen examples of these, including jealousy, factionalism, envy, and immorality (Gal 5:19–21).

In contrast to the sinful and divisive marks in the community, St. Paul also enumerates several "fruits of the Spirit," which both speak to the Spirit's presence and reflect the values of the reign of God proclaimed by Christ.[19] These include "love, joy, peace, patience, kindness, goodness, faithfulness, gentleness, [and] self-control" (Gal 5:22–23). To these nine the Catholic tradition, working from the Latin Vulgate translation, adds generosity, modesty, and chastity.

While the references to the effects of the Holy Spirit in St. Paul primarily concern persons at an individual level, they may also be applied collectively to the discernment of grace within Christian movements. For example, movements or actions of movements that lead to or inspire immorality, division, idolatry, or a sense of collective pride clearly cannot be considered to be reflecting grace. Something of God, by contrast, can be seen in the actions of movements that inspire genuine virtues, such as love, kindness, and peace.

In his study of the Holy Spirit through the lens of liberation theology José Comblin offers his own list of visible signs or fruits of the Sprit's effects in communities. Drawing from the lived experiences of basic Christian communities in Latin America in the wake of Vatican II he identifies five communal experiences of the Spirit. Since

---

[18] See also 1 Corinthians 12:4–6.

[19] Charles E. Bouchard, "Recovering the Gifts of the Holy Spirit in Moral Theology," *Theological Studies* 63, no. 3 (2002): 539–58.

FRUITS AND EXPERIENCES OF THE SPIRIT

Fruits of the Spirit according to St. Paul (Gal 5:22–23)
- charity
- joy
- peace
- patience
- kindness
- goodness
- gentleness
- self-control
- faithfulness
- modesty*
- generosity*
- chastity*

Effects of the Spirit in Communities according to José Comblin
- action
- freedom
- speech
- community
- life

*Added in the Catholic tradition.

basic Christian communities are themselves a social movement, the analysis here is worth examining.

The first experience outlined by Comblin is *action*. At their best, Christian social movements are involved in dynamic actions that move and transform people in powerful ways. Comblin points to the role of the Spirit in motivating members of basic Christian communities, people who had previously been marginalized from society and the church, to take action. Through the experience of the Spirit in the community, they suddenly "begin to act; they discover that they themselves are capable of action."[20] Communities not only inspire and support personal action, but they also facilitate collective action at the local, national, and global levels.

Action relates to a second mark of the Spirit's presence in the community, *freedom*. God, as liberation theologians remind the church,

---

[20] Comblin, *The Holy Spirit and Liberation*, 21.

is deeply concerned with human freedom and liberation in the face of many forms of sinful oppression and structural violence. Through the experience of the Spirit in Christian social movements, people often discover what it means to be free in light of Christ's liberating action. This, however, is not an individualistic notion of freedom, a freedom primarily *from* something. Rather, the gifts of the Spirit inspire a sense a positive freedom, a freedom *for* God, for the reign of God, and for social relationships that are in line with the gospel. As such, it is a freedom that means "collaborating in a community" with others for common goals.[21] This type of freedom can be threatening to those in positions of power. Indeed, one of the marks of an oppressive political regime is the tendency to prevent people from gathering freely in communities. For example, in the 1980s many Christian social movements were prevented from meeting under both the communist governments in Eastern Europe and right-wing dictators in Latin America. By gathering people into groups and empowering them to work for the reign of God, Christian social movements embody this sense of positive freedom in profoundly personal and social ways.

Third, the Holy Spirit often manifests itself in Christian social movements through the gift of *speech*. For Comblin, this can be miraculous. Through Christian communities, people who are often prevented from speaking in public are enabled to speak. This can take many forms from the hopeful messages of prophets and social visionaries to the public denunciations of human rights abuses. The speech of the marginalized and the poor can also be threatening to those in positions of power. Consider, for example, the public speech of the Madres de Plaza de Mayo, a movement of women in Argentina organized in the 1970s to demand justice for their children who were "disappeared" under the military dictatorship. In isolation, taking the risk to speak out against structures of sin is intimidating at best. It is not easy to risk one's own life by speaking out for justice. Through the workings of the Spirit in communities, people discover a new confidence and are empowered to speak and witness to the gospel. This is a sign of the same force that empowered the biblical prophets to denounce injustices thousands of years ago.

---

[21] Ibid., 64.

Fourth, the Spirit is experienced in Christian social movements through the experience of *community*. Finding, forming, and sustaining genuine communities is not easy, particularly in individualistic cultures and in the face of what Pope Francis describes as the "globalization of indifference." Such a task demands grace and the unifying force of God's love. When people who would not otherwise do so join together and form a community, often at a personal cost, there is something of God at work. Consider the many different examples of this, including the communities of the L'Arche movement where people with and without intellectual disabilities share a common life; the communities of the Jesuit Volunteer Corps, where young adults choose to live together for a year or more as they serve local nonprofits; and the emerging intentional Christian communities of the new monasticism movement.

Finally, for Comblin, the Spirit is evident in the experience of *life*. For many involved in Christian social movements as either members or recipients of services, their involvement with the movement is life giving. In some cases, such as the disaster relief services offered by World Vision, the healthcare services offered by the Medical Mission Sisters, and the urgent human rights advocacy efforts of Pax Romana, the experience of Christian social movements is literally life saving. In other cases this experience of life is subtler. Participation in a social movement can also be life enriching. The experience of a movement, many feel, makes their lives better and helps them to discover what it means to be a person created in the image and likeness of God.

With the two lists articulated by St. Paul and José Comblin we can identify at least seventeen fruits or experiences of God's action in communities. There are likely to be other values or effects that can be included. Like the identification of the different pairs of movement vices above, the enumeration of the different fruits of grace is limited. No fruit will look exactly the same in every movement. They do not necessarily tell movements what to do or how to address specific problems, and the human beings doing the discernment will always be fallible. Nevertheless, being attentive to these and other effects of God's grace within a community can offer some criteria for movements as they seek to discern how best to live out their grace-filled missions in a changing world.

In their embodiment of charism and their opposition to the three manifestations of social sin, Christian social movements, among other structures, can be described as potential manifestations of structural grace. Again, this is not to suggest that these structures have moral agency; nor is it to say that they are perfect. Rather, the language of social grace can help movements recognize that their good work has theological value in light of God's loving action.

By helping movements acknowledge the dynamic presence of God's grace in the liberating actions of God's people, a framework of structural grace can aid movements to discern how to best embody that gift in their identities, missions, and organizational structure. In a 2014 homily to a meeting of Italian charismatic movements, Pope Francis speaks to this. After describing the charismatic movement as "a current of grace" in the world, he offered advice that might be applied to all movements involved in the process of discernment and renewal:

> Be stewards of the grace of God, avoid the danger of excessive organization, go out into the streets to evangelize. Remember that the Church was born with an outward bound spirit that morning of Pentecost. Move closer to the poor and touch in their flesh the wounds of Jesus. Please do not imprison the Holy Spirit! Live with freedom! Look for the unity of the Renewal, which comes from the Trinity.[22]

---

[22] Pope Francis, "Pope to Charismatic Renewal: Be Stewards Not 'Inspectors' of God's Grace," AsiaNews, June 2, 2014, www.asianews.it.

Chapter 8

Conclusion

Movement Self-Care

All persons and institutions embody multiple identities
simultaneously. Discerning the core characteristics of one's
identity is an ongoing process attuned to place and time.
. . . While Catholic identity is neither fixed nor complete,
it does have roots. And it should be perceptible to others.
We ask, Who do we say we are? in order to discern who
we are called to be, and what we ought to do in new situ-
ations.

—KAREN SUE SMITH,
A SUMMARY: CARITAS IN COMMUNION

As we move further into the twenty-first century, Christian social
movements, like the church as a whole, will continue to face challenges as they seek to live out the gospel in the world. The distinctive
experiences of Jesuit Refugee Service, the Young Christian Workers,
and Plowshares raise important questions in relation to movement
identity, mission, and organization.

While the changing demographics of global Christianity and
the growing complexities of the world's problems have given
these questions new urgency, these are not entirely new. In 1991, a
conference of leaders from Catholic health care, educational, and
social-service agencies convened at Fordham University to reflect
on common challenges of maintaining identity in the context of
pluralism. Participants were asked to envision what the future of

171

Catholic institutional ministries in the United States would look like in 2015.[1]

In response to the conference's preliminary report Cardinal Joseph Bernardin of Chicago summed up the challenges facing the church's social institutions in this way:

> Catholic colleges and universities, health care institutions and social service agencies already live with one foot firmly planted in the Catholic Church and the other in our pluralistic society. It should come as no surprise, then, when the competing vision and value system of the "tectonic" plates on which they stand are in tension with one another, and shifts in the plates cause tremors which create anxiety and are, at times, seen as threats.[2]

Bernardin's words still ring true for the current realities of many Christian social movements and movement organizations. Much of the potential of Christian social movements, as Chapter 1 detailed, lies precisely in this mediating role. At their best, Christian social movements and their structures serve as visible signs of God's love and the gospel in a broken world. Christian institutions from NGOs and hospitals to clubs and charities represent, to use the words of Doris Gottemoeller, RSM, the *"inculturation of the faith in a pluralistic environment."*[3] They are often what come to mind when considering the presence of the church in public life. Nevertheless, this mediating position also makes their mission fraught with dangers, risks, and questions.

The ways in which movements respond to these fundamental questions of identity, mission, and organization profoundly shape how the church as a whole will respond to human suffering, sin, and indifference in the world today. Examining the experiences of Christian social movements through the dual lenses of missiology and pneumatology, four main conclusions surface from this book

---

[1] Charles Fahey and Mary Ann Lewis, *The Future of Catholic Institutional Ministries: A Continuing Conversation* (Bronx, NY: Third Age Center of Fordham University, 1992); Thomas Narn, "Catholic Health Care Must Stand in the Middle," *Health Progress* 94, no. 4 (August 2013): 87–89.

[2] Joseph Bernardin, "Catholic Institutions and Their Identity," *Origins* 21, no. 2 (1991): 33–36.

[3] Doris Gottemoeller, "History of Catholic Institutions in the United States," *New Theology Review* 14, no. 2 (2001): 27.

that, it is to be hoped, can aid those movements and movement structures on the "fault lines" of church and society to better respond to the call of the gospel.

First, *action for justice is an integral dimension of what it means to be church in the world.* As with many Christian movements, all three case studies were deeply shaped by the new justice consciousness that arose in the decade following the Second Vatican Council. This new appreciation for mission is perhaps best summarized by the text of the 1971 Synod of Bishops and can be seen in many other statements elaborated by the major meetings of social movements, bishops' conferences, and Christian churches during this period. These include the 1968 statement of the Catonsville Nine, the *Declaration of Principles* of 1975 of the IYCW World Council, and "Decree 4" of GC 32 of the Society of Jesus in 1974–1975.

While some may lament the increased awareness of the church's obligation to justice and peace, this new approach to mission continues to inspire impressive actions in defense of the rights of human beings on the margins of society, including refugees and young workers. It would not be an exaggeration to claim that Christian social movements inspired by the church's turn to justice have transformed the world.[4]

There are, of course, dangers to adopting a strong position in favor of social action, as this book has shown. No movement is perfect. In the pursuit of justice, movements or even parts of movements can turn away from their founding Christian identity. Both Plowshares and the IYCW have experienced this with some of their European expressions. The reasons for the shift away from explicit Christian identity are multifaceted. For some activists, a movement's religious identity can be seen as a liability. Religious identity can be an obstacle to obtaining funding from external donors. Others associated with the movement "may have great problems with the institutional . . . Church today."[5] Resistance can also arise from a point of view which sees religion as a conservative force that stands in the way of real proposals for social change. While this last point has some

---

[4] Consider the impact of Christian social movements in the "third wave of democracy." See Monica Duffy Toft, Daniel Philpott, and Timothy Samuel Shah, *God's Century: Resurgent Religion and Global Politics* (New York: W. W. Norton, 2011).

[5] Charles E. Curran, "The Catholic Identity of Catholic Institutions," *Theological Studies* 58, no. 1 (1997): 108.

merit, religion need not be a conservative force, as Sharon Erickson Nepstad and Stellan Vinthagen have shown in their comparative study of the Plowshares movement. At least within Plowshares, the loss of an explicitly Christian identity and the theology of prophetic resistance actually resulted in the movement becoming less radical.

In other cases the loss of Christian identity is more subtle. Peter Steinfels has described this phenomona as an unintentional "drift" where organizations keep the religious symbolism and name but ultimately make decisions that lead to a "hollowing out" of their Catholic identity.[6]

This is a particular concern for movement organizations in the United States and Europe founded by movements of vowed religious in which the number of members of the sponsoring movement is decreasing. A more robust and holistic missiological framework that attends to both the horizontal and vertical demands of faith will go a long way to help movements maintain their Christian identity and mission. It may also help organizations to clarify what relationships, if any, they wish to maintain with the sponsoring movement and the wider church. There are many possible degrees of relationship between a specific organization and its sponsoring/founding movement. Being clear about this is essential in the formation of a clear identity.

Second, *from the point of view of Christian faith, it is apparent that something of God is at work in the life of Christian social movements.* Movements, in other words, are more than just collectives of well-meaning individuals somehow linked to the church. A pneumatological lens reveals the different ways in which Christian social movements embody or reflect God's love or grace in their collective actions for the global common good. This is particularly evident in the ways in which they embody specific graces (charisms) and in their struggle to overcome the structures of sin that divide the human family.

Again, this does not mean that everything they do is graced or perfect. On the contrary, a framework of structural grace provides movements with discernment tools and goals to work toward in their process of continual reform. Much like individual Christians and the church universal, Christian social movements must always

---

[6] Peter Steinfels, *A People Adrift: The Crisis of the Roman Catholic Church in America* (New York: Simon and Schuster, 2013), 114.

be careful of collective pride. Like the church as a whole, they are always in need of reform.

Third, *there is more than one way of organizing a Christian social movement.* No one movement or type of movement can claim a monopoly over the church's social mission. The diversity of styles, structures, and areas of focus in ecclesial responses to social injustice is a great asset for the body of Christ and its mission of proclaiming the reign of God. For example, one of the problems with the pre-conciliar model of Catholic action—distinct from *specialized* Catholic action—was its insistence on a uniformed, centralized structure and model.

Here, again, a theology of social grace informed by the Pauline notion of charism can help. The multiple expressions of God's grace within the Christian community should not simply be tolerated but should be promoted. No one movement can do everything. No one model of movement organizing will solve all the world's problems. Reconciling the lofty ideals of catholicity within a human community often divided into ideological blocks, however, is much easier said than done.[7] At the very least, movements with different methods and priories ought to strive, in the words of Cardinal Bernardin, "not to stand against each other when the protection *and* the promotion of life are at stake."[8]

Fourth, *forming a culture of discernment with participatory structures for communal discernment is absolutely essential for Christian social movements and social movement organizations.* Discerning the best ways to respond to questions of identity, mission, and organization is not easy for Christian social movements. Navigating around the pairs of "social movement vices" enumerated in the previous chapter demands constant attention.

Making time and mobilizing resources to explicitly address such questions, however, is often not considered a priority for movements passionate about social concerns. Such efforts can easily be seen as superfluous or secondary to the real mission and the urgent tasks

---

[7] Bradford E. Hinze, *Practices of Dialogue in the Roman Catholic Church: Aims and Obstacles, Lessons and Laments* (New York: Continuum, 2006).

[8] Joseph Bernardin, "A Consistent Ethic of Life: Continuing the Dialogue, The William Wade Lecture Series, St. Louis University, March 11, 1984," in *The Seamless Garment: Writings on the Consistent Ethic of Life*, ed. Thomas Narn (Maryknoll, NY: Orbis Books, 2008), 17.

at hand needed to sustain an organization. A similar dynamic happens at the individual level. Many socially engaged people devote so much of their time, talent, and treasure to the urgent tasks and to-do lists that "must get done" that they neglect their own needs and well-being. This can be a recipe for disaster, because it easily leads to burn out, bitterness, and other effects that are ultimately counter-productive to the cause.

Concerned about these dangers for socially engaged Christians, Jesuit theologian James Keenan has proposed self-care as a virtue for people active in the church and social justice causes. In addition to responsibilities toward others, as demanded by the virtues of justice and fidelity, we also have specific responsibilities toward ourselves. Love of God and love of neighbor, as the Christian tradition has long expressed, cannot be separated from love of self.[9]

The same virtue can be applied collectively at the movement level. Spending time and devoting resources to address issues of movement identity, mission, and organization are not superfluous. They are critical ways for any movement to take care of itself, its mission, and its members. In other words, in order to promote the common good, Christian social movements must be concerned about the good of their own movement. Movement self-care ought not to be confused with fundraising, building an endowment, recruitment, redrafting the mission statement, or the maintenance of programing. All of these are important and necessary elements. Movement self-care, however, goes deeper. Within the context of communal discernment, movement self-care involves, among other things, attending to three resources that are too often neglected: people, narratives, and relationships.

RESOURCES FOR MISSION

People

People are an essential resource for movements. Engaged and empowered members and competent leaders can make or break a movement. How do members and leaders understand and relate

---

[9] James F. Keenan, "Proposing Cardinal Virtues," *Theological Studies*, no. 56 (1995): 709–29; James F. Keenan, *Virtues for Ordinary Christians* (Lanham, MD: Rowman and Littlefield, 1996).

to movement identity, mission, and organization? How are new members or new staff of an organization trained in the sponsoring movement's mission? How are those involved in the movement and the movement organization supported, treated, and invited to participate in decision making?

These are all important questions that need to be addressed by movements in their own specific contexts. Finding, developing, and retaining the right people who are committed to the mission of the movement will go a long way. In the process of member and staff recruitment, being straightforward and clear about the movement's identity and mission is critically important. Communicating clearly the mission and identity to new members does not have to conflict with commitments to diversity and inclusiveness. New members or staff, at the very least, should know what they are joining.

For some Christian groups, such as religious congregations and new ecclesial movements, long processes of formation (for example, novitiates) offer effective introductions to the life and vision of the movement.[10] The formation of a Jesuit priest or brother, for example, can last over a decade. Living in religious communities with other members reinforces this training throughout the person's lifetime. Most Christian social movements, however, do not engage in prolonged processes of initiation, and most do not require their members to live in a community setting. In many cases people join a movement simply by feeling drawn to its goals, showing up at events, or getting involved in small ways. Training becomes more complex for those movement organizations, such as hospitals and educational institutions, where staff often seek employment without any reference to the Christian mission or the sponsoring movement's identity. In such cases mission-related topics are sometimes reduced to one agenda item among many in new staff orientations. For example, when I began graduate school, the institution's Catholic and Jesuit identity was presented at the orientation very briefly and was overshadowed by other important information such as healthcare, housing, and benefits. In speaking with other students after the program, it was evident that those unfamiliar with the Jesuit tradition did not

---

[10] See Patricia Wittberg, *The Rise and Fall of Catholic Religious Orders: A Social Movement Perspective* (Albany: State University of New York Press, 1994).

understand what was presented. One was surprised to learn that the Jesuits are a Catholic or Christian group!

There are strengths and weaknesses to various approaches to initiating members into a movement's life and charism. Clearly, longer and more robust initiation processes will engender greater commitment and dedication to the cause. By contrast, movements with looser initiation requirements allowing for multiple degrees of participation are often able to engage more people and to be more inclusive. There are strengths and weakness to both models. No matter what is chosen, movements have a responsibility to introduce new members to the charism, spirituality, history, and structure of the movement. Movements and movement organizations need to be upfront and honest about their identity, especially to those who may be unfamiliar with the tradition. Training materials, identity documents, and declarations of principles are useful tools in sustaining a movement's mission and identity. Yet, they have little meaning if movement members do not know them.

Leadership formation is essential for movement sustainability over time.[11] Without welcoming new generations, how can any movement be expected to adapt and grow in new contexts? Leadership trainings and programs specifically designed for younger generations can go a long way, but alone they are not enough. They need to be coupled with opportunities for newer members to take on leadership roles within the community. Finding ways to give young members leadership roles, even if that means risking mistakes, is vital for leadership development.

For many movements, such as the YCW and other lay movements, identity and mission are greatly aided by the presence of committed chaplains or mission officers. While traditionally a role for priests and religious, chaplains are increasingly lay people. Chaplains do more than lead prayer and provide spiritual direction. They are often important voices on behalf of the movement mission and identity. For movements with high leadership turnover, chaplains can also play a role in continuity. For example, in my role in the International Movement of Catholic Students, I was lucky enough to benefit from the wisdom and guidance of a dynamic South African Dominican

---

[11] See Zeni Fox and Regina M. Bechtle, *Called and Chosen: Toward a Spirituality for Lay Leaders* (Lanham, MD: Rowman and Littlefield, 2005).

priest who had already served for four years as international chaplain and who brought with him decades of experience with the movement. His wisdom and guidance were essential in helping leadership to balance the competing demands placed on our mission.

Many hospitals, universities, and other movement organizations have sought to fulfill this role by appointing a vice-president for mission and/or creating committees for mission. These positions have become increasingly important for movement organizations sponsored by vowed religious experiencing changing demographics. Such roles ought to go beyond tokenism. Vice-presidents of mission need to have roles in the life of the organization, including the formation of new recruits, direct involvement in decision making, and discernment of future plans. Every Christian social movement and organization, even the most diffuse, ought to have a person or a group of people specifically charged with the responsibility to study, promote, and adapt the mission of the movement. A recent document by the Reid Group and the Association of Catholic Colleges and Universities in the United States, for example, highlights several best practices for mission officers, including the creation of "a representational campus-wide advisory committee to serve as conversation partners with the mission officer" and the "dedication of a portion of each Board of Trustees meeting to unique dimensions of the mission."[12] While these suggestions make sense at big institutions, smaller movements can also learn from such initiatives.

Narratives

How and why was the movement founded? What are the stories that sustain a movement's vision and capture the imagination of new members? What are the experiences of success and failure that can continue to guide movements today? Communal narratives are important; they shape the imaginations of the people involved. The history of a movement, its development over time, and the motivation of its founding members speak volumes to movement mission and identity. Like people, narratives can often be overlooked in the face of social problems. Speaking of the power of stories in the

---

[12] Association of Catholic Colleges and Universities and The Reid Group, *Mission Officer*, Strengthening Catholic Identity Brochure Series (Washington, DC: ACCU, 2011).

formation of identity in American Catholic healthcare, M. Therese Lysaught writes:

> We are all shaped by particular stories and narratives. Often, the stories that most powerfully drive our actions do so implicitly. We adopt them from the world around us and they shape our lives and actions without our realizing it. As such, we are always shaped by multiple stories. Operative in our own institutions are the narratives of medicine and the various professions; free market economics; American identity; cultural stories about health, illness, poverty and death; local histories; as well as the stories of our founding religious orders, the longer history of Catholic health care and the broader Catholic tradition as well. Some of these stories may overlap; often they are in conflict. Getting one's stories straight is a first step in clarifying identity.[13]

Like any resource, communal narratives need to be cultivated and developed. This can happen in several different ways in a movement's life. First, communities need to make time for members and former members to tell their stories. The lived experiences of charismatic leaders—from Dorothy Day and the Berrigan brothers to Pedro Arrupe and Chiara Lubich—are important motivating and pedagogical forces for members. Biographies, films, artwork, and interviews with these figures help to shape the way movements understand the past, present, and future.

But these are not the only stories. Often some of the most powerful narratives come from "regular" members of the movement. When I was in graduate school, I participated in a program for graduate students called Veritas and Vinum. Every semester, over wine and cheese, we asked one or two professors or university administrators to share their stories about how faith influences their professional life. This helped to flesh out the mission of the school in deeply personal ways. The program was modeled after a similar program for undergraduates, Agape Latte, sponsored by the Boston College Center for the Church in the Twenty-first Century. In the life of many movements there are far too few spaces like these where members

---

[13] M. Therese Lysaught, *Caritas in Communion: Theological Foundations of Catholic Health Care* (Washington, DC: Catholic Health Association, 2013), 14.

of communities can share their stories with one another in a communal environment.

Second, more historical and scholarly research is needed to record people's experiences within the movement. Far too often the stories, struggles, and achievements of movements are lost or forgotten. Many movements have no serious plans for recording and archiving their activities. Without getting lost in an idealized past, major movements and movement organizations would benefit from engaging some sort of historian or volunteer team of scholars who can look after the historical patrimony of the movement. I know of several church movements, in particular youth movements, that have lost major portions of their archival materials to new leaders who did not understand their importance.

Third, narratives can be developed through events and times that commemorate the past. Annual celebrations of the movement's founding date, special events on the feast day of the founder, commemorations of important movement milestones (for example, centenaries), and special days set aside by the United Nations for the movement causes (for example, human rights day) can all serve as important times to communicate stories of the past while also looking to the future. Such days can also serve to unite the movement in common actions across the world. The IYCW, for instance, mobilizes YCW members around May Day actions for worker rights. Each movement should consider a special day to celebrate each year if it does not have one already.

Annual commemorations of the founding mission can also be very helpful for movement organizations, including those with diverse constituents. For example, the Cardinal Cushing Centers in Massachusetts, an organization for children and adults with intellectual disabilities, recently started to organize a Franciscan Values Festival to honor the charism and vision of the Sisters of St. Francis of Assisi, who founded the organization but are no longer actively present on staff. As part of the day-long event, clients, staff, and other community members learned about the different Franciscan values that are embodied in the organization's mission. In a similar way Manhattan College in New York City, an institution founded by the Brothers of the Christian Schools, organized a "mission month" in 2014 to draw attention to the college's core Lasallian principles. Rather than limiting the mission-related events to one event or one day, the month-long celebration highlighted Lasallian principles through dozens of events on campus, including service projects and interreligious prayer services. Like similar events at many other movement organizations, both these programs were specifically designed so that even non-Christians would be able to connect with the founding movement's mission in some way.

Liturgies, regular moments of prayer, and eucharistic celebrations also offer movements important spaces to encounter and live out their own specific narratives and to encounter the great Christian narratives in scripture and salvation history. There is often an inclination, I have found, to relegate these spaces to a secondary status. In the annual meeting of a movement organization, it can be tempting to focus on the business agenda and neglect the need for prayer. Finding a way to integrate liturgical celebrations in some way into the life of the movement can help to strengthen the movement's life and work as it celebrates what God is doing in its midst.

Finally, movements can also celebrate narratives through art and music. Much can be learned about a person or a group by the ways it decorates its spaces. Walking into a house or institution sponsored by a religious congregation, for instance, it is not uncommon to see paintings, photos, or statues depicting important leaders from the movement, key events in the movement's history, and even photos of the present leadership (for example, local bishop, pope, superior). Other movements use images, songs, and symbols that become emblematic of their cause and social commitments. Expressive symbols such as peace signs, protest songs from the civil rights movement, or icons of prophetic figures (for example, Martin Luther King, Jr.; Archbishop Romero) communicate the values of a movement and form the moral imagination and outlook of members. Whether expressed through stories, celebrations, historical research, or artwork, these narratives are a key component for Christian social movements to discern who they are and what they need to do in the future.

Relationships

A final set of resources for movements that demands greater attention is relationships. Relationships matter. As communal and social beings, the identity of any human group is formed in and through relationships. Relationships among members are the glue that keeps a movement together. In every community, of course, conflicts, tensions, and disagreements are bound to arise. Developing practices to address conflicts before they surface or get out of hand is a good idea for any movement.

Within each relationship there are different power dynamics at play. Even the best Christian movements are not immune to this reality. Left unchecked, this can destroy a movement and unhinge it from its identity and mission. Even power accumulated with the best of charitable intentions, as José Comblin warns, can end up turning against the core mission of the organization.[14] Christian movements need to seek out models of relating that go beyond corporate-business models and that value mutuality, respect, inclusion, and participation.

External relationships are an important resource for Christian social movements. Whom they choose to partner with can say much about who movements are and what they aspire to be. No movement can "go it alone." The problems facing the world are far too great for any one community to address by itself.

Like the resources of people and narratives, relational resources demand attention and time. External relationships can be just and life giving or exploitative and counter to the gospel mission. Consequently, movements must be discerning about whom they partner with, whom they receive money from, and how power is distributed in these relationships.

Relationships with governments are among the most complex and possibly dangerous relationships for movements. As we have seen, not all movements approach government structures in the same way. Those with a more prophetic style, such as Plowshares, are generally opposed to entering into any kind of relationships with governments. Other movements institutionalize themselves with organizations formally recognized by local authorities and see lobbying governments and/or the United Nations as a necessary means for living out their mission.

Receiving government money in the form of grants or contracts can assist groups in working toward their goals, but it can also raise

---

[14] José Comblin, *The Holy Spirit and Liberation*, trans. Paul Burns, Theology and Liberation (Maryknoll, NY: Orbis Books, 1989), 114.

many questions for movement organizations. Many structures are highly dependent on this source of financial support either directly or indirectly. A large number of Christian social movements around the world depend upon support from Christian development agencies in Europe and North America. Many of these agencies receive substantial funding from their national government sources. But, at times, this support can come at a price. Consider MISEREOR, the German Catholic Bishops' Organization for Development Cooperation. This agency, which identifies itself as a movement, like its Protestant sister organizations, has been a critical source of financial support for the social initiatives of Christian social movements around the world. While some of its funding comes from parish campaigns throughout Germany during Lent, the majority, two-thirds, comes from German tax dollars.

Like the other agencies that receive support from the German government in this way, MISEREOR must pledge that "no pastoral or missionary measures" are promoted with public funds.[15] While understandable, this can create strange situations in which grant recipients are forced to distinguish between justice/development work and missionary/pastoral activities. If movements or organizations understand charitable and justice work to be integral to their Christian identity, is it really possible to distinguish between what is religious and what is not? Can this even lead to the problematic disconnect between mission and justice addressed in Chapter 5?

In other countries the situation can be even more complex. In the United States major Christian social organizations, such as World Vision, Catholic Relief Services, and Catholic Charities USA, receive extensive portions of their budgets from US government funds. As with MISEREOR, careful provisions are made to ensure that public money does not promote so-called "religious" programs. These relationships, however, have recently come under scrutiny in public debates on contraception, the separation of church and state, and gay marriage. Should government funds, for instance, be provided to groups that do not support gay marriage? Should Christian groups receive funding from governmental agencies that also support artificial methods of family planning? These debates have raised serious

---

[15] MISEREOR, *With Righteous Anger and Tenderness at the Side of the Poor* (Aachen: MISEREOR, 2010), 14, www.misereor.org.

questions, from both inside and outside the church, on the nature and limits of the relationships between Christian movements and the US government.

This is not the place to examine these questions. Others have written about them specifically. No matter where the sources come from, Christian social movements that receive external support from governments, private foundations, and wealthy individuals will always encounter power dynamics within these relationship. At times, these may result in conflicts between the identity and mission of the movement and the expectations of the donors. These power dynamics must be measured and named in some way. Done well, such partnerships can maximize and strengthen the mission of the movement and its social impact while also meeting the needs of the donor. Movement organizations often require such external support. Structured poorly, these relationships can result in the damage to both public trust and the mission of the recipient.

Perhaps the most important relationship for any Christian social movement is its relationship with people who are poor and communities of the poor. Without romanticizing the brutal realities of poverty, the Christian tradition draws attention to the privileged place of the poor in God's relationship with creation. All Christian communities, including social movements, are challenged to develop genuine relationships with the poor—not as objects of pity or service, but as human beings and partners in a shared mission to build social arrangements that are more reflective of God's reign. The gospel, as liberation theologians remind us, is quite clear on the obligation of all Christians to the poor. Like many socially engaged individuals, some Christian social movements lack any real relationship with the poor. This can be very dangerous, especially if such a movement is asked to speak about the realities of poverty. Without any real relationship, those words lose legitimacy and become almost meaningless. Marie Dennis, an active leader in many Christian social movements, sums it up this way: "If what we have, where we live, and how we spend, or don't spend our time keeps us from having friends who are poor, then we need to rethink what we have, where we live, and how we spend out time."[16] Likewise, if a Christian social

---

[16] Marie Dennis, *Diversity of Vocations* (Maryknoll, NY: Orbis Books, 2008), 94.

movement lacks any real relationships to the poor, then it needs to rethink seriously its identity, mission, and organization.

MOVEMENTS FOR THE REIGN OF GOD

In their actions aimed at social transformation, Christian social movements are an important way in which the church fulfills its sacramental vocation to be a "sign and instrument" in the world (LG, no. 1). In the face of suffering, sin, and what Pope Francis has described as the "globalization of indifference," Christian social movements from many churches are among the most active agents working for positive social change.

In the end, what difference does it make for ecclesial movements to understand themselves as participating in the mission of the church? Developing a more robust missiological framework, or what Pope Francis describes as "ministry in a missionary key," will not only engender a greater appreciation for such movements in the life of the church, but it can also aid ecclesial movements to better discern how to navigate the complex ethical and organizational questions that they face as they seek to be church in the world (EG, no. 33).

Focusing on grace and the church's mission for the reign of God also brings perspective to the broader context. There is more at stake than any one movement, any report to a donor, or any single project. There is even more at stake than the very survival of a movement or movement organization. Movements, if they do indeed reflect God's grace, in other words, do not exist for themselves but for the common good and the reign of God. In his apostolic exhortation on mission, Pope Francis reminds Christians and the church of their true goal:

Reading the Scriptures also makes it clear that the Gospel is not merely about our personal relationship with God. Nor should our loving response to God be seen simply as an accumulation of small personal gestures to individuals in need, a kind of "charity à la carte," or a series of acts aimed solely at easing our conscience. The Gospel is about the kingdom of God (cf. *Lk* 4:43); it is about loving God who reigns in our world. To the extent that he reigns within us, the life of society will be a setting for universal fraternity, justice, peace and dignity. Both

Christian preaching and life, then, are meant to have an impact on society. We are seeking God's kingdom: "Seek first God's kingdom and his righteousness, and all these things will be given to you as well" (*Mt* 6:33). Jesus' mission is to inaugurate the kingdom of his Father; he commands his disciples to proclaim the good news that "the kingdom of heaven is at hand" (*Mt* 10:7). (EG, no. 180)

Adopting this type of perspective illuminates both the role and responsibility of Christian social movements. Individual acts of faith and charity, while important, are not sufficient to serve the reign of God. Isolated individuals, for example, cannot overcome the structures of sin, domination, and oppression that stand in opposition to God's reign. Indeed, much of the power of structures of sin rests in their ability to make people indifferent, passive, and isolated. In the context of globalization, organized action and communal responses to grace are playing an increasingly important role in the life of the church as servants of God's reign.

Ultimately, however, it is not about them. Acknowledging this fact can liberate movement members and leaders from obsessive concerns about the movement's survival. It is about God and those who are at the heart of God's reign: the poor and the marginalized. As structures of the church, movements must never forget the simple truth that they exist "to serve and not to be served."[17]

In recent years the Christian church has celebrated the fiftieth anniversary of the Second Vatican Council. Vatican II's vision, as the three case studies in this book demonstrate, continues to influence the church's response to social questions around the world. What will the state of Christian social movements look like in another fifty years? While it is impossible to answer that question clearly in any detail, it is certain that the reality will not be the same as it is right now. Not all the movements and movement organizations that currently exist will remain. Some will disappear. Others that were once Christian will no longer remain connected to the faith. This will mean difficult decisions and moments for the life of the church. Managing these changes will take work. But it will also mean new opportunities. New movements and forms of organization will most

---

[17] Comblin, *The Holy Spirit and Liberation*, 94.

certainly arise in the life of the church, likely in surprising ways. Whatever happens, I am confident that God's grace will continue to manifest itself in powerful ways throughout movements in the church.

Acknowledgments

I have been privileged to get to know a number of Christian social movements as a member, recipient of services, and elected leader. In my four years as president of the International Movement of Catholic Students (Pax Romana) I learned much from the commitment and dedication of empowered student leaders around the world; my teammates, Zobel Behalal and Mike Deeb, OP; our sister movements, the International Young Catholic Students and the International Catholic Movement for Intellectual and Cultural Affairs; and our partners in the Conference of International Catholic Organizations and the Forum of Catholic Inspired NGOs. These movements and their leadership taught me much about how God works through human communities.

This book is dedicated to the many vowed religious women and men who support so many Christian social movements. Each day I grow in admiration of the prophetic work undertaken by these individuals, often at the margins of society and the church. From education to social justice advocacy, these movements have improved the lives of millions. For that, we should all be grateful.

I can think of many individuals who offer so much of their time, talents, and treasures to the life of church movements; they include Margareta Lemon; Christopher Malano; Michelle Sardone; Luis Maria Goicoechea; Javier Iguiniz; Philippe Ledouble; Elisabeth Muller; Adrian Pereira; Antoine Songag; Dorothy Farley, OP; Jojo Fung, SJ; Stefan Gigacz; Bridget Lally; Bishop François Lapierre; Maryanne Loughry, RSM; Matthew Malone, SJ; Thomas Marti, MM; Fratern Masawe, SJ; Erika Meyer; Michael Place; Leo Shea, MM; Daniel Villanueva, SJ; Fredrick Wamalwa; and Bishop Peter Rosazza.

If, as this book suggests, the Christian experience is a fundamentally social one, then Christian theology must also be a social experience. This project is a result of many hours of conversation and exploration

189

in a community of learning. I am profoundly grateful to all those who have supported me, including my colleagues at Manhattan College and, in particular, Mehnaz Afridi; Robert Berger, FSC; Jawanza Clark; William Clyde; Jack Curran, FSC; Joseph Fahey; Thomas Ferguson; Philip Francis; Lois Harr; Natalia Imperatori-Lee; Robert M. Geraci; Stephen Kaplan; Brennan O'Donnell; Michele Saracino; Claudia Setzer; and Andrew Skotnicki. Much of this project would not have been possible without Manhattan College's support to its faculty for academic research.

I am also thankful to my mentors and friends in the wider theological community, including David Hollenbach, SJ; Lisa Sowle Cahill; Thomas Massaro, SJ; Elizabeth Johnson, CSJ; Bradford Hinze; James Keenan, SJ; Mark Massa, SJ; Stephen Okey; Meghan Clark; Amanda Osheim; Daniel Cosacchi; Benjamin Durheim; Katherine Greiner; Kevin Johnson; Nichole Flores Henry; Michael Jaycox; Eric Martin; Megan McCabe; René Micallef, SJ; Jill O'Brien; David Turnbloom; and Gonzalo Villagrán, SJ. Many ideas in this project have developed as a result of many years of fruitful conversation with my fellow scholars. Both Patricia Wittberg, SC, and Massimo Faggioli served as important conversation partners in the development of this project.

My scholarship and research would not have been possible without the support of my family. I particularly would like to express my deepest gratitude to Beth Glauber Ahern, for her constant encouragement, patience, and inspiration. Thank you also to my parents, John and Clare Ahern, and my siblings, Shawn and Zoe, for the many years of support and care.

Finally, I would like to acknowledge all those at Orbis Books who made this project a reality, including Robert Ellsberg, Michael Leach, and James Keane. For over forty years Orbis Books, an integral part of the Maryknoll movement, has been a critically important resource for both Christian scholarship and Christian social movements. Thank you.

Selected Bibliography

Jesuit Refugee Service

JRS: www.jrs.net
The Jesuit Curia in Rome: www.sjweb.info

Alonso, Pablo, Jacques Hares, Elias Lopez, Lluis Magrina, and Danielle Vella, eds. *God in Exile: Towards a Shared Spirituality with Refugees*. Rome: Jesuit Refugee Service, 2005.
Anderson, Mary B. *Do No Harm: How Aid Can Support Peace—or War*. Boulder, CO: Lynne Rienner Publishers, 1999.
Arrupe, Pedro. "Men for Others." Valencia: Creighton University Online Ministries, 1973. www.creighton.edu.
Au, Wilkie. "Ignatian Service, Gratitude and Love in Action." *Studies in the Spirituality of Jesuits* 40, no. 2 (Summer 2008).
Barnett, Michael N., and Thomas G. Weiss, eds. *Humanitarianism in Question: Politics, Power, Ethics*. Ithaca, NY: Cornell University, 2008.
Dulles, Avery. "Faith, Justice, and the Jesuit Mission." In *Assembly 1989: Jesuit Ministry in Higher Education*, 19–25. Washington, DC: Jesuit Conference, 1990.
Pope Francis. *Address to the "Astalli Centre," the Jesuit Refugee Service in Rome*. Rome: Libreria Editrice Vaticana, 2013. www.vatican.va.
Greene, Tom. "Observations of the Social Apostolate, Justice and the Decrees of General Congregations 31 to 35." *Promotio Justitiae*, no. 108 (2012).
Hollenbach, David. "Faith, Justice, and the Jesuit Mission: A Response to Avery Dulles." In *Assembly 1989: Jesuit Ministry in Higher Education*, 26–29. Washington, DC: Jesuit Conference, 1990.
Jesuit Refugee Service. "The Charter of Jesuit Refugee Service," March 19, 2000. www.jrs.net.
John Paul II. "Allocution to the Jesuit Provincials." Vatican City: Libreria Editrice Vaticana, 1982. www.vatican.va.
———. "Who Is the Priest? Remarks of Pope John Paul II during Ordination Ceremonies in Rio de Janeiro." *Origins* 10, no. 9 (July 31, 1980).
O'Brien, Kevin. "Consolation in Action: The Jesuit Refugee Service and the Ministry of Accompaniment." *Studies in the Spirituality of Jesuits* 37, no. 4 (Winter 2005).

Orobator, Agbonkhianmeghe E. "Justice for the Displaced: The Challenge of a Christian Understanding." In *Driven from Home: Protecting the Rights of Forced Migrants*, edited by David Hollenbach, 37–54. Washington, DC: Georgetown University Press, 2010.

Padberg, John W., ed. *Jesuit Life and Mission Today: The Decrees of the 31st–35th General Congregations of the Society of Jesus*. Jesuit Primary Sources in English Translation 25. St. Louis, MO: Institute of Jesuit Sources, 2009.

Rieff, David. *A Bed for the Night: Humanitarianism in Crisis*. New York: Simon and Schuster, 2002.

Tripole, Martin R. *Faith beyond Justice: Widening the Perspective*. Saint Louis: Institute of Jesuit Sources, 1994.

Valcárcel, Amaya, ed. *The Wound of the Border: Twenty-five Years with the Refugees*. Rome: Jesuit Refugee Service, 2005.

Valcárcel, Amaya, and Danielle Vella, eds. *Advocacy in Jesuit Refugee Service*. Rome: Jesuit Refugee Service, 2011.

Vella, Danielle, ed. *Everybody's Challenge: Essential Documents of Jesuit Refugee Service, 1980–2000*. Rome: Jesuit Refugee Service, 2000.

Villanueva, Daniel. "The Jesuit Way of Going Global: Outlines for a Public Presence of the Society of Jesus in a Globalized World in the Light of Lessons Learned from the Jesuit Refugee Service." STL Thesis, Weston Jesuit School of Theology, 2008.

Young Christian Workers

Cardijn Online: www.josephcardijn.com
International Young Christian Workers: www.joci.org
International Coordination of Young Christian Workers: www.cijoc.org

Bidegaín, Anna Maria. *From Catholic Action to Liberation Theology: The Historical Process of the Laity in Latin America in the Twentieth Century*. Working Paper 48. Notre Dame, IN: Kellogg Institute, University of Notre Dame, 1985.

Cardijn, Joseph. "1911 Worker Organisation in England." *Cardijn Online*, 1911. www.josephcardijn.com.

———. "The Three Truths." Presented at the First International Study Week of the YCW, Brussels, August 26, 1935. www.josephcardijn.com.

Congar, Yves. *Lay People in the Church: A Study for a Theology of Laity*. Translated by Donald Attwater. Westminster, MD: Newman, 1956.

D'Sami, Bernard. "The Impact of *Gaudium et Spes* on the Social Mission of the Church in Asia with Particular Reference to Catholic Students and Workers Movements." In *The Call to Justice: The Legacy of* Gaudium et Spes *Forty Years Later*. Rome, 2005.

De La Bedoyere, Michael. *The Cardijn Story: A Study of the Life of Mgr. Joseph Cardijn and the Young Christian Workers' Movement Which He Founded*. Milwaukee, WI: The Bruce Publishing Company, 1959.

Dussel, Enrique D. *A History of the Church in Latin America: Colonialism to Liberation (1492–1979)*. Translated by Alan Neely. Grand Rapids, MI: Eerdmans, 1981.

———. "Recent Latin American Theology." In *The Church in Latin America, 1492–1992*, edited by Enrique D. Dussel, translated by Paul Burns, 1:391–402. A History of the Church in the Third World. Maryknoll, NY: Orbis Books, 1992.

Fievez, Marguerite, Jacques Meert, and Roger Aubert. *Life and Times of Joseph Cardijn*. Translated by Edward Mitchinson. London: Young Christian Workers, 1974.

Glorieux, Achille. "Histoire Du Décret." In *L'apostolat des Laïcs: Décret "Apostolicam Actuositatem,"* edited by Yves Congar, 91–140. Unam Sanctam 75. Paris: Editions du Cerf, 1970.

Goldie, Rosemary. *From a Roman Window: Five Decades of the World, the Church and the Laity*. Melbourne: HarperCollins Melbourne, 1998.

———. "Lay Participation in the Work of Vatican II." *Miscellanea Lateranense*, no. 40–41 (1975–74): 503–25.

Hari, Albert. *IYCW: International Young Christian Workers, Seventy-five Years of Action*. Edited by Fondation internationale Cardijn. Strasbourg: Signe, 2000.

International Co-ordination of Young Christian Worker Movements. *ICYCW Declaration of Principles*. Rome: CIJOC-ICYCW, 2004. www.cijoc.org.

Minvielle, Bernard. *L'Apostolat des laïcs à la veille du concile (1949–1959): histoire des congrès mondiaux de 1951 et 1957*. Fribourg, Switzerland: Editions Universitaires, 2001.

Ninth International Council of the IYCW. *Declaration of Principles*. Brussels: International Young Christian Workers, 1995.

Roussel, Luc. "The YCW and the Vatican: From Confidence to Incomprehension and Rupture 1945–1985." In *The First Steps towards a History of the IYCW*. Brussels: International Young Christian Workers, 1997.

Smith, Christian. *The Emergence of Liberation Theology: Radical Religion and Social Movement Theory*. Chicago: University of Chicago, 1991.

Plowshares

Jonah House: www.jonahhouse.org
Trident Ploughshares: www.tridentploughshares.org

Berrigan, Daniel. *To Dwell in Peace: An Autobiography*. San Francisco: Harper and Row, 1987.

Berrigan, Philip. *Fighting the Lamb's War: Skirmishes with the American Empire: The Autobiography of Philip Berrigan*. Monroe, ME: Common Courage Press, 1996.

———. *Prison Journals of a Priest Revolutionary*. New York: Holt, Rinehart, and Winston, 1970.

Berrigan, Philip, and Elizabeth McAlister. *The Time's Discipline: The Beatitudes and Nuclear Resistance*. Baltimore: Fortkamp, 1989.

Boertje-Obed, Greg, Megan Rice, and Michael Walli. "A Statement for the Y-12 Facility." Transform Now Plowshares. 2014. http://transformnowplowshares.wordpress.com.

Dear, John. "Jesus and Civil Disobedience." Father John Dear, 1994. www.fatherjohndear.org.

———. *The Sacrament of Civil Disobedience*. Baltimore: Fortkamp, 1994.

Forest, Jim. *All Is Grace: A Biography of Dorothy Day*. Maryknoll, NY: Orbis Books, 2011.

Klejment, Anne. *American Catholic Pacifism: The Influence of Dorothy Day and the Catholic Worker Movement*. Westport, CT: Praeger, 1996.

———. "War Resistance and Property Destruction: The Catonsville Nine Draft Board Raid and Catholic Worker Pacifism." In *A Revolution of the Heart: Essays on the Catholic Worker*, edited by Patrick G. Coy, 272–312. Philadelphia: Temple University Press, 1988.

Laffin, Arthur J. *The Plowshares Disarmament Chronology, 1980–2003*. Marion, SD: Rose Hill Books, 2003.

Laffin, Arthur J., and Anne Montgomery. *Swords into Plowshares: Nonviolent Direct Action for Disarmament*. San Francisco: Perennial Library, 1987.

Nepstad, Sharon Erickson. *Religion and War Resistance in the Plowshares Movement*. New York: Cambridge University, 2008.

Nepstad, Sharon Erickson, and Stellan Vinthagen. "Strategic Changes and Cultural Adaptations: Explaining Differential Outcomes in the International Plowshares Movement." *International Journal of Peace Studies* 13, no. 1 (2008).

Peters, Shawn Francis. *The Catonsville Nine: A Story of Faith and Resistance in the Vietnam Era*. New York: Oxford University Press, 2012.

Wilcox, Fred A. *Uncommon Martyrs: The Plowshares Movement and the Catholic Left*. Bloomington, IN: iUniverse, 1991.

Christian Social Movements and Organizations

Ahern, Kevin "Structures of Hope in a Fractured World: The Ministry of the International Catholic Youth Movements." In Concilium 2010/1: Ministries in the Church, edited by Susan Ross, Diego Irarrázaval, and Paul Murr, 76–84.

Appleby, R. Scott. *The Ambivalence of the Sacred: Religion, Violence, and Reconciliation*. Lanham, MD: Rowman and Littlefield, 2000.

Bartoli, Andrea. "Forgiveness and Reconciliation in the Mozambique Peace Process." In *Forgiveness and Reconciliation: Religion, Public Policy, and Conflict Transformation*, edited by Raymond G. Helmick and Rodney L. Petersen, 316–81. Philadelphia: Templeton, 2001.

Bellin, Eva. "Faith in Politics: New Trends in the Study of Religion and Politics." *World Politics* 60, no. 2 (January 2008): 315–47.

Berger, Peter L., and Richard John Neuhaus. *To Empower People: The Role of Mediating Structures in Public Policy*. Studies in Political and Social Processes 139. Washington, DC: American Enterprise Institute for Public Policy Research, 1977.

Buechler, Steven M. *Social Movements in Advanced Capitalism: The Political Economy and Cultural Construction of Social Activism*. New York: Oxford University Press, 2000.

Campbell, Simone. *A Nun on the Bus: How All of Us Can Create Hope, Change, and Community*. New York: HarperOne, 2014.

Casanova, José. *Public Religions in the Modern World*. Chicago: University of Chicago Press, 1994.

Diamond, Louise, and John McDonald. *Multi-Track Diplomacy: A Systems Approach to Peace*. 3rd edition. West Hartford, CT: Kumarian Press, 1996.

Hannigan, John A. "Social Movement Theory and the Sociology of Religion: Toward a New Synthesis." *Sociological Analysis* 52, no. 4 (Winter 1991): 311–31.

Hehir, J. Bryan. "Overview." In *Religion in World Affairs*, 11–24. DACOR Bacon House Foundation, 1995.

———. "Religious Activism for Human Rights: A Christian Case Study." In *Religious Human Rights in Global Perspective: Religious Perspectives*, edited by John Witte and Johan David Van der Vyver, 97–119. Boston: Martinus Nijhoff Publishers, 1996.

Hollenbach, David. "Sustaining Catholic Social Engagement: A Key Role for Movements in the Church Today." Edited by Cheryl Handel and Kathleen Shields. *Journal of Catholic Social Thought* 10, no. 2 (2013): 431–47.

Huntington, Samuel P. *The Third Wave: Democratization in the Late Twentieth Century*. Norman: University of Oklahoma Press, 1991.

Johnston, Douglas M., and Cynthia Sampson, eds. *Religion: The Missing Dimension of Statecraft*. New York: Oxford University Press, 1994.

Keck, Margaret E., and Kathryn Sikkink. *Activists beyond Borders: Advocacy Networks in International Politics*. Ithaca, NY: Cornell University Press, 1998.

Leahy, Brendan. *Ecclesial Movements and Communities: Origins, Significance, and Issues*. Hyde Park, NY: New City Press, 2011.

McDonald, John. "Further Exploration of Track Two Diplomacy." In *Timing the De-Escalation of International Conflicts*, edited by Louis Kriesberg and Stuart J. Thorson, 201–20. Syracuse, NY: Syracuse University Press, 1991.

Melloni, Alberto, ed. *"Movements" in the Church*. Concilium 2003/3. London: SCM, 2003.

196 Selected Bibliography

Pontifical Council for the Laity, ed. *The Beauty of Being a Christian: Movements in the Church.* Laity Today 2. Vatican City: Pontificium Consilium pro Laicis, 2006.

———., ed. *Movements in the Church: Proceedings of the World Congress of the Ecclesial Movements, Rome, 27–29 May 1998.* Laity Today 2. Vatican City: Pontificium Consilium pro Laicis, 1999.

Musto, Ronald G. *The Catholic Peace Tradition.* Maryknoll, NY: Orbis Books, 1986.

Schneiders, Sandra M. *New Wineskins: Re-Imagining Religious Life Today.* New York: Paulist Press, 1986.

Smith, Jackie, Charles Chatfield, and Ron Pagnucco, eds. *Transnational Social Movements and Global Politics: Solidarity beyond the State.* Syracuse, NY: Syracuse University Press, 1997.

Sugranyes de Franch, Ramon. *Le Christ Dans Le Monde: Les Organisations Internationales Catholiques.* Paris: Fayard, 1972.

Toft, Monica Duffy, Daniel Philpott, and Timothy Samuel Shah. *God's Century: Resurgent Religion and Global Politics.* New York: W. W. Norton and Company, 2011.

Van Stichel, Ellen. "Movements Struggling for Justice within the Church: A Theological Response to John Coleman's Sociological Approach." Edited by Cheryl Handel and Kathleen Shields. *Journal of Catholic Social Thought* 10, no. 2 (2013): 281–93.

Vanier, Jean. "The Rise of Catholic Movements." *The Tablet,* March 15, 1997.

Verstraeten, Johan. "Catholic Social Thought and the Movements: Towards Social Discernment and a Transformative Presence in the World." Edited by Cheryl Handel and Kathleen Shields. *Journal of Catholic Social Thought* 10, no. 2 (2013): 231–39.

Wittberg, Patricia, *The Rise and Fall of Catholic Religious Orders: A Social Movement Perspective.* Albany: State University of New York Press, 1994.

———. "Faith-Based Umbrella Organizations: Implications for Religious Identity." *Nonprofit and Voluntary Sector Quarterly* 42, no. 3 (June 2013): 540–62.

Zahn, Gordon C. "Social Movements and Catholic Social Thought." In *One Hundred Years of Catholic Social Thought: Celebration and Challenge,* edited by John A. Coleman, 43–54. Maryknoll, NY: Orbis Books, 1991.

Zald, Mayer N., and Roberta Ash. "Social Movement Organizations: Growth, Decay, and Change." *Social Forces* 44, no. 3 (March 1, 1966): 327–41.

Catholic Institutional Identity

Bernardin, Joseph. "A Consistent Ethic of Life: Continuing the Dialogue, The William Wade Lecture Series, St. Louis University, March 11, 1984."

In *The Seamless Garment: Writings on the Consistent Ethic of Life*, edited by Thomas Narn. Maryknoll, NY: Orbis Books, 2008.

———. "Catholic Institutions and Their Identity." *Origins* 21, no. 2 (1991): 33–36.

Curran, Charles E. "The Catholic Identity of Catholic Institutions." *Theological Studies* 58, no. 1 (1997): 90–108.

Fahey, Charles, and Mary Ann Lewis. *The Future of Catholic Institutional Ministries: A Continuing Conversation*. [Bronx, NY]: Third Age Center of Fordham University, 1992.

Fox, Zeni, and Regina M. Bechtle. *Called and Chosen: Toward a Spirituality for Lay Leaders*. Lanham, MD: Rowman and Littlefield, 2005.

Gottemoeller, Doris. "History of Catholic Institutions in the United States." *New Theology Review* 14, no. 2 (2001): 16–27.

Heyer, Kristin E. *Prophetic and Public: The Social Witness of US Catholicism*. Moral Traditions Series. Washington, DC: Georgetown University Press, 2006.

Lysaught, M. Therese. *Caritas in Communion: Theological Foundations of Catholic Health Care*. Washington, DC: Catholic Health Association, 2013. www.chausa.org.

Narn, Thomas. "Catholic Health Care Must Stand in the Middle." *Health Progress* 94, no. 4 (August 2013): 87–89.

Orsy, Ladislas M. *Toward a Theological Evaluation of Communal Discernment*. St. Louis: American Assistancy Seminar on Jesuit Spirituality, 1973.

Smith, Karen Sue. "A Summary: Caritas in Communion." *Health Progress* 94, no. 4 (August 2013): 80–86.

Steinfels, Peter. *A People Adrift: The Crisis of the Roman Catholic Church in America*. New York: Simon and Schuster, 2013.

Structural Grace

Boff, Leonardo. *Church: Charism and Power: Liberation Theology and the Institutional Church*. Translated by John W. Dierchsmeier. New York: Crossroad, 1985.

Bouchard, Charles E. "Recovering the Gifts of the Holy Spirit in Moral Theology." *Theological Studies* 63, no. 3 (2002): 539–58.

Comblin, José. "Grace." In *Mysterium Liberationis: Fundamental Concepts of Liberation Theology*, edited by Ignacio Ellacuría and Jon Sobrino, 522–31. Maryknoll, NY: Orbis Books, 1993.

———. *The Holy Spirit and Liberation*. Translated by Paul Burns. Theology and Liberation. Maryknoll, NY: Orbis Books, 1989.

Daly, Daniel J. "Structures of Virtue and Vice." *New Blackfriars* 92, no. 1039 (2011): 341–57.

Duquoc, Christian, and Casiano Floristán Floristán Samanes, eds. *Charisms in the Church*. Concilium. New York: Seabury, 1978.

Francis. "Pope to Charismatic Renewal: Be Stewards Not 'Inspectors' of God's Grace." AsiaNews, June 2, 2014. www.asianews.it.

Haight, Roger. *The Experience and Language of Grace*. New York: Paulist Press, 1979.

Henriot, Peter J. "Social Sin and Conversion: A Theology of the Church's Involvement." *Chicago Studies* 11 (1972): 115–30.

Koupal, William. "Charism: A Relational Concept." *Worship* 42, no. 9 (1968): 539–45.

Küng, Hans. "The Charismatic Structure of the Church." In *The Church and Ecumenism*, 41–61. New York: Paulist Press, 1965.

Lane, Dermot A. *Foundations for a Social Theology: Praxis, Process, and Salvation*. New York: Paulist Press, 1984.

Nolan, Albert. *God in South Africa: The Challenge of the Gospel*. Cape Town: D. Philip, 1988.

O'Keefe, Mark. *What Are They Saying about Social Sin?* New York: Paulist Press, 1990.

Rahner, Karl. *The Dynamic Element in the Church*. Translated by W. J. O'Hara. New York: Herder and Herder, 1964.

Mission

Benedict XVI. "Address of His Holiness Benedict XVI to Representatives of the Holy See; to International Organizations and to Participants in the Forum of Catholic-Inspired Non-Governmental Organizations." *The Holy See*, December 1, 2007. www.vatican.va.

———. *"Motu Proprio" On the Service of Charity*. Vatican City: Libreria Editrice Vaticana, 2012. www.vatican.va.

Bevans, Stephen B., and Roger Schroeder *Constants in Context: A Theology of Mission for Today*. Maryknoll, NY: Orbis Books, 2004.

Boff, Leonardo. *Church: Charism and Power: Liberation Theology and the Institutional Church*. Translated by John W. Dierchsmeier. New York: Crossroad, 1985.

Bosch, David Jacobus. *Transforming Mission: Paradigm Shifts in Theology of Mission*. American Society of Missiology Series 16. Maryknoll, NY: Orbis Books, 1991.

Cahill, Lisa Sowle. "*Caritas in Veritate*: Benedict's Global Reorientation." *Theological Studies* 71, no. 2 (June 1, 2010): 291–319.

Congregation for the Doctrine of the Faith. *Doctrinal Note on Some Aspects of Evangelization*. Vatican City: Libreria Editrice Vaticana, 2007. www.vatican.va.

Elsbernd, Mary. "What Ever Happened to *Octogesima Adveniens*?" *Theological Studies* 56, no. 1 (March 1995): 39–60.

Gutiérrez, Gustavo. *A Theology of Liberation: History, Politics, and Salvation*. Maryknoll, NY: Orbis Books, 1988.

Hinze, Bradford E. *Practices of Dialogue in the Roman Catholic Church: Aims and Obstacles, Lessons and Laments*. New York: Continuum, 2006.

Keenan, James F. "Proposing Cardinal Virtues." *Theological Studies*, no. 56 (1995): 709–29.

———. *Virtues for Ordinary Christians*. Lanham, MD: Rowman and Littlefield, 1996.

Maritain, Jacques. *Integral Humanism: Temporal and Spiritual Problems of a New Christendom*. Translated by Joseph W. Evans. New York: Scribner and Sons, 1968.

Murphy, Charles M. "Action for Justice as Constitutive of the Preaching of the Gospel: What Did the 1971 Synod Mean?" In *Readings in Moral Theology No. 5: Official Catholic Social Teaching*, edited by Charles E. Curran and Richard A. McCormick, 150–68. New York: Paulist Press, 1986.

———. "Charity, Not Justice, as Constitutive of the Church's Mission." *Theological Studies* 68, no. 2 (2007): 274–86.

Index

201

JC-HEM. *See* Jesuit Commons: Higher Education at the Margins
JECI. *See* International Young Catholic Students
Jesuit Commons: Higher Education at the Margins, 52–53
Jesuit Refugee Service, 7, 35, 39, 86, 87, 105, 109, 124
  accompaniment and, 49–51, 158
  advocacy work of, 53–56
  campaigning against landmine use, 55
  committed to peace and reconciliation, 136
  educational focus of, 52–53
  embodying God's grace, 127
  establishment of, 48, 141
  ethical transformation and, 134
  holding public leaders accountable, 135
  identity of, maintaining, 161
  as Jesuit work, 60–61
  non-Jesuits role in, 61
  personifying Ignatian charism, 141
  policy research and analysis by, 55–56
  relationship of, with the Jesuits, 61
  responding to Syrian civil war, 43
  scope of activities, 51–53
  service operations of, guidelines for, 61
  structure of, 48–49, 158, 161
Jesuits (Society of Jesus), 7, 34, 118
  committed to social justice, 45
  criticism of, 120
  general congregations of, 45. *See also* general congregations
  identity of, 57, 60
  maintaining oversight of JRS, 158
  mission of, 43–46
  rearticulating sense of mission, 114–15
  refugees and, 43, 47–48. *See also* Jesuit Refugee Service
  renewal of, after Vatican II, 45–46, 141
  suppression of, 154–55
Jesuit Secondary Education Association, 33
Jesuit Volunteer Corps, 4, 169
Jesus, civil disobedience by, 92–93
Jeunes Organisés et Combatifs (Youth Organized and Competitive), 77, 78
Jeunesse Ouvrière Crétienne (JOC), 64, 68, 70, 77. *See also* Young Christian Workers
Jeunesse syndicaliste (Young Trade Unionists), 67
Jeyaku, Balendran, 125
Jeyaku, Vipoosika, 125
JIIC. *See* International Independent Christian Youth
JOC. *See* Young Christian Workers
JOC Europe, 82
JOCF, 68. *See also* Young Christian Workers
JOCI, *See* International Young Christian Workers
jocists, focused on organized action, 79
  model of, 69
  mystique of, 77
John XXIII, 26–27, 70, 131
John Paul II, 15, 119
  on charisms, 139–40, 157
  on the church's unity and diversity, 163–64
  critical of liberation theology, 27
  critical of turn toward justice, 118, 121
  on gifts of the Spirit, 139
  on grace, 136
  on mission, 122, 159

of the poor, 122
secular movement for, 115
liberation theology, 14, 27, 65, 71,
72, 131, 142
fruits of the Spirit and, 166–69
jocist youth movements and,
71–72
life, as fruit of the Spirit, 170
like to like, apostolate of, 78
liturgies, 182
locals, empowerment of, 23
Lubich, Chiara, 180
Lumen Gentium (Vatican II), 112,
139
Lutheran World Federation, 43n3
Lysaught, M. Therese, 180

Maas, Elmer, 87
Madres de Plaza de Mayo, 125,
168
Mahesan, Praveen, 125–26, 135
Maiden protest movement, 96
Mandela, Nelson, 72–73
Manhattan College, 181–82
Manhattan Project, 86
Manhattanville College, 159
Marist College, 159
Maritain, Jacques, 113
Marx, Karl, 16
Mater et Magistra (John XXIII),
26–27, 70
Maurin, Peter, 64, 97
McAlister, Elizabeth, 99, 103
McAuley, Catherine, 5
Médecins Sans Frontières, 59
Medical Mission Sisters, 170
Meert, Jacques, 67
Melloni, Alberto, 31
Melville, Marjorie Bradford, 98
Melville, Thomas, 98
Mengel, James, 98
Mercier, Désiré-Joseph, 67
Merton, Thomas, 98
Merton (Thomas) Center (Pittsburgh, PA), 88–89

"Message for the Celebration of
the World Day of Peace: Fraternity, the Foundation and
Pathway to Peace" (Francis),
14–15
method, truth of, 79
MIAMSI. *See* International Movement of Apostolate in the
Independent Social Milieus
MIDADE. *See* International
Movement of Apostolate of
Children
Middle Ages, Christian social
movements in, 24–25
MIEC-Pax Romana. *See* International Movement of Catholic
Students
migrants, 1, 3–4. *See also* displacement, forced; refugees
deaths of, 2
as source of energy for Christian
communities, 37
migration, Christian social movements' involvement with, 13
MIIC-Pax Romana. *See* International Catholic Movement
for Intellectual and Cultural
Affairs
MIJARC. *See* International Movement of Catholic Agricultural
and Rural Youth
military orders, 24
millennialism, 24
Miller, David, 97
Mingst, Karen, 19n12
Mische, George, 98
MISEREOR, German Catholic
Bishops' Organization for
Development Cooperation,
184
missiology, 110, 186
mission
complexity of, 118, 122
dialogical approach to, 122–23
diversity in, 159

YCS France, 114
YCW. *See* Young Christian Workers
YCW Australia, 80
YCW Philippines, 80
YMCA. *See* Young Men's Christian Association
Young Christian Students, 72
Young Christian Workers, 7, 27, 34, 35, 64, 70, 86, 87, 105, 109, 131
    addressing young workers' realities, 136
    Congar on, 114
    educational role of, 134
    embodying God's grace, 127
    federated structure of, 162
    financial and logistical support for, 124
    goal of, 76, 77
    holding public leaders accountable, 135
    identity of, 76–77, 82, 103
    mission of, 77, 141

    national movements of, autonomy of, 161
    origins of, 66
    participation in, 65
    split in, 74–76, 83
    spread of, 68
    structure of, 84, 157
    support for, 84
    style of, 67, 141
    vision of, 65, 72–73, 78
Young Men's Christian Association, 43n3, 159
young people's movements, leadership transitions in, 83
Young Women's Christian Association, 4
youth organizations, role of, 78
Y-12 National Security Complex (Oak Ridge, TN), 86
YWCA. *See* Young Women's Christian Association

Zahn, Gordon, 26
Zelter, Angie, 94